THE LAST EMPEROR OF MEXICO

The LAST EMPEROR *of* MEXICO

A Disaster in the New World

EDWARD SHAWCROSS

faber

First published in the UK in 2022
by Faber & Faber Ltd
Bloomsbury House
74–77 Great Russell Street
London WC1B 3DA

First published in the USA in 2021
by Basic Books
Hachette Book Group
1290 Avenue of the Americas
New York, NY 10104

Printed in the UK by CPI Group (UK) Ltd, Croydon, CR0 4YY

A CIP record for this book
is available from the British Library

ISBN 978–0–571–36057–4

MIX
Paper from
responsible sources
FSC
www.fsc.org   FSC® C171272

2   4   6   8   10   9   7   5   3   1

For Hannah and Ena

CONTENTS

PROLOGUE

I n the spring of 1867, three men awaited their fate. They were imprisoned in a former convent amidst the shell-shattered, sun-scorched streets of Querétaro, a provincial town some 130 miles northwest of Mexico City. The nuns' chambers made perfect cells. But a heavy guard kept watch: these were dangerous political prisoners, leaders of a faction in a civil war that had ravaged Mexico for nearly ten years. All three had been charged with treason. The sentence was death.

One of them, Miguel Miramón, was a former Mexican president. At least, he had been president to his supporters in the Conservative Party—his opponents had never recognised his appointment. Born in Mexico City to an affluent family that could trace its roots back to aristocratic marquises, Miramón was only twenty-six when appointed head of state. Urbane and charming, he was devoted to the army, the church, and his wife. He was the epitome of the conservative cause that he had once led.

His fellow prisoner Tomás Mejía was an Otomí, an indigenous people from the Sierra Gorda range. So harsh and remote was this region that it was not fully brought under Spanish rule until the 1740s, more than two hundred years after Spain first colonised

Mexico. Forty-seven years old, Mejía typified a strand of deeply pious and fiercely independent indigenous peoples who had supported the conservatives. Although both men disputed the charges of treason against them, they had been fanatical devotees for more than a decade of the now defeated Conservative Party.

The third man was different. Tall, with blue eyes, fair hair, and a distinctive beard obsessively parted in the middle, he had been in Mexico for only three years. He claimed he was a liberal, not a conservative. He also claimed he was the emperor of Mexico. A scion of one of the oldest and most illustrious royal families in Europe, Ferdinand Maximilian had been born into imperial splendour in Vienna, a Habsburg archduke. Now, sick, emaciated, and separated from friends and family, Maximilian's world had shrunk to a four-by-six-foot cell in a devastated Mexican town.

THE STORY OF how a Habsburg archduke came to be emperor of Mexico is a strange one. President Ulysses S. Grant saw it as outrageous, nothing short of an act of war against the United States. Karl Marx labelled the initial military intervention that paved the way for a kingdom in North America as one of the most monstrous enterprises in the annals of international history. Adolphe Thiers, president of the French Third Republic, called the Mexican empire a madness without parallel since Don Quixote. These three men held vastly different political convictions, yet they were united in their sheer incredulity at the hubris that had brought Maximilian to Mexico.

On one level, the story of Maximilian is that of a frustrated second son, convinced of his own destiny, but – unlike his older brother, the emperor of Austria, Franz Joseph – with no empire to rule. On a geopolitical level, the tale is that of dynastic Europe's challenge to the republican Americas, the Old World reasserting itself against the New. For the conspiracy that brought Maximilian across the Atlantic was hatched in Mexico but incubated in the court of Napoleon III, emperor of the French. Posing the century's greatest challenge to the Monroe Doctrine, the US policy that prohibited European intervention in the Americas after the collapse of the Spanish empire some forty years earlier, it was French troops that invaded Mexico in 1862 and carved out a kingdom for Maximilian to rule.

What followed was a monumental struggle, pitting emperors against presidents, monarchies against republics, and Europe against the United States. The outcome would determine who controlled the Western Hemisphere and its system of government for the next century and beyond.

The story would approach its denouement in the cramped cells of Querétaro.

But the saga had its roots some twenty years before.

1

THE PLOT AGAINST MEXICO

On the morning of September 14, 1847, US troops marched through the streets of a foreign capital for the first time in history. Hours before, the soldiers had been engaged in savage fighting against the Mexican army. Now making their way to the centre of Mexico City in their torn and bloodstained uniforms, with their commanding officer wearing only one boot after losing the other in battle, the US forces took possession of the enormous main square, today known as the Zócalo.

At seven o'clock, the Stars and Stripes were unfurled over the National Palace, the official residence of Mexico's presidents. One hour later, General Winfield Scott, commander in chief of the US expeditionary force, led his troops in triumph to join the advance guard outside the former seat of Mexico's government. Against the backdrop of the looming cathedral that dominates the north of the square, a military band played "Yankee Doodle."

For many Mexicans, this was too great a humiliation. Citizens began to make their way to the Zócalo, staring with hostility at the foreign invaders. As the US troops began to disperse, a shot rang out from the rooftops, and a musket ball tore into the leg of an American officer. Soon more shots were fired, and stones and bottles rained down from the buildings on the panicking soldiers as the mob unleashed its fury.

Three days of fighting followed. The men and women of Mexico City fought bravely, but hopelessly. US artillery destroyed the houses where gunmen were hiding; howitzers opened fire on the crowds. After order was ruthlessly restored, a Mexican observer lamented that the capital's beauty was now matched only by its misfortune. This was not Mexican hyperbole; a US soldier who took part in the repression described "bloodshed and brutality such as I trust I will never see again", adding that "its horrors will never be forgotten in Mexico."[1] He was right.

While the violence was shocking, it came as no surprise to José María Gutiérrez de Estrada. A Mexican politician, he had predicted exactly this scenario in a pamphlet published seven years earlier. "If we do not change our ways", he had warned in 1840, then "we will see the stars of the US flag wave over our National Palace" and, worse, "Protestant services celebrated in our splendid Catholic cathedral."[2] No one listened. Branded a traitor, Gutiérrez de Estrada had been forced to flee the country, and the publisher who printed his work was thrown in prison. This was because the work contained an idea so dangerous, it had to be suppressed: Mexico should have a foreign king.

Born into the Mexican political class, Gutiérrez de Estrada spoke and wrote in the verbose style of an eighteenth-century Spanish aristocrat. Patrician, unsmiling, and nostalgic for the colonial past, he was a typical member of the creole elite, the descendants of Spanish immigrants, who dominated political and economic life in nineteenth-century Mexico. Having married into the most illustrious circles of Mexican high society, he had served in various government posts, including as foreign minister.

What turned him from establishment politician to exiled pariah was witnessing political violence firsthand. After years travelling abroad, Gutiérrez de Estrada had returned to Mexico City in the summer of 1840 in time to see rebels storm the National Palace, take the president hostage, and attempt to seize power. Twelve days of carnage ensued—some seven hundred people died—before government forces used artillery to bombard the palace, ending the revolt. An Englishwoman living in the city recorded the events in her diary: "People come running up the street. . . . The cannon are roaring now. . . . They are ringing the tocsin—things seem to be getting serious." They were. Soon cannons lined the streets, while soldiers were "firing indiscriminately on all who pass." She added that Count José María Justo Gómez de la Cortina had been wounded.[3] This was Gutiérrez de Estrada's father-in-law.

Had this been the first time that violence shook Mexico in recent memory, Gutiérrez de Estrada might not have been moved to publish his ideas; however, the country had experienced numerous revolts since independence in 1821. By 1840 only one president—there had been eleven already—had served out his full term in office. Violence was more important than the ballot box.

In 1840 Gutiérrez de Estrada diagnosed what he saw as the disease at the heart of the Mexican state: republicanism. Mexico, he believed, should have been a monarchy. His argument drew on the unique circumstances of Mexican history. After a long struggle against its colonial master, Spain, Mexico emerged as an independent nation in 1821. It did so under a former officer in the royalist army, Agustín de Iturbide, who changed sides and declared the new nation-state not a republic to be ruled by a president but an empire that required an emperor.

In so doing, he put Mexico in distinguished company. "Emperor" was a title transcending "king", and "empire" here meant a political state. In the early nineteenth century, Austria, Russia, and France, for example, were, or had been, empires ruled by emperors. It was not because these emperors governed territories beyond their national borders—although they also did this—that they laid claim to the title, but because these monarchs considered themselves greater than kings and their states more important than mere kingdoms.

Mexico certainly possessed scale and immense potential. With some 137,000 inhabitants in 1803, Mexico City was larger at the time than Philadelphia and New York combined, unrivalled in the Americas in the sciences and arts, and graced by some of the finest architecture anywhere on the globe. For nearly three hundred years, it had been the centre of the Spanish empire in the Western Hemisphere. Before Washington, DC, existed, Mexico City was a bustling metropolis, controlling territory that stretched from Panama to California, from Florida to the Philippines. Anyone who read the writings of famed explorer and scientist Alexander von Humboldt, who travelled through the region between 1799 and 1804, detailing its fabulous wealth in precious metals, would have understood Iturbide's confidence, concluding that Mexico might come to rival the United States as the greatest power in North America.

When Humboldt journeyed through Mexico, it was still under Spanish rule. In 1519 the Spanish king, Charles I, inherited the lands of the Habsburg Monarchy from his grandfather and was elected Holy Roman emperor. Now Charles V, he governed territory spanning Spain, much of Italy, the Netherlands, and central Europe, including Austria. This made him one of the most powerful men in the world, and his domains dramatically increased the same year he became emperor when an adventurer named Hernán Cortés led a small band of Spaniards to invade Mexico and, in the name of the Habsburgs, subjugate the wealthy Mexica, today better known as the Aztecs. Spanish technology, local indigenous allies, and disease aided Cortés in a brutal conquest.

This history resulted in a complex society in Mexico. Spanish colonialism imposed a European veneer on a far older Mesoamerican culture that stretched back thousands of years. In towns, the cathedrals, government buildings, and ordered streets set out in a grid reminded visitors of Spain. So did the dominance of the Catholic religion, which missionaries had spread, often violently, across the region. But sheltered in the enormity of Mexico, life in remote spots continued as it had for centuries before Cortés arrived. Spanish was not spoken; small Christian shrines were the only indication of European influence.

According to nineteenth-century estimates, the population of Mexico in 1810 was about 6 million, split between about 1 million Spaniards or creoles; some 1.5 million of mixed heritage known as mestizos; and roughly 3.5 million indigenous people. By the mid-nineteenth century, the total population had risen to perhaps 8 million, but these neat figures belied a heterogeneous population that was as diverse as Mexico's geography and unevenly spread across it. Millions lived in the fertile central valleys near Mexico City, while only tens of thousands, if that, peopled far-flung regions like Texas or California. Moreover, from the tropical peninsula of Yucatán to the harsh northern deserts, the indigenous peoples of Mexico spoke different languages, had varying interests, and formed anything but a homogenous group.

It was on Mexico's indigenous history, not its Spanish past, that Iturbide rested his main claim to empire. The Aztecs were the last in a long line of indigenous peoples who enslaved most of central Mexico before the Spanish arrived in the sixteenth century. For those under the Aztecs, paying heavy tribute, often with their lives as human sacrifices to Aztec gods, this empire was no antediluvian paradise; however, the sophistication of Aztec culture combined with their resistance to Cortés's Spanish invaders led Iturbide to recall them in 1821, arguing that independent Mexico was now the inheritor of their empire.

There was, therefore, nothing outlandish about Iturbide's declaration that Mexico should be a monarchy. After all, Mexico had been governed under Spanish kings for hundreds of years; monarchy was the system under which all major European powers flourished and had existed in Mexico before Europeans even arrived. Indeed, had Iturbide embraced the federal republican system, then largely unknown in Mexico and an experiment barely thirty years old in the United States, it is unlikely he would have gained the support he did. Besides, what many of those who objected to Spanish rule disliked was that they were governed from across the Atlantic. With a European monarch in Mexico, heading a Mexican government with a Mexican constitution limiting his powers and elected Mexican representatives helping him govern, Mexico would be independent. In 1822 Brazil adopted a similar model and was ruled by its emperors as an independent nation-state until 1889.

The genius of Iturbide's plan was that it united disparate forces in Mexico long enough to defeat Spain's armies. Mexico's struggle for independence began in 1810, but after a savage eleven-year conflict against its colonial master, and at the cost of some two hundred thousand lives, it had yet to succeed. Some in Mexico wanted to throw off all vestiges of Spanish rule, others wanted self-government within the Spanish empire, and still others wanted an independent nation-state, but with close ties to Spain combined with protection for colonial institutions such as the army and the Catholic Church. The genius of Iturbide's manifesto, declared in February 1821, was that it united these groups under one banner. At the head of a triumphant army, which had vanquished Spanish royalists, Iturbide marched into Mexico City on September 27. There was, however, one flaw in his plan: Who would rule this new kingdom?

In theory, the plan answered this: Ferdinand VII, king of Spain, was offered the crown. No one expected him to accept—the plan required that he come to Mexico in person—but provision was made for this eventuality. If he refused, then the throne would be offered to one of his relations. However, Ferdinand wanted nothing less than the complete reconquest of one of the richest parts of the Spanish empire and rejected Iturbide's offer for himself and his family. The new Mexican empire now had no monarch. Iturbide's solution was to crown himself the first emperor of Mexico in July 1822.

His reign was short. With dizzying speed he went from liberator to dictator and then abdicated in March 1823. Forced into exile, he returned in 1824 under the belief that he would be welcomed back as a hero. This was a mistake. Within weeks, he was arrested and shot for treason. In three years of independence, Mexico had executed its first emperor and independence hero and transformed from an empire into a federal republic, proclaimed in the same year Iturbide was shot. This system proved little more successful than its predecessor, subject as it was to numerous armed revolts and constitutional changes.

In Gutiérrez de Estrada's view, the instability Mexico suffered from 1824 was because the nation had adopted a form of government alien to its traditions. As a royalist, he argued that the disastrous denouement of Iturbide's empire did not discredit monarchy; rather, his assumption of the crown was Mexico's original sin. For emperor, the nation required not a Mexican army officer, but a European of royal blood. Exiled for this belief, Gutiérrez de Estrada launched a one-man mission to turn his dream into reality by lobbying European courts. "Time is pressing", wrote Gutiérrez de Estrada in 1846 to the foreign minister of the Austrian Empire. "A moment's pause and it will be too late". If "republican anarchy" continued in Mexico, the country would "cease to exist" and be annexed to the United States.[4]

Gutiérrez de Estrada was right: it was too late. The United States was covetous of Mexico's vast, sparsely populated northern territory, and thus relations with the United States had been problematic from the outset. They got worse after 1836 when Texas, part of Mexico, declared itself an independent republic, with many US citizens fighting and then defeating the Mexican army sent to end this insurrection. Next, in 1845 Texas was annexed and became a state in the Union, yet President James Polk craved more of Mexico's lands. Weeks after Gutiérrez de Estrada wrote his letter, Polk spuriously claimed that American blood had been spilt on American soil during a border skirmish and declared war on Mexico in April 1846.

Poorly trained, ill-equipped, and badly led, the Mexican army lost every major battle it fought. US troops occupied Mexico, leaving only at a formidably high price. The 1848 Treaty of Guadalupe stands as one of the most unequal agreements in history, gaining for the United States all or parts of (Alta) California, New Mexico,

Arizona, Utah, Wyoming, and Colorado. In return, Mexico received $15 million and the withdrawal of US soldiers. Even the American who negotiated the treaty was astonished by its greed, calling it "a thing for every right minded American to be ashamed of, and I was ashamed of it, most cordially and intensely ashamed of it."[5] After an illegal war, the United States had become a continental empire with access to the Pacific, fashioning a momentous transformation of international power at Mexico's expense.

The end of US occupation did not bring peace in Mexico. Instead, what followed was a war of ideas between two political parties convinced that their vision for Mexico would provide its unique salvation. On one side, the Conservative Party argued that US republicanism was an exotic seed planted in Mexican soil to corrupt its traditions. They insisted that unless Catholic Mexico maintained the power of the church, rejected radical democracy, and allied itself with monarchical Europe, then the Protestant United States would take what remained of the nation. On the other side, Mexico's liberals concluded that the disgrace of the US-Mexican War was not because Mexico was too republican, but because it was not republican enough. The only way to forge a powerful Mexico, they argued, was to break the power of the Catholic Church, sweep away colonial institutions, and embrace change.

In 1855 these liberals came to power in a revolution that aimed at radical reform of Mexican society. Their principal target was the Catholic Church, which not only wielded immense religious authority, but was also the nation's largest landowner. To break the church's spiritual and temporal hold on the population, and conveniently enrich the government treasury at the same time, liberals nationalised church property so it could be sold to private buyers. For conservatives, this proved the impiety that lay at the heart of the radical liberal agenda. It was an act that they would never forgive.

Nor, to the horror of conservatives, were the liberals finished. They wanted to calcify their reforms through a new constitution, which confirmed the sale of church property. What angered conservatives

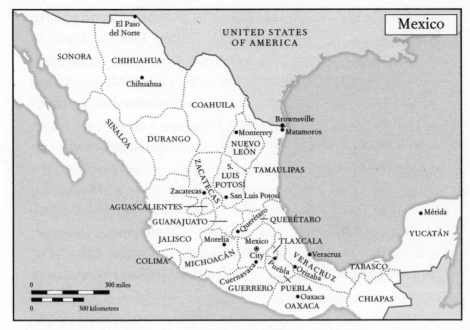

Mexico circa 1854

even more was what it did not say. For the first time in Mexican history, the nation's charter failed to declare Catholicism as the state religion to the exclusion of all others. The constitution enacted in 1857, conservatives fumed, was a revolutionary attack on property and faith. The archbishop of Mexico warned that he would excommunicate anyone who swore allegiance to it. Determined to overturn the new constitution, in December 1857, conservatives launched a coup d'état and deposed the liberal president. Civil war had begun.

During what was known as the War of Reform, conservative hopes lay with a young military commander, Miguel Miramón. He loathed the United States. Ten years earlier, aged fourteen, he was one of many cadets who volunteered to defend Chapultepec Castle, which guarded the approach to Mexico City from the invading US Army. At five on the morning of September 12, 1847, the first shells from US heavy artillery smashed into the masonry of this eighteenth-century palace, which had been designed to house Spanish viceroys in luxury—not withstand mortar fire. Miramón and his comrades took cover as best they could until the shelling stopped that night.

The next morning, the infantry assault began. Situated on a hill, Chapultepec was surrounded as US troops swarmed from all sides. In the intense hand-to-hand combat that followed, the outnumbered and poorly armed Mexicans were pushed back into the castle. Most never got out. US troops killed them as they tried to flee or surrender. Inside, the young Miramón had fought desperately until a musket ball struck his face and he fell to the floor. A soldier rushed forward to bayonet him, but a US officer swooped in to pick up Miramón and carry him to a hospital. Six of Miramón's classmates were not so lucky. Later, myth had it that these *niños héroes* (child heroes) wrapped themselves in the Mexican flag and leapt to their deaths rather than surrender.

A decade later, conservatives were confident that Miramón would give them victory, not least because the liberals were led by a lawyer, not a general. As head of the Mexican Supreme Court, Benito Juárez was constitutionally next in line for the presidency. After the conservative coup d'état, he escaped Mexico City to set up a rival government at the port of Veracruz.

Unlike Miramón, Juárez was born into rural poverty. He grew up far from Mexico City in San Pablo Guelatao, Oaxaca, a tiny village with no school and only around twenty families in the foothills of desolate mountains. Life there had been largely unchanged since the Zapotec peoples first settled the area some two thousand years before the Spanish conquest. Juárez's parents died before he was three, and he was raised by an uncle, one of the few people in the village who knew Spanish. Determined to better himself, Juárez began to learn the language, bringing a whip to lessons and urging his uncle to beat him whenever he got anything wrong. Juárez, however, was soon put to work in the fields, and the long, hard days meant he made little progress with his studies. Staring into the distant horizons surrounding his village, he knew that if he stayed his life would never change. So, at the age of twelve, he walked the sixty miles to the state capital.

Here, in Oaxaca City, he found menial work. In return, Juárez was given lodging and enrolled in school. One of the only paths out of poverty for indigenous Mexicans was the church, and after mastering Spanish (though imperfectly, as he admitted), Juárez joined a seminary to train as a priest. This was a repugnant choice for Juárez, who held a contemptuously low opinion of the church. He was saved from a life of God—and existential *mauvaise foi*—when a liberal and secular university opened in 1828. There he trained as a lawyer, a profession he practiced with moderate success, but it was only a stepping-stone to his true calling in the Liberal Party.

What made Juárez exceptional was his political career. Neither a brilliant speaker nor a great writer, he had a fascination for power and an extraordinary gift for holding on to it. Before the 1850s he held high office, but he was forced into exile in 1853 after one of Mexico's by now regular revolts. Reduced to poverty in New Orleans, he made a living selling cigars on Bourbon Street, before returning to Mexico in 1855, when the liberal revolt put his party in power. From this point, his rise was meteoric. He went from minister to head of the Supreme Court and then in 1858 to president. This austere, taciturn republican believed it his destiny to break the church's power, implement liberal reforms, and, after conservatives had suspended it, restore the 1857 constitution. The only way to do this was to defeat Miramón, who held the capital.

This three-year civil war between a wealthy creole and an indigenous Zapotec was not only a struggle for the future of Mexico but a geopolitical battleground as well. The United States backed Juárez, believing that a liberal victory would allow US investments and businesses to develop the nation, delivering the country to US control far more easily, and profitably, than annexation. This would not be permitted under the conservatives, who were wary of US influence and looked to Europe, but they received little more than diplomatic sympathy from across the Atlantic.

The war lasted three years. Miramón nearly won—would have won, he claimed—had not the US Navy intervened in the conflict to stop a conservative flotilla from resupplying his army while besieging Juárez at Veracruz. Whatever the truth of Miramón's claims, however, in January 1861 the liberals entered Mexico City. Many conservative leaders, including Miramón, fled to Europe. Others refused to surrender, retreating into the wilderness of Mexico, biding their time until the chance came to exact revenge.

Celebrations of Juárez's triumph proved short-lived. His government was bankrupt. Mexico owed Britain, France, and Spain millions of pounds, with the most owed to London. Worse, the British government itself had been robbed during the civil war when armed forces broke into the British legation and stole $660,000 worth of silver. For the British, it did not matter that a leading conservative general had committed this crime; the Mexican government, now led by Juárez, was responsible. Besides, the British were hardly enamoured with Juárez's liberals, who had seized a convoy of silver worth $1 million, much of it owned by British nationals, to fund their war effort.

The new British representative to Mexico, Sir Charles Wyke, therefore drew up a list of demands for Juárez's government. Far from meeting them, on July 17, 1861, Mexico's congress suspended foreign-debt repayment. Furious, Wyke in turn suspended diplomatic relations on July 25 and fired off a letter to Britain's foreign secretary, Lord John Russell, in which he argued that refusing to honour its debt was "only a solitary instance of the many acts of cruelty and injustice" of which this "wretched government" had been guilty. It was all the more deplorable, continued Wyke, because Juárez was "constantly talking of liberty and toleration and the blessings of a constitutional system." For the Englishman, this was the worst kind of hypocrisy: "I know nothing more detestable than this species of tyranny under the guise of freedom; it is like a prostitute boasting of her virtue."[6]

Britain was not the only aggrieved nation. France had recently sent Dubois de Saligny as its representative to Mexico. Saligny was an odd choice. Vain, arrogant, and obstreperous, he had shown a singular talent for offending nearly everyone he met. His only important previous diplomatic experience had been fifteen years before as chargé d'affaires to the ephemeral Republic of Texas. Here, only two years into the post, he broke relations with the republic over an incident known as the Pig War. While waiting for the construction of a new legation in Austin, Saligny had lodged at a hotel owned by Richard Bullock, who also raised pigs. Once Saligny moved to his new residence, some of these pigs, perhaps missing the Frenchman, wandered over to the new property, knocked over fences, devoured what they could in the garden, and, most shocking for the diplomat, managed to get inside the building, where they happily chewed the fine French linen for dessert.

For Saligny, the honour of France had been engaged. He ordered his servant to shoot any pig that invaded French territory; this one-sided conflict resulted in several dead hogs. Once Bullock found out that his animals had been killed, he thrashed Saligny's servant in the street. Bullock then cornered the Frenchman and threatened to mete out the same punishment unless compensated for the loss of porcine life. Saligny raised this private dispute to the level of international diplomacy, demanding Bullock be punished for assault. When the Texan government refused, Saligny broke off diplomatic relations, left the republic, and threatened that France was ready to invade. This was entirely false. In 1845 Saligny was recalled to Paris. On his return, the foreign minister explained that while France could afford to be wrong, it could never afford to be ridiculous.

Understandably, Saligny languished in obscurity for nearly fifteen years, and there was much speculation as to why he was sent to Mexico. One theory was that, in return for pressing the dubious claims of some European banking houses who had loaned money on outrageous terms during the civil war, he would get a cut of whatever Juárez's government repaid. Saligny offered his own interpretation for his appointment: he was there to cause trouble. The French government, tired of Mexico's hostility towards European powers, Saligny claimed, wanted a pretext for intervention. And the French diplomat was the kind of man who excelled at creating one.

Indeed, he exceeded even his own high expectations because on the night of August 14, 1861, as he was readying for bed, he heard cries of "Death to the French!" and "Death to the French minister!" outside in the streets. Two hours previously, on the veranda of the French legation, he remembered that had he smelt gunpowder and had felt something brush past his arm. Concluding that an attempt had been made on his life, Saligny recommended that France send forces to Mexico. As with Wyke, the diplomatic basis for this was the July 17 law suspending payments on foreign debt, which Saligny described as a "veritable act of suicide".[7] This time, it was more serious than pigs; the French Foreign Ministry agreed with him, as did the Spanish government, to which Mexico also owed money. After only a few months in power, Juárez had so antagonised France, Britain, and Spain, the three major European naval powers, that they agreed to a combined military intervention in Mexico.

They were free to do so because another civil war in North America started months after the Mexican one finished. Fearing that the newly elected Republican president, Abraham Lincoln, would abolish slavery, seven southern states formed the Confederacy and seceded from the Union. Lincoln was determined to end this rebellion, but when war broke out in April 1861 four more states joined the Confederacy, marking the start of the American Civil War.

While this conflict tore the United States apart, some in Europe spied an opportunity. Normally, any European interference would meet with determined resistance from Washington, guided by the Monroe Doctrine. Formulated in 1823 by President James Monroe, this doctrine, which quickly became a popular cornerstone of US foreign policy, claimed hegemony over the Americas and warned European governments against intervention on the continent. In Europe the policy was dismissed as US arrogance. But if European statesmen sneered contemptuously at the United States and its pretensions to suzerainty over the Americas, none had seriously challenged it.

On October 31, 1861, that changed. Britain, Spain, and France signed the Convention of London, which stated that they were compelled by Juárez's conduct to send military forces to Mexico. Gutiérrez de Estrada and the defeated conservatives who had fled to Europe saw an opening. What if they could convince the monarchies of Europe that Mexico was an ideological and geopolitical battleground where victory could roll back US dominion and republicanism in North America? Put simply, replacing a hostile republic with a sympathetic monarchy would safeguard European interests in the Americas far better than a one-off intervention to collect unpaid debts.

A few weeks before the three powers agreed to intervene in Mexico, Miguel Miramón, now a refugee from the Mexican civil war, arrived in Paris with his wife, Concepción Lombardo. Shortly afterwards, as befitted Paris, they were invited to a soirée. Concepción was left dazzled by the extraordinary, radiant beauty of the hostess, who at thirty-seven years old had "conserved all the freshness of youth" in a white dress, adorned with lace and a pearl necklace formed of several threads that came down to her waist. Her outfit was finished with two diamond earrings. As the hostess turned, Concepción admired her neck, her beautiful eyes, and her light-coloured hair, "which fell like golden rain over her back". The whole effect, she concluded, combined to form "the most beautiful creature that I have ever seen".[8]

Concepción had just met Empress Eugenie, wife of Louis-Napoleon, better known as Napoleon III, emperor of the French. Also attending the party were the emperor himself, the French foreign minister, and at least a platoon of French generals, alongside women of the court in the voluminous crinoline dresses fashionable at the time. In short, the elite of Parisian society were gathered in their finery at the Tuileries, the imperial palace on the right bank of the Seine. But Miramón and Concepción were not there for the glamour of the occasion. They were being drawn into a world of international conspiracy and intrigue centred around a man who revelled in secretive deals, back channels, and disinformation. This man also happened to be the ruler of France.

That he was had come as a shock to the French political elite more than a decade earlier. In February 1848, weeks after the United States forced Mexico to sign away half its national territory, revolution had broken out in Paris before spreading across Europe. Mindful of what happened to French kings who outstayed their welcome, the French monarch, Louis Philippe, abdicated. His regime was replaced by the Second Republic, the nightmare that the powers of Europe had feared for more than fifty years. The First Republic, founded in 1792, had executed French king Louis XVI and his Austrian wife, Marie Antoinette; fought revolutionary wars across Europe; and killed some thirty thousand of its own citizens in what became known as the Terror. In 1848, with much of Europe already in revolt, all eyes had turned fearfully, or hopefully, depending on one's politics, towards Paris and the December presidential elections to see if radicals would win and unleash an even bloodier repeat performance.

On December 20, 1848, disbelieving deputies had watched as the new president of France shuffled into place to make his inaugural speech before the National Assembly. Dressed in white tie, with heavy sideburns, a moustache, and a well-disciplined goatee under a large nose, his head down and slouched into his shoulders, he spoke in a faltering voice with a slight foreign accent. This was not the grandeur of French republicanism or the spectre of revolution; rather, it was the nephew of the former emperor Napoleon Bonaparte, known as Louis-Napoleon.

If anything, this was more terrifying for European royalty. The original Napoleon Bonaparte may have tamed the radicalism of the French Revolution, but he extended the power of France across the Continent. After a series of stunning victories, he overthrew the republic he had vowed to protect and proclaimed himself emperor of the French in 1804. Then he defeated the Austrians, Russians, and Prussians with startling speed, and Europe became the hinterland of a continental empire centred in Paris. But it was a perilous edifice maintained through constant war and propped up with satellite kingdoms, over many of which Napoleon's brothers ruled.

One of these brothers, Louis, married Napoleon's stepdaughter, Hortense de Beauharnais. They had three sons; the youngest, born in 1808, was imaginatively called Louis-Napoleon. The fall of his uncle's empire after defeat at the Battle of Waterloo in 1815 meant that Louis-Napoleon grew up in exile—hence the accent to his French. Seeking adventure as a young man, he went to Italy, where, in smoke-filled taverns, he plotted with liberal nationalists to unite the disparate states that then ruled the peninsula. This movement was crushed, its ringleaders condemned to die, and Louis-Napoleon barely escaped with his life, but he never lost his love for conspiracy, intrigue, and, above all, bold gambles.

He soon had plenty of practice at all three. In the early 1830s, with other candidates now either dead or uninterested, Louis-Napoleon seized the Bonapartist legacy, claiming to be next in line to any future empire. Few took him seriously, but this inheritance weighed heavily on him. "From time to time," he explained, "men are created whom I call volunteers of providence, in whose hands are placed the destiny of their countries. I believe I am one of those men. If I am wrong, I can perish uselessly. If I am right, then providence will put me into a position to fulfil my mission."[9]

Disappointed with the progress of Providence, in 1836 Louis-Napoleon took matters into his own hands and launched a coup d'état. It was a humiliation; a supposedly loyal Bonapartist regiment failed to rally, and Louis-Napoleon was arrested. The French government, more embarrassed than angry, agreed to his exile on the condition that he promise never to return to France. Thus, in 1840, when he returned to France and made another attempt, by sea across the Channel, and, supposedly, with a tame vulture tied to the mast of the ship in lieu of an eagle, the French government took it more seriously.

Failure is too grand a word for this comic opera. Once again, the local garrison refused to back the cause. On seeing the futility of the situation, Louis-Napoleon tried to row back to the boat that had carried him from England, but capsized and had to be fished out of the waves. Soaking wet, he was arrested on the beach. This time, in

October 1840, Louis-Napoleon was locked up in a fortress. Unde-terred, six years later, while the prison was undergoing construction, Louis-Napoleon dressed in the clothes of a workman, picked up a wooden plank, put it over his shoulder, and walked out the front gate before fleeing to London.

And there it would have ended had it not been for the provi-dential moment Louis-Napoleon had been waiting for: the Euro-pean revolutions of 1848. After the abdication of the French king, a republic was hastily proclaimed and elections announced. Despite no experience of democratic politics, or a political party to support him, Louis-Napoleon grandiosely told a cousin, "I'm going to Paris. A republic has been proclaimed. I must be its master." His cousin responded, "You are dreaming, as usual".[10] Louis-Napoleon won the election by a landslide.

The name "Napoleon" proved enormously popular with voters, but the man who bore this legend was hated by the French political elite. Indeed, political thinker Alexis de Tocqueville compared Louis-Napoleon to a "dwarf" who "on the summit of a great wave is able to scale a high cliff which a giant placed on dry ground would not be able to climb". Writer and politician Victor Hugo penned a series of vitriolic attacks on Louis-Napoleon, one titled *Napoléon le pétit*, exhorting the French to "look at this hog wallowing in his own slime on a lion's skin".[11] Even Adolphe Thiers, leader of conservative pol-iticians in France who supported Louis-Napoleon, thought him an idiot who could be easily controlled. Certainly, Louis-Napoleon did not seem to have his uncle's drive—except when it came to women. Indeed, his mistress at this time—and financial backer—was a noto-rious English courtesan and failed actress, a combination too much even for French politics. To the relief of many, the constitution of the republic limited the presidency to one four-year term.

Louis-Napoleon, however, was not going to allow a constitution he had sworn to uphold get in the way of destiny. Third-time lucky, after nearly three years as president, on December 2, 1851, he led a coup d'état and made himself president for ten years. President, though, was not a title grand enough for a Bonaparte, and a year later he declared himself emperor of the French, creating the Second Empire (his uncle's was the first). For the second time in French history, a Bonaparte had ended the republican experiment, and it was the coup d'état of December 2, 1851, that moved Karl Marx to write: "the first time as tragedy, the second time as farce."[12]

Napoleon III's unique insight, and it was unique at the time, was that conservatism could be popular—for millions of Frenchmen, there was nothing farcical about the new regime. Rather than seeing democratic politics as resulting in left-wing radical change, Napoleon III understood that, carefully managed, the people could legitimise an authoritarian regime through the ballot box. To that end, he appealed directly to French voters, holding two plebiscites, the first asking the French people to endorse his coup d'état and the second on whether he should be emperor. He overwhelmingly won both; more than seven million voted "yes", over 90 percent of the all-male electorate. Declaring it the will of the people, Louis-Napoleon became Napoleon III on December 2, 1852.

As Napoleon III practiced it, Bonapartism aimed to plough a middle way between liberalism and conservatism. In this, he built on the example of the recently overthrown king Louis Philippe, lover of the centrist *juste milieu*, but Napoleon III was willing to go further and base his regime on direct democracy as expressed through universal male suffrage. As one of his aphorisms supposedly went, "Do not fear the people, they are more conservative than you".[13]

The first decade of his rule was an astonishing success. The economy rapidly expanded, allowing the emperor to embark on a foreign policy designed to restore France to glory. First, he ended France's isolation in Europe after the Napoleonic Wars, allying with Britain in the Crimean War of 1853–1856 and defeating Russia. Next, in 1859, he personally commanded an army that vanquished the Austrian emperor, Franz Joseph, in Italy. Furthermore, the long, brutal conquest of Algeria, begun in 1830, officially ended in 1858 with local resistance crushed. Europe and North Africa were not the limit of the emperor's ambition. French troops occupied Saigon, slowly drawing Indochina—modern-day Laos, Cambodia, and Vietnam—into the French empire. At the same time, France again allied with Britain to defeat China in the Second Opium War. Napoleon III was instrumental, too, in funding the construction of the Suez Canal, opened in 1869.

Bar his uncle, he had the greatest global ambition of any modern French ruler, and by 1861 Paris could confidently claim to be the centre of an imperial superpower with a global reach second only to Britain. With the transformation of Paris under Georges-Eugène Haussmann, the wide boulevards, grand apartments, and monumental train stations of the capital reflected the confidence—and modernity—of the regime.

Napoleon III now turned his gaze towards the Americas. In Mexico he already had many admirers. Conservatives there saw him as the man who had saved France and Europe from radicals bent on destroying peace, order, and religion during the 1848 revolutions. Lest Mexico sink further into the abyss, they argued, it must imitate Napoleon III's example of strong authoritarian government. What drew them most to France, however, was fear of US expansion. Nothing indicated that 1848 had sated Washington's appetite for territory. As President James Buchanan made clear to the Senate in 1858, "It is beyond question the destiny of our race to spread themselves over the continent of North America".[14] In this speech, he merely echoed the manifest-destiny views of many in the United States who believed the time was apposite for the United States to enter the world stage and rival European power.

Keenly aware of these public statements, Mexican conservatives believed they were locked in a global struggle: not only did the United States want to destroy Mexico, but it also intended to export republicanism to Europe. As a conservative foreign minister lamented to a French diplomat, Washington supported the "rebels of Hungary", the "reds of Italy", the "socialists of France", the "disloyal subjects of Spain", as well as the "scum of Mexican politics".[15] Conservatives called the expansion of the United States combined with the spread of republicanism the "Western question". Just as France had stopped Russian expansion in the Crimean War, so too should it intervene in the Americas to save Mexico.

In this they were preaching to the converted. Napoleon III saw the rise of US power through the prism of pan-Latinism, a doctrine that tied the fate of Mexico and its "Latin" culture to France. Indeed, so terrified were many thinkers about further US aggression that in the 1850s they invented a new term, *Latin America*, which was designed to rally southern Catholic peoples in the face of the expected northern Protestant onslaught. The term quickly caught on. Soon after a French journalist used it in print in 1856, a Colombian living in Paris wrote a poem warning that the Anglo-Saxons, as he referred to the United States, were the mortal enemies of Latin Americans; a Chilean politician made a speech in France that Latin America was already in the jaws of the Saxon boa constrictor; and a Frenchman, Michel Chevalier, cautioned that Mexico, "one of the most beautiful jewels in the Catholic and Latin crown," was about to "fall into the hands of the invading Anglo-Saxons."[16]

Chevalier, an economist and journalist, was one of the first to think in pan-Latinist terms. He accepted the idea current at the time that Europe was broken down into different races, such as Anglo-Saxon, Latin, and Slavs; however, his claim to originality lay in extending these racial distinctions to the New World. The United States and Canada, he argued, were Anglo-Saxon; Mexico southward was Latin. Chevalier further believed that because of cultural and historical differences between Catholicism and Protestantism, Anglo-Saxon nations were suited to democracy, whereas Latin states should be monarchies.

French thinkers pushed and popularised the term *Latin America*, demarcating a new sphere of French influence. At the stroke of a pen, French claims to hegemony crossed the Atlantic; however, as Chevalier and many others noted, the United States threatened "Latin" America. French policy must, therefore, Chevalier insisted, "put up a barrier to the imminent invasion of the entire American continent by the United States" and so "save from irreparable ruin not only Mexico, but also the whole Spanish branch of Latin civilisation in the New World."[17] Mexico, then, was the front line in a conflict between Europe and the Americas, republicanism and monarchism, the Old World versus the New. And Chevalier had argued this not only in the press. As one of Napoleon III's closest and most trusted advisers, he made the case directly to the emperor.

Using the new science of statistics, another of Napoleon III's advisers starkly outlined the urgency of stopping the United States. He noted that its population had been 2 million in 1763, was 32 million in 1863, and calculated that in 1963 it would be 512 million. The United States would need more land for these people and would absorb Mexico, cross over the Isthmus of Panama, and invade South America. "Jealous of Europe, enemies of the old world, it would be capable of trying to enslave the universe," he wrote. Stopping this was the boldest idea "of our century, I would say further, of modern times".[18]

Mexico, most observers agreed, was not strong enough to resist US expansion on its own, but how was a country as large as Mexico to be put under French control when it had taken France eighteen years and some 100,000 troops to subjugate an area of Algeria, half the size and considerably closer? Empress Eugenie provided the answer.

Although Eugenie de Montijo, Countess of Teba, was a Spanish aristocrat, she was considered a poor choice of wife for Napoleon III. Charming, yes, but too informal for an empress and, besides, not from one of Europe's ruling families, thus bringing no dynastic lustre to the arriviste regime. Yet the emperor had fallen in love and so, against the wishes of family and advisers, had married her in 1853. Napoleon III's love may not have stretched to remaining faithful, but their marriage was founded on genuine affection. As no one had greater access to the all-powerful emperor, the union also afforded Eugenie an active political role. It was through her that Gutiérrez de

Estrada's Mexican monarchists found themselves at the heart of the French court.

Alongside Gutiérrez de Estrada, the most important of this coterie was José Manuel Hidalgo y Esnaurrízar. Born in Mexico, he was descended from a noble Spanish family and had spent most of his life in Europe as a diplomat. Although he could not openly declare it for fear of losing his job, Hidalgo privately believed that if Mexico were to survive, it must fulfil the original plan for independence and become a monarchy under a European emperor. His views were a badly kept secret, though, and Gutiérrez de Estrada cultivated him as a fellow traveller. Hidalgo was posted as a diplomat to Spain in 1853; amongst the exalted circles he moved in was the salon of the Countess of Montijo, Eugenie's mother.

In 1857 the radical new Mexican constitution was proclaimed, requiring all government employees to swear allegiance. Explaining he could not do so in good conscience, Hidalgo was dismissed from his post and made his way to Paris, stopping off at the small French town of Bayonne. There, covered in dust from the coach ride, Hidalgo had what he saw as a providential encounter. On the same day, Sunday, August 30, 1857, Eugenie, staying in nearby Biarritz, was driving with her family to a local bullfight.

Recognising Hidalgo, who was dutifully saluting in the street, the empress beckoned the Mexican towards the imperial carriage and invited him to spend the next day with her at the beach. Seizing this opportunity, Hidalgo discussed Mexico with Eugenie. He explained that anarchy reigned, the Catholic Church was threatened, and the only way to save Mexico, and the Latin race, from the United States was to found a monarchy. Hidalgo played on Eugenie's sympathies. A devout Catholic, Eugenie was also a strong believer, as befitted the wife of an empress, in the dangers of republicanism. She was so moved by Mexico's plight that she promised to raise the issue with Napoleon III.

When civil war broke out in Mexico, conservatives appointed Hidalgo as secretary to their legation in France, a key brief of his position to secure European intervention for his government. Hidalgo's closeness to Eugenie meant that he could bring the matter in person to the emperor. In 1858 she arranged for Hidalgo to stay at the Château de Compiègne, the imperial couple's autumn residence. There, after lunch, Hidalgo spoke with Napoleon III. Hidalgo pleaded his case. Though Napoleon III sympathised with the monarchist's arguments, he replied that France could do nothing alone because of US opposition.

For Hidalgo, then, the American Civil War was not a tragedy but an opportunity. And from there, events continued to turn in his favour. That summer, Eugenie was again in Biarritz, accompanied by her husband. The imperial couple had constructed a luxurious villa there, built in the shape of the letter *E* in honour of the empress. In September, Hidalgo was invited to join them. There, with no telegram communication between Europe and Mexico—news took up to six weeks to cross the Atlantic—Hidalgo received letters explaining that the British had suspended relations with Juárez's government and that Saligny had broken them on behalf of Napoleon III's own. After dinner, Hidalgo approached the empress. He told her, "Your Majesty, I have just received some very interesting letters; events are moving in our direction, and I hope that our idea of intervention and of an empire may become a reality. I should like to tell the emperor." Eugenie abruptly left the room, quickly returned, and beckoned Hidalgo to follow her. "Tell the emperor what you have just told me," she said.

Napoleon III was in his study, reading a letter from the king of Siam (modern-day Thailand). He set it on the table in front of him, stood up, lit a cigarette, and looked expectantly at Hidalgo. "Sir", said Hidalgo, "I have for some time lost all hope of seeing those ideas realised about which I had the honour of speaking to your majesty some four years ago; but England, together with France and Spain, is now irritated by Juárez's policy, and they are going to send warships to [Mexico]. And so, Your Majesty, we have what we needed: English intervention. France will not be acting alone, which is what Your Majesty always wanted to avoid". With Britain, Spain, and France on board, continued Hidalgo, the overwhelming majority in Mexico would rise up to "annihilate the demagogues and proclaim a monarchy, which alone can save the country." Hidalgo added that the American Civil War meant that Washington was powerless to interfere.

Napoleon III had not yet received dispatches from his foreign minister, though. "If England and Spain are prepared to act, and the interests of France demand it, I will also join them", he replied. "For the rest, as you say, the state of affairs in the United States is very propitious." And so, amidst clouds of cigarette smoke, in the study of an opulent villa on the southwest coast of France, without even the knowledge of the French foreign minister, the momentous decision was made to establish a monarchy in Mexico.

What attracted Napoleon III to the scheme was the prospect of a fabulously wealthy Latin empire on the cheap. Unlike Algeria, where French colonialism relied on military repression and direct rule from the metropole, Mexican monarchists would provide France with collaborating elites drawn towards a French vision of pan-Latinism, monarchy, and European power to undertake the expensive task of creating and administering the new kingdom. Owing its existence to France, Napoleon III envisaged that this nominally independent Mexican kingdom would repay its debt through favourable terms of trade, mining concessions, and transit rights, while French investors and businesses would reap the benefits of developing resource-rich Mexico, famed for its wealth in precious metals. French power would also radiate from Mexico; as the political benefits of monarchy became apparent, other unstable Latin American states would look to Paris as their model, rolling back the republican experiment in the Americas. In short, Napoleon III's plan for Mexico had all the benefits of colonialism for France at only a fraction of the cost. At least, that was the theory. There remained, however, the question of who would sit on this imaginary throne.

Hidalgo said, "Will Your Majesty allow me to ask whether you have a candidate in view?" Lighting another cigarette, the emperor replied, "I have none". After dismissing the possibility of a Spanish prince and then running through some minor German royals, Hidalgo changed tack. Might an Austrian archduke accept the crown? "But which archduke?" Eugenie enquired.[19]

2

THE ARCHDUKE AND
THE PRINCESS

Ferdinand Maximilian was an archduke in the royal house of the Habsburgs, one of the oldest dynasties in Europe. Many centuries earlier, the Habsburgs had been a global power, and memories of their imperial glory captivated Maximilian as a child. In the palaces where he grew up, the ceilings, walls, and even sundials were adorned with the acrostic AEIOU—Latin for "All the world is subject to Austria". This was no boast. In the sixteenth century, under Charles V, Mexico had become a Habsburg dominion, and his empire soon expanded to include much of both North and South America, the Philippines, as well as parts of India and Africa. Legend had it that Hercules inscribed the motto "Non plus ultra"— "Nothing further beyond"—on the straits of Gibraltar to mark the end of the known world. Such was Charles V's ambition that he dropped the "nothing" and simply adopted "Plus ultra" as his personal motto.

Three centuries later, however, Austria was a declining nineteenth-century power struggling to hold on to its central and eastern European heartlands, its pretensions to global supremacy long abandoned.

In 1556 Charles V had divided his empire between his son Philip II, who retained the Spanish possessions, and his brother, who controlled the traditional central European territories. By 1700 the Spanish branch of the Habsburgs died out, leaving only the Austrian line. Sitting at the centre of Europe, the Austrian Empire, as it was officially titled from 1806, was a stultifying bastion of royalism and conservatism: an absolute monarchy reigning over a multitude of different nationalities, the antithesis of the democratic nation-state that the French Revolution embodied. What held this precarious patchwork of kingdoms together was loyalty to the Habsburgs. Repressive at home, abroad Austria was the lynchpin of the so-called Holy Alliance, upholding Catholicism and monarchy against atheism and republicanism.

Unfortunately for a regime predicated upon the majesty of monarchy, mid-nineteenth-century Austria had a less than magisterial emperor. Cursed by debilitating bouts of epilepsy, Ferdinand had an unnaturally large head on top of a withered body. He became emperor in 1835, but his health problems meant he governed in name only and few expected his reign to be a long one. Given that Ferdinand was unable to have children, the throne would pass to his younger brother, Franz Karl.

Physically and mentally fine, Franz Karl was considered a mediocre individual, not least by his own wife, Princess Sophie of Bavaria. Sophie was only nineteen when she married into the stifling Habsburg court. After leaving her family behind, she was desperately lonely and had five miscarriages before giving birth to a son, Franz Joseph, in 1830. During her early years in Austria, her best friend was a fellow outsider, Napoléon François Joseph Charles Bonaparte, the son of Napoleon Bonaparte through his second marriage to an Austrian archduchess. Briefly titled Napoleon II, then the Duke of Reichstadt, after his father's defeat at Waterloo he was brought up a virtual prisoner in Vienna's imperial palaces. Here he found a kindred spirit in Sophie, whose husband preferred hunting, fishing, and military matters. In contrast, the duke accompanied Sophie to the opera and the theatre and read with her the latest French novels—until he contracted tuberculosis and after an agonisingly painful few weeks died, age twenty-one, in July 1832. The last time he smiled was reportedly when he heard the news that Sophie had given birth to a baby boy, Maximilian, two weeks earlier. Unfounded rumours soon circulated that the duke was the father and Maximilian was not a Habsburg, but a Bonaparte.

After the death of her friend, Sophie had another two sons, but she was especially dedicated to the two eldest, "Franzi" and "Maxi". A devout Catholic and ardent royalist, Sophie hated liberalism. Thus, her ideas for educating her children accorded with Habsburg tradition, which, as befitted one of the oldest dynasties in Europe, was modelled on a system developed in the Middle Ages. Children were in the hands of a governess until the age of six, when their formal education began, which was overseen by a male tutor until the age of eighteen. Finally, in theory at least, the father would serve as their guide to politics and statecraft.

Less than two years separated Maximilian and Franz Joseph, and they were educated together alongside their younger brother, Karl Ludwig, who was born in 1833. Their governess instilled in them the virtues of the Catholic faith alongside other more tangible traits, such as tidiness and punctuality. Franz Joseph excelled in these qualities, making sure to clear away his toys every night before bed. In contrast, Maximilian had a tendency to daydream. The boys' differences soon showed in other areas as well. A military upbringing was key to Habsburg life, and Sophie took her sons to parades in Vienna. After his first, Franz Joseph declared that he had never seen anything more beautiful, whereas the spectacle bored Maximilian. He preferred the Schönbrunn zoo, full of exotic animals. Hating the cold, Maximilian spent time enraptured amongst tropical plants housed in the palace's warm conservatories rather than watch military drill outside.

Sophie was more successful imbuing Maximilian with a love of literature. She invited writers to perform for the young archdukes,

Hans Christian Andersen even reading fairy tales to the boys. These performances made an impression on Maximilian. In his studies, his favourite tutor was an Englishman, Charles Gaulis Clairmont, who had excellent credentials as a literature teacher—he was brother to Claire Clairmont, Mary Shelley's stepsister and Byron's lover. Whereas Maximilian delighted in poetry and languages, quoting long passages of Shelley in English, Franz Joseph found them difficult and dull. When old enough, Maximilian would accompany his mother to the theatre, as the Duke of Reichstadt once had. Maximilian's love of arts reminded Sophie of herself, and she pandered to his imaginative and unruly spirit, which contrasted sharply with that of Franz Joseph, who took after his father and loved order and routine.

Yet despite their differences, the two brothers were extremely close. When Maximilian was ill, for instance, and confined to his room, Franz Joseph wrote him letters, telling him about the new toys they would play with when his brother was better. As a boy and then as a teenager, Maximilian looked up to, respected, and trusted his older brother.

A somewhat idyllic childhood ended when the boys entered the next stage of their education. Their tutor was charged with inculcating the conservative values that upheld the monarchy. God and the divine right of kings were at the heart of the curriculum, but these two concepts would not fill the punishing fifty hours a week that made up Maximilian's timetable. Only the hour after he woke up and the one before he went to bed were free. He rose at six and went to sleep at eight. The relentless seven days of study a week focussed on languages, geography, history, and natural sciences. Dancing, horse riding, and military drill were also on the syllabus.

Excelling in subjects he liked, Maximilian became a talented linguist, speaking French, Italian, Spanish, and English fluently. He also enjoyed literature and history. In other subjects, however, he was less enthusiastic. His mother complained that he hated everything that he found hard or did not enjoy. She knew that this attitude did not endear him to his teachers, writing that Maximilian was lazy and that his wild imagination meant he would talk excitedly about whatever notion caught his fancy. Sophie admitted that Franz Joseph was the better behaved of the two; however, Maximilian still won everyone over with his personality. She loved his playfulness, even as his restlessness made her worry about his future.

He enjoyed humour, too: teasing and practical jokes were Maximilian's comic metier. He made fun of teachers he did not like, whereas Franz Joseph displayed perfect deference. Maximilian also loved playing tricks. Dining with the emperor, Maximilian would pretend to sneeze, knowing that poor Ferdinand would say "Bless you" every time. On one occasion Maximilian dressed up in women's clothes and was introduced to his aunt as the princess of Modena, a ruse that worked until he let out a genuine sneeze, unbecoming of an elegant princess. On another occasion, after watching a performance of the opera *La sonnambula*, he reenacted the drama on the parapets of Schönbrunn, complete with a woman's nightdress and candle, much to the amusement of palace guards below.

Mischievous yet good-natured, Maximilian grew into an affable and charismatic, if contradictory, young man. He cut an impressive figure, tall for the time at around six feet, with a fair complexion, blue eyes, prominent sideburns, blondish hair, and a distinctive forked beard. "His eyes, which were of a bright china blue, beamed with kindness on whomsoever they rested", an acquaintance noted. "He looked and was a gentleman. His manner was attractive; he had the faculty of making one feel at ease", wrote another. But his character was complex, his actions inconsistent. Outgoing and gregarious when he wanted to be, he was also introspective and bound— sometimes crippled—by rigid ideas about honour and Habsburg etiquette. Although a dreamer by nature, he was acutely aware of how a young Habsburg should behave and so desperately wanted to live by the rules that as an adult he carried a well-thumbed card with twenty-seven aphorisms to encourage good conduct. One, written in English, simply read "Take it coolly"; other maxims included "Be kind to everyone," "Two hours' exercise daily," and "Nothing lasts forever".[1]

Just before Maximilian turned sixteen, in March 1848, his education was interrupted when news of the February Revolution in Paris reached Vienna. The cafés came alive with criticism of the Habsburg regime, but it was in another part of the empire, Hungary, where the first insurrection began. On March 3 a fiery nationalist, Lajos Kossuth, delivered a scathing attack. Criticising everything Maximilian had been brought up to believe, Kossuth declared that Habsburg absolutism was the "pestilential air which dulls our nerves and paralyses our spirits".[2] Within days this incendiary speech was clandestinely printed and distributed throughout the land, especially Vienna, where liberals, radicals, and students now demanded freedom of the press, the right to protest, and a democratic constitution.

On March 13 thousands took to the streets and marched on the Hofburg, the imperial palace at the heart of Vienna. Here the government met the masses with cannons and bayonets. The soldiers were showered with insults and, more painfully, makeshift missiles, including furniture thrown from apartments lining the streets. When a stone hit the commander, a regimental officer ordered the soldiers to open fire.

The crack of muskets announced that revolution had begun. Four civilians were killed, and a woman was trampled to death as the crowd stampeded away from the advancing troops. Further clashes raged through the night, lit by plumes of fire shooting from vandalised gas streetlights. To placate the crowds, the government announced the resignation of an unpopular minister, architect of conservative Europe Klemens von Metternich. This was followed by a proclamation that Emperor Ferdinand had agreed to grant a constitution.

Yet despite these concessions, the government lost control of its capital, and on May 17, 1848, the imperial family quietly slipped out of Vienna. Maximilian, still only fifteen, rode out alongside his parents to safety. For his mother, the humiliation was unbearable. She could have borne the loss of one of her children more easily, she told Maximilian, than the ignominy of submitting to a mass of students. Struck by the unpopularity of the autocratic regime as he rode through the hostile streets of Vienna, the humiliation of abandoning the capital and the palpable feeling of his mother's shame left a deep impression on Maximilian.

Incredible as it was to Sophie, the revolt continued to spread throughout Habsburg lands. Crucially, though, the army remained loyal. Franz Joseph, serving in the Austrian province of Lombardy-Venetia in northern Italy, played a leading part in putting down the popular insurrection. Compared with the ineffectual emperor, Ferdinand, fleeing his capital, Maximilian's older brother seemed a man of action behind whom the forces of order could rally. Seizing the initiative, Sophie organised a plan with leading generals and aristocrats: Ferdinand would abdicate, but not in favour of Franz Karl, who was next in line, but for his son Franz Joseph. Her husband, Sophie had concluded, was incapable of putting down the revolution. She convinced Franz Karl of this as well. So secret was the plan that not even Maximilian knew of it until the last moment.

On December 2, 1848, Maximilian watched as his brother was crowned emperor of Austria, surrounded by his family as well as the most distinguished aristocrats and clergy of the empire. For Maximilian, any joy he felt at Franz Joseph's coronation was tempered by the transformation in their formerly close relationship. No longer the playful younger brother, Maximilian was now next in line for the throne, and Franz Joseph recognised him as a potential rival. Moreover, as head of the Habsburgs, Franz Joseph in his official role now placed Maximilian in a subordinate position: he would have to request an audience to speak to his brother and required permission for any major decision, such as marriage, and Franz Joseph controlled his career as well.

More immediately, though, Maximilian was shocked at how his brother began his reign. Franz Joseph had promised to govern in the name of liberty and rights. Instead, he launched a vengeful crackdown across his empire, inviting Russian troops into Hungary to put down the rebels there, while permitting the arbitrary imprisonment, torture, and often execution of anyone suspected of insurrection. These measures restored order, but as his brother crushed the unrest and reneged on the promised constitution, Maximilian was appalled. His education had instilled a deep respect for Habsburg traditions, but he had also developed a sympathy for liberalism and political reform and urged clemency. Later he wrote about the summary executions, "We call our age the Age of Enlightenment, but there are cities in Europe where future men will look back with horror and amazement at the injustice of tribunals, which in the spirit of vengeance condemned to death those whose only crime lay in wanting something different to the arbitrary rule of governments which placed themselves above the law."[3] Alarmingly for his brother, Maximilian did not keep his criticisms private. Furthermore, his outgoing personality made him popular with Viennese society, especially in contrast to the stern, cold formality of his older brother. Franz Joseph's advisers made it clear to him that a likable, liberal prince was best kept far from Vienna—and even further from power.

While out for a stroll one day in Vienna, Franz Joseph realised how close Maximilian was to the throne. As the emperor walked along the city's fortifications, he stopped to watch military exercises on a parade ground below. A Hungarian revolutionary spotted his moment. He rushed at the emperor, knife readied to plunge into his back, but as the would-be assassin ran towards Franz Joseph an onlooker screamed. When Franz Joseph turned to see what was happening, the assailant's dagger was deflected towards the emperor's neck. Although Franz Joseph was badly wounded, his stiff military collar had absorbed the blow. Away from Vienna at the time, when Maximilian heard the news he hurried to his brother's sickbed. Exhausted, tired, and emotional, Maximilian was met with hostile indifference. Franz Joseph accused him of deserting his post without permission, interpreting his brother's haste to return to Vienna as eagerness to seize the imperial crown. In fact, a distraught Sophie had asked Maximilian to come, but the emperor wanted his brother nowhere near the capital.

For Franz Joseph, the incident vindicated an earlier decision to channel Maximilian's energies into the navy. Long sea voyages were the perfect occupation for an ambitious, popular younger brother, and the navy was a joke. Historically a land power, in 1815 Austria was confirmed to be in control of the former Venetian Republic's territory, now organised into the province of Lombardy-Venetia. With this came the remnants of the Venetian fleet, which became the Austrian Navy. Predominantly crewed by Italians with little loyalty to the Habsburgs, the fleet had disgraced itself in the eyes of Vienna by siding with the revolutionaries in 1848, who dreamt of a united Italy.

A naval career was not, however, quite the snub that it might have been for someone else. For many years, Maximilian had harboured dreams of becoming a sailor. Describing his first voyage, he wrote of his excitement at fulfilling a long-held ambition when boarding, as the national anthem played, the *Novara*. This frigate, named after an Austrian victory in Italy during the revolutionary wars of 1848–1849, was the pride of the Habsburg navy.

Maximilian impressed in his role, performing well as an officer and, in 1854, was appointed commander in chief of the Austrian Navy. At the age of twenty-two, he was young for the post, but he gained the respect of his fellow officers, working tirelessly to modernise the small fleet. With steam replacing sail and ironclads beginning to make wooden ships irrelevant, Maximilian embraced these technologies and persuaded his brother to grant the necessary funds. As commander in chief, Maximilian proved a capable administrator who relished modernity and change and transformed a makeshift fleet into a respected navy.

Another advantage of pushing Maximilian into the navy was that he would be based at the Adriatic port of Trieste, far from Vienna. Trieste was a cosmopolitan city with shipping links throughout the Mediterranean and beyond, and Maximilian grew to love the region so much that he decided to make it his permanent home, commissioning the construction of a castle a few miles outside the city. With building work beginning in 1856, he named the spot Miramar, in celebration of the magnificent view overlooking the sky-blue Adriatic, and involved himself in every detail. The site was a barren rock, but Maximilian transformed it into a bucolic paradise, with tall, shady trees and exotic plants. A keen natural scientist and lover of botany, he delighted in turning his imagination into reality, although the cost nearly bankrupted him.

What most defined Maximilian was the weight he attached to his dynasty, and he channelled this reverence into his castle, a fantastical, neo-Gothic exterior creating the impression of a medieval fairy tale. The interiors were decorated according to Maximilian's exacting plans, many of the rooms showing off his storied ancestors. Hanging from one wall, for instance, was an enormous illustrated genealogical painting that traced his ancestry back to the first Habsburg monarch, Rudolph I, whose reign began in 1218. On the opposite wall was a map of the world with the legendary Emperor Charles V at the centre. Everywhere the power of monarchy was celebrated. In the "Royal Room," there were fifteen portraits of the leading rulers of Europe; in the adjacent "Audience Chamber," Franz Joseph had centre stage. As a younger brother, Maximilian's own portrait could never hang in these rooms, but that did not stop him from dreaming of power: he commissioned a picture of himself in medieval Habsburg regalia, wearing a crimson imperial cloak with an eagle hovering above him.

Regardless of what he chose to hang on his walls, his role was not to govern but to serve. Given his brother's charm, Franz Joseph frequently put Maximilian to work as a diplomat, sailing the Mediterranean, showing the Austrian flag, and projecting Habsburg power. These journeys appealed to Maximilian's wanderlust, taking him to Jerusalem, Egypt, Greece, and Gibraltar, amongst other places, where his experiences ranged from Ottoman slave markets to tea parties with British officers and their wives.

Maximilian's travels reminded him of former Habsburg glories. During one trip to Spain, the sun beat down on the archduke as he sat in an amphitheatre watching a bullfight under a flawless blue sky. As the bull entered the arena, Maximilian roared with the crowd. The bull soon knocked over the horse of a picador. With fireworks burning from the bull's horns, the fighters eventually subdued the frenzied animal before the matador turned to Maximilian in his box, announcing the coup de grâce would be in honour of the Austrian aristocrat. The crowd fell silent, turning as one towards Maximilian. "A strange feeling" came over me, he wrote, as his imagination "fancied myself back in the fine old times, when the Hapsburgs were the rulers of this noble people."

To further sate his veneration for his ancestors, Maximilian visited the tomb of his namesake and the man who first brought the New World under Spanish rule, Ferdinand II of Aragon, grandfather of Charles V. Kneeling before the grave, Maximilian recalled how, even amongst the Spanish, "I was, as a legitimate relative, closest to the poor deceased, closer than the rulers and princes of the land; there I felt that, even after centuries, the feeling of being related takes hold, and a melancholic lamenting moved my soul". Rather than looking inward and protecting what Austria had left, Franz Joseph's preoccupation as emperor, Maximilian dreamt of former glories across the oceans, "a time when Spain, under the wings of the eagle [the Habsburg emblem], was on the highest pinnacle of power, and the greatest empire of the world; days when a mighty Hapsburger spoke the words, 'plus ultra'".[4]

IT WAS ON a diplomatic mission to France in May 1856 that Maximilian met a man who had turned a dream of becoming an emperor into a reality, Napoleon III. Describing the encounter for his brother, Maximilian penned an underwhelming portrait, highlighting Napoleon III's "short, unimposing stature, his exterior, which is utterly lacking in nobility, his shuffling gait, his ugly hands and the sly, inquiring glance of his lustreless eyes". The French emperor was socially awkward too, displaying "an insuperable embarrass-ment" and, at dinner, "was so ill at ease that the conversation was never entertaining". Maximilian felt he knew why: the emperor was embarrassed "in the presence of a prince of more ancient lineage". For his part, Napoleon III was indeed nervous. His empire was still young, visits from illustrious ruling houses were rare, and he was, no doubt, curious as to whether there was any truth to the rumours that Maximilian was the true heir of the Bonaparte name.

Of more concern to Maximilian were the easy manners of impe-rial France compared to the arcane rules, discipline, and deference of the Habsburg court, which he knew and loved obsessively. Empress Eugenie was overly friendly with her court ladies, even shaking their hands, which, the archduke related to his brother, was "a little shock-ing to our conceptions of imperial etiquette." Napoleon III spoke in a "reckless way" in front of his servants, "typical of a parvenu", and did not understand that one must "be careful not to expose oneself before those in subordinate positions".

Maximilian soon changed his mind about the French emperor. He left Paris with a favourable impression, recalling Napoleon III's "great calm and noble simplicity of character". Maximilian praised his "frankness and amiability" as well as his ability to "speak well and with animation, and the impression is heightened by a certain flash of the eyes."[5] The feeling was mutual. Maximilian charmed Napoleon III and Eugenie.

From Paris, Maximilian found himself disgusted by another court, Belgium's. Like much of Europe, Belgium's territory had once been ruled by Maximilian's ancestors and became independent only in 1831. After yet another revolution spread from France in 1830, the French-speaking Belgians, then part of the Netherlands, had rebelled against their Dutch rulers. With the nightmare of the French revolu-tionary armies and the first Napoleon still fresh in their minds, the major powers of Europe had then invented Belgium to put Europe back into a conservative sleep and prevent France from annexing the territory. If Napoleon III was a parvenu emperor, Belgium was a parvenu nation. "The higher nobility in the land", Maximilian noted with abhorrence, "rubs shoulders with its own tailors and cobblers."[6]

In nineteenth-century Europe, a new nation required a new king, and Leopold Saxe-Coburg-Saalfeld, the youngest son of a duke from a minor German dynasty, had been chosen for the Belgian throne. Maximilian's initial estimation of Leopold was low, not least because Leopold had cornered Maximilian and "involved me in an interminable political conversation" after a long dinner with the Belgian royal family. Unfortunately, it did not end there. Leopold ended the monologue with a promise to give "a lecture on political science and the balance of Europe; an offer which I received in yawning spirit."[7]

But the Belgian court did hold a more propitious encounter for Maximilian. Before he was king, Leopold had been married to Princess Charlotte of Wales, the only daughter of British king George IV. A year later, she died in childbirth. Leopold then married Louise-Marie, the daughter of the French king, Louis Philippe. She had four children, three sons and a daughter, Charlotte, named after Leopold's dead first wife. Better known to history as Carlota, Charlotte was considered one of the most beautiful princesses in Europe, and no doubt this is what first caught Maximilian's attention. Only sixteen when Maximilian saw her, she was slender and diminutive, her pale face framed with dark hair and liquid eyes. She was also clever. Like Maximilian, she was a talented linguist, but unlike him she had a practical intelligence, excelling at arithmetic as a student. She also read history—she boasted she could recite all the kings and queens of England—and philosophy as a young girl for pleasure.

She was serious, determined, and fiercely ambitious. At thirteen she had declared her two favourite subjects were religion and Plutarch, but chastised herself for not being "sufficiently keen on my studies". She resolved to study harder. "When I try to reason with myself," she wrote, "it makes no sense. It is very wicked of me to be so little grateful towards god for all the spiritual and material blessings he has given me. The only thing I want is what I cannot have, which proves that I must have a very twisted mind. I cannot conquer my laziness and I fall so easily, making resolutions which I cannot keep."[8]

So severe was she that she held her sister-in-law Marie-Henriette in contempt for her frivolity. In part, this was because Carlota disliked her eldest brother, later Leopold II, but, also because Carlota claimed that Marie-Henriette gave her headaches, always talking about the concerts she was organising. "It is insipid!" Carlota complained. Every day, she continued, Marie-Henriette would excitedly discuss whatever opera singer was coming next. "It bores me to death!"[9] It was shameful, thought Carlota, to have nothing but music in one's life.

It had been the death of her mother, Louise-Marie, that turned a playful child into a severe teenager. In the summer of 1850, when Carlota was only ten years old, she had fallen ill with whooping cough; her mother spent weeks at her bedside, nursing her. But the strain was too much for Louise-Marie, who had tuberculosis, and she died months later. Her father, Louis Philippe, had died only a few months earlier, which meant that Carlota's grandmother Marie-Amelie suffered the double tragedy of losing her husband and daughter. Carlota's concern was not for herself, but for her grandmother. Carlota wrote to her that she would do everything possible to replace what had been lost. This was, of course, an impossible burden for a ten-year-old, but Carlota would take on any responsibility to help those she loved. After the death of her mother and grandfather, she became devoted to her father, Leopold.

Like Napoleon III, Carlota was also driven by fate. Whereas the French emperor thought the secular forces of history intended him for greatness, though, it was divine Providence that gave Carlota her mission. A deeply pious Catholic, she believed that she was destined to carry out God's work. As the daughter of a Belgian king and granddaughter of a French king, Carlota was also born to rule; however, as a woman in the nineteenth century, she would need a husband if she hoped to play a leading political role commensurate with her ambitions. To that end, there were few bachelors more eligible than Maximilian.

When the elegant, charismatic, and sophisticated Maximilian swept into her life, Carlota was immediately impressed. Having read much but seen little, she was mesmerised by colourful stories of his foreign travels. They spent hours enjoying each other's company. "The archduke is charming in all respects", she wrote to her closest confidante. Physically, "I find him attractive, and morally he leaves nothing to be desired, that's all there is to say", she concluded with characteristic directness. "Our hearts always understand each other more and more", she wrote. That their views and sentiments were almost as one, she added, amounted to "true happiness".[10]

As the seriousness of the relationship became apparent, Leopold asked his niece the queen of England, Victoria, to appraise Maximilian during a visit he made to London. After spending time with him, she wrote to her uncle, "I cannot say how much we like the archduke; he is charming, so clever, natural, kind and amiable". Crucially for the queen, he was also "so English in his feelings and likings." Physically, "with the exception of his mouth and chin", which for the Habsburgs tended to be quite a large exception, Victoria found him "good-looking". She skirted over the mouth and chin issue, falling back on the time-honoured method of praising personality: "I think one does not the least care for that, as he is so very kind and clever and pleasant". In short, she concluded, "I am sure he will make [Carlota] happy, and is quite worthy of her."[11]

Despite Victoria's endorsement, Maximilian was neither Victoria's nor Leopold's preferred choice as a husband for Carlota, but the young princess was determined to marry whom she wanted, and what she wanted she usually got. After some haggling over finances, Leopold and Franz Joseph, who both had to approve the marriage, consented, and the wedding was held in Brussels on July 27, 1857. Carlota had just turned seventeen, Maximilian twenty-five. As befitted two of the most aristocratic people in Europe, the celebrations were extravagant. A week of festivities was organised, with lavish dinners, extravagant balls, and a public party where, according to the *Times*, some sixty thousand people attended and broke out into loud cheers when the couple appeared before them.

After the celebrations, a tearful Carlota said good-bye to her family before visiting her mother's tomb, praying for an hour while Maximilian waited. Then they travelled to Vienna, where Maximilian's mother immediately warmed to Carlota, although the other Habsburgs looked down on a mere Belgian princess. The wife of Franz Joseph, Elisabeth, was especially disdainful, adding more strain to the brothers' relationship. Their time in Vienna, though, was brief, for Leopold had written to Franz Joseph requesting that Maximilian be appointed to a prominent position. Franz Joseph agreed, making his brother the governor of one of the richest provinces in the empire, Lombardy-Venetia in Italy.

Despite its prestige, this position was a poisoned chalice. Although wealthy, Lombardy-Venetia was a hotbed of revolutionary intrigue and nationalist sedition. In 1848–1849, the province had nearly broken away from autocratic Austrian rule in favour of a liberal Italian nationalism. Johann Strauss's Radetzky March celebrates the crushing of this revolution, but foreign domination—sustained through the torture, imprisonment, and execution of opponents—stirred up hatred for Austria in those who still dreamed of Italian unification. Maximilian, already known in the region, and more liberal than Franz Joseph, was chosen in part to placate public opinion, but he was constrained in his efforts by his brother. Maximilian's role was limited; he was more ambassador than governor—real power, Franz Joseph ensured, remained in Vienna.

Maximilian was well aware that the people he governed saw the Habsburgs as foreign tyrants. His response was to try to win over hostile Italians by touring his kingdom and showing them the pomp and majesty of the Habsburg court. In this he was lucky to have Carlota, the epitome of regal elegance, wearing a rich crimson silk dress with white lace and a tiara of roses and diamonds when they made their entry into the capital of the province, Milan. Equally important, unlike her husband, who found formal social engagements tedious, Carlota relished the receptions, dinners, and balls, regaling everyone with her style and intelligence. If the entry into Milan had been triumphal, however, another arrival at Venice had been met by ominously silent crowds.

Maximilian, therefore, was determined to show that his governorship marked a radical departure from Austrian repression. Believing a liberal approach would unite the local nobility behind the dynasty, he delighted in being a patron of the arts and revelled in the Renaissance splendour of northern Italy, inviting artists and architects to his court. To further boost the regime's popularity, he frequently went out and met the people, implemented economic reforms to alleviate poverty, and drew up plans to change radically how the province was governed to placate nationalist sentiment. Instead of absolute control from Vienna, he proposed the province should have a senate, which would advise a governor entrusted with greater power.

After a year in the role, Maximilian went to Vienna to explain his reforms to Franz Joseph. They were dismissed out of hand. The emperor bluntly stated that his brother had been blinded to the wider interests of Austria. Rather than more freedom, what was needed in Lombardy-Venetia was greater repression. Franz Joseph ordered his brother to expand the secret police, arrest dissidents, and close down universities suspected of radicalism. This, Maximilian believed, would merely fuel revolution in northern Italy; however, there was nothing he could do. Writing to Sophie, he complained that his brother had managed to unite the region against Austria. "I am not afraid, for that is not the way of the Habsburgs, but I am silent and ashamed".[12] His plans constantly frustrated, he now lived in fear of crowds insulting him and Carlota or, worse, assassination. He was, he lamented, at the head of a moribund government whose ideas he could not defend, but duty prevented him from abandoning his post.

Soon the chaos Maximilian predicted was unleashed. Again it came from France, but, this time, the drama started with a night at the opera. On January 14, 1858, Napoleon III and Eugenie attended a charity gala at the Salle Le Peletier, the imperial opera house. As their carriage approached the theatre on the narrow street, an explosion rocked the coach, and one of the horses collapsed. A second and then a third explosion threw the entire carriage against the wall of the street, shrapnel hitting one of the companions opposite the emperor in the neck. Blood stained the empress's white dress; another piece of shrapnel had pierced the emperor's top hat. Then a man rushed the carriage, a dagger in one hand, a revolver in the other. A policeman intercepted him. The assassination attempt was over, but the streets were littered with wounded and dead horses and soldiers.

The failed assassination had been orchestrated by Italian nationalists. Their ringleader, Felice Orsini, was tried, convicted, and sentenced to death in February 1858. The assassin was a hero to many Italians. His trial whipped up nationalist fervour throughout Lombardy-Venetia, leading to demonstrations. In the face of these events, Maximilian showed great personal courage, often confronting protestors in person. On one occasion, arms locked with Carlota, he walked out to meet the crowds in Venice and then marched through the streets, facing down those who were hostile and rallying supporters. As more people began to follow Maximilian and Carlota, the streets became crowded, leaving no room for protestors. Soon afterwards, however, Maximilian felt it was no longer safe for Carlota and in the winter of 1858 sent her to Belgium, the first time they had been separated since their marriage.

Though Maximilian wanted to deal leniently with the dissidents, Franz Joseph had other ideas. The Austrian secret police, acting on orders from Vienna, broke up meetings and arrested suspects. When Maximilian then asked to be granted extraordinary civilian and military powers in order to preserve what he had tried to achieve in the previous two years, Franz Joseph instead sidelined him in favour of a military governor and then sacked him on April 19, 1859.

Two days after Maximilian's dismissal, Austria was at war with the northern Italian state Piedmont and, more seriously, France. The

Orsini assassination attempt had not only stirred up nationalist fury in Lombardy-Venetia, but also reminded Napoleon III of his own youthful involvement with Italian revolutionaries. The French emperor arranged a secret meeting with the prime minister of Piedmont and agreed to commit two hundred thousand French troops to drive the Austrians out of Italy. The French then crossed the Alps and defeated Habsburg forces at the battle of Magenta, prompting Franz Joseph, who had loved playing with toy soldiers as a child, to take personal command of the army. Joining his brother, Maximilian arrived in time to witness his defeat at the battle of Solferino. Commanding the victorious French army was Napoleon III, who routed the Austrians and forced Franz Joseph into a humiliating treaty, losing Lombardy. With Maximilian already shaken by Franz Joseph's treatment, this disgrace of Habsburg Austria at the hands of arriviste Bonapartist France deeply traumatised him.

Disillusioned with Europe, Maximilian now indulged his wanderlust and escaped for a few months to Brazil. Seeing the coast of Latin America for the first time, he combined a romantic quest for the unknown with the weight of his ancestry, reminiscing, "It seems to me to be a legend that I should be the first lineal descendent of Ferdinand and Isabella, to whom from childhood upwards it has been a daydream to visit this continent, now holding so important a place in the history of mankind."[13]

Excited by the New World, he returned even more disenchanted to the Old. Increasingly pessimistic, his only solace was with Carlota at his fairy-tale castle. Time away was difficult, especially visiting his family in Vienna. For him, the capital was cold, grey, and tedious. The empire's catastrophic defeat to France had resulted in profound changes, with Franz Joseph forced to adopt a federal constitution not dissimilar to what Maximilian had proposed for Lombardy-Venetia. For his archconservative mother, this was an abomination. Family dinners were tense and joyless. Moreover, Maximilian and Carlota found Franz Joseph's wife, Elisabeth, insufferable, petulant, and dismissive. Matters were not helped by the fact that on a visit to Miramar, Elisabeth's English sheepdog had attacked and killed Carlota's little lapdog, a present from her cousin Queen Victoria. An unrepentant Elisabeth merely remarked that she hated small dogs.

The rigid conservatism of his mother and older brother intensely frustrated Maximilian. If the monarchy were to survive, Maximilian believed, it must be dynamic and popular and embrace change. Rather than his Habsburg family, Maximilian now turned his affections towards his father-in-law. In contrast to Austria, Leopold seemed the embodiment of modern royalty. After all, Leopold ruled over Belgium as a constitutional monarch, with a parliament and a free press. Under this system, Belgium had not only weathered the 1848 revolutions when more powerful monarchies had fallen, but undergone rapid industrialisation. As a result, Maximilian's father-in-law wielded influence greater than anyone expected of such a small country. Maximilian was also an anglophile, impressed with British parliamentary democracy. Nor was it lost on him that the French empire, nominally based on the will of the people, had defeated not only his autocratic brother but also the embodiment of absolutist power, Russia. If Maximilian were ever to rule, Belgium, Britain, and France would be his models, not what he saw as the decrepit Austrian Empire.

Increasingly defining himself against his Habsburg family, Maximilian carefully cultivated his image as a modern, liberal man, a lover of literature, the arts, and science. Franz Joseph's subjects used to say that the only book he opened was the army list. By contrast, Maximilian read for pleasure and penned numerous poems published privately for the Viennese court as well as lengthy travel writings imbued with German romanticism. With its *Weltschmerz* (world weariness), nostalgia for the past, and love for the exotic, this movement reflected Maximilian's outlook. And these musings were a further chance to air his liberal views. After visiting Brazil, for instance, he railed against slavery, which was still practised in this Latin American kingdom.

Maximilian was convinced not only that he was born for greatness, but that he had already demonstrated significant talent as a leader. Many agreed with him. In the Austrian Navy, for instance, a loyal cadre of young officers hero-worshipped him as an officer-savant, while his governorship of Lombardy-Venetia was praised by friends and enemies alike. Maximilian had founded museums, supported the arts, and championed science, commissioning the frigate *Novara* to go on a celebrated voyage, the first Austrian ship to circumnavigate the globe. These events, however, had all taken place in the 1850s. With the work on Miramar completed in 1861, Maximilian no longer had a project, let alone a means of exercising what he felt were his considerable abilities.

And it was not just Maximilian who felt he was destined for greater things. Carlota, fiercely ambitious for herself and her husband, urged him on. In 1860 she wrote to a close confidante that "the day will come" when "Maximilian will be once again placed in a high position, I want to say that he would be a governor because he has been created for this and blessed by providence with everything that makes people happy. It seems to me impossible that these gifts should remain buried forever after having shone for scarcely three years."[14] Yet Franz Joseph, suspicious of his brother's popularity and what he saw as dangerously liberal views, would never give Maximilian such a role.

Bereft of purpose, Maximilian suffered debilitating bouts of depression, which left him in a state of mental paralysis for days. These fugues proved especially bad when away from Carlota. Without her, everything seemed empty and barren, and he found it difficult to work and be amongst people. The word he used to describe his mental state was *melancholy*. On one occasion, after spending time away from Carlota with his family in Vienna, he wrote to her, "I cannot tell you everything my poor heart felt as I prayed for you, my angel, and how sad it was not to be near you, my rock and my only centre. Last night, alone, I wanted to cry and was more sad and melancholic than in a long time."[15]

For the first Easter after his dismissal as governor of Lombardy-Venetia, he remarked that he would celebrate the holiday at a small local church amongst peasants and fishermen. "How different to previous years", he wrote to his wife. "Sic transit gloria mundi [Thus passes the glory of the world]".[16] Moreover, Carlota was less enamoured with Miramar than her husband. What stretched out ahead of them, she felt, was infinite boredom, staring at the sea from a rock until old age. In the autumn of 1861, José María Gutiérrez de Estrada offered a glorious future that could end Maximilian's life as a dilettante and Carlota's ennui.

THE THREE QUALITIES that most drew Gutiérrez de Estrada to Maximilian were that he was a Habsburg, a Catholic, and, above all, available. On July 4, 1861, therefore, Gutiérrez de Estrada wrote to Richard Metternich, Austrian ambassador to France, son of the great diplomat, and a favourite of Eugenie in Paris. Gutiérrez de Estrada reiterated what he had long argued—monarchy was the only system that could save Mexico—before enquiring whether Maximilian might consider becoming emperor. Metternich forwarded the letter to Count Johann Bernhard von Rechberg, the Austrian foreign minister. Metternich explained that in his opinion, the plan was "not without grandeur", but from a practical point of view it was "deplorable and discouraging".[17]

Rechberg agreed, replying that it would be an "incontestable advantage and a striking triumph to the see the monarchical principle, so shaken in Europe, restored in the New World." Moreover, Austria would be happy to see such a glorious mission fall to the Habsburgs, but, as Gutiérrez de Estrada himself admitted, success would depend on the major naval powers. "We have not had any positive indications," Rechberg continued, that Britain and France would support a "restoration of the monarchical principle in Mexico". Nonetheless, Rechberg added, "We do not, however, want to discourage this diplomat", but only make known to him that Austria could not yet commit to an enterprise that required "conditions more favourable than the present."[18]

After his drawing-room discussion with Eugenie and José Manuel Hidalgo y Esnaurrízar in September, Napoleon III was now firmly, though unofficially, trying to achieve those favourable conditions. The first battles of the American Civil War had confirmed his belief that the conflict between the Union and Confederacy would not be resolved quickly. With Washington powerless to intervene, Napoleon III needed to act fast to claim suzerainty of Latin America and reclaim Mexico for monarchical Europe, but he still required a monarch. Although careful to present Maximilian as the only choice, Napoleon III had, in fact, considered many other candidates. The French emperor liked Maximilian, thought he was a competent individual, and understood the prestige of the Habsburg name, but, as with Gutiérrez de Estrada, what especially marked the archduke out for the position was that he seemed the most likely to accept—that and the insistence of Eugenie, who was certain Maximilian was their man. Making informal overtures through Metternich, Napoleon III thus let it be known that France would support Maximilian's candidature if convenient in Vienna. If so, France would ensure Britain and Spain backed the scheme.

Armed with these vague promises, Rechberg put the matter before Franz Joseph, who would have to give permission before Maximilian could accept the crown. For Franz Joseph, frequently and unfavourably compared to his popular younger brother, it would be no great loss to see the underemployed Maximilian in Mexico. The emperor, therefore, instructed his foreign minister to go to Miramar and suggest the idea in person.

Maximilian found this first discussion intoxicating. As he explained after hearing the idea, "I shall always, and in every circumstance of life, be found ready to make every sacrifice, however heavy it may be, for Austria". By taking the throne, Maximilian continued, "I by no means underestimate the great advantage this would be to

Austria, in reviving the lustre" of the Habsburgs. Whereas others were advancing, Austria was retreating after the humiliating defeat to France in Italy. Maximilian claimed, "None see more clearly than I that it is the duty of our house to wipe out this stain."[19] Estranged from his brother, believing that his natural ability to govern had been thwarted in Lombardy-Venetia, and disillusioned with his lack of opportunity in Europe, power and glory in Mexico captivated him.

Maximilian, however, made no decisions without consulting Carlota. Indeed, critics said that he made no decisions whatsoever; his wife did. Carlota was as enraptured as her husband, believing Providence had delivered them the Mexican crown. "Such a beautiful thing", she wrote to her brother, adding, "Max has all the talents necessary to rule a great empire". She had also bought into the idea of Habsburg destiny, writing that Maximilian might bring "order and civilisation" to the place where Hernán Cortés had "first carried the flame of the faith in the name of Charles V".[20]

Carlota's father, Leopold, also supported the idea. Maximilian wrote to him in October, forwarding all the information he had received on Mexico. Despite having never been there and without any knowledge whatsoever about the country, Leopold pronounced Mexico perfectly suited to monarchy. The view of Carlota's older brother was even clearer: "Mexico is a magnificent country", he wrote to his sister. "If I had a son of age I would try to make him king of Mexico".[21]

Placing people on thrones, especially Habsburgs, was a time-honoured European tradition, nor was it merely an archaic practice. As a newly founded monarchy, Leopold's Belgium provided one example for Maximilian and Carlota, while Sweden and Greece had recently had foreign rulers invited, or imposed, upon them. Mexican monarchists went further back in history to justify their calls for a foreign king, using the example of 1688 and the Glorious Revolution in England when Parliament asked William of Orange to take the throne, albeit with the assistance of some fifteen thousand foreign troops. Additionally, because of US hostility to their scheme,

Mexican conservatives delighted in arguing that even the United States owed its independence to French intervention because in the eighteenth century French king Louis XVI sent men and ships to help defeat British forces in America.

As keen students of history, these examples encouraged Maximilian and Carlota, but the list of present-day supporters was just as impressive. With the emperor and empress of the French, the king of the Belgians, the Austrian Foreign Ministry, and Maximilian's own brother now all backing the idea of placing them on the Mexican throne, the scheme did not seem outlandish. Confidentially, Maximilian let it be known to Gutiérrez de Estrada that he was interested.

Nonetheless, Maximilian had reservations. He feared that the United States might invade his new kingdom, and, even if it did not, he worried that a monarchy would be unpopular in republican Mexico. He therefore placed two conditions on definitive acceptance. First, Britain and France must sign a military alliance protecting the new kingdom. Second, the Mexican people must declare in his favour through a vote.

Desperate to convince Maximilian of the popularity of monarchy, Gutiérrez de Estrada cobbled together a petition signed by like-minded Mexicans. It was not, however, quite the expression of the nation that it purported to be, signed, as it was, by only six names, one of whom was Gutiérrez de Estrada's son. Knowing this was not enough, the Mexican monarchist bombarded the archduke with letters asking for a personal interview where he could allay doubts. Still circumspect, and wishing to avoid public scandal, Maximilian instead sent his secretary to Paris to discuss Gutiérrez de Estrada's vision.

Returning to Miramar impressed, Maximilian's agent debriefed the archduke. Gutiérrez de Estrada had indeed been persuasive, arguing that with the genius of Napoleon III and the backing of Mexican patriots, the affair was destined to succeed. Excited, that same day, October 12, Maximilian himself wrote to Gutiérrez de Estrada. Maximilian praised the zeal and devotion that the émigré had given to a cause "worthy of all my attention". He concluded with a terrible pun: "I hope that with the help of god these patriotic efforts . . . will end by being crowned with success."[22]

Meanwhile, Napoleon III was not taking any chances. His plan was now so advanced, and Maximilian so indispensable to its success, that the emperor stepped in, engaging his officials to dispel any fears the archduke had over the popularity of monarchy in Mexico. Private briefings designed to be reported back to Vienna were arranged. An Austrian diplomat was told that upon the arrival of French, Spanish, and British forces, the population would "rise up and declare" itself for monarchy. "All the information we have received", a French minister said, "supports this". For his part, Napoleon III wrote in a letter he knew would be shown to Maximilian that "as soon as our squadrons appear before Veracruz, a considerable party in Mexico is ready to seize power, to call a national assembly and to proclaim a monarchy."[23]

Having finally secured a monarch after twenty-one years of trying, albeit for a still imaginary kingdom, Gutiérrez de Estrada was determined not to lose Maximilian's interest. Aware that he needed to name as many backers as possible, he co-opted the powerful Mexican bishop Pelagio Antonio de Labastida y Dávalos, who, though exiled in Europe, wielded great influence over the Mexican clergy. Gutiérrez de Estrada also sent agents to Mexico to rally the Conservative Party behind monarchy, while making sure that he kept Maximilian informed of all these plans through letters that now named an assortment of Mexican monarchists. Eventually, the briefings from Paris combined with Gutiérrez de Estrada's relentless campaign saw Maximilian put caution to one side: he invited the Mexican monarchist to spend Christmas at Miramar.

There, when they met, Gutiérrez de Estrada spent hours flattering the archduke, painting him as the saviour of Mexico. Describing the meeting afterwards, Gutiérrez de Estrada reached the full heights of his grandiose obsequiousness. Before meeting Maximilian, the Mexican wrote, he already held the archduke in high regard, but after "being witness to noble and rare qualities which are found in such great number and to such a high degree in your imperial majesty, this esteem and sympathy have become the most noble admiration, the most perfect devotion and, dare I say it, the most cordial and the most enthusiastic attachment." He continued, "I will never forget the fortunate moment where, for the first time, I saw your imperial highness". In case the point was not coming across, Gutiérrez de Estrada added that along with his wedding—he did not stipulate which one, for he had been married three times—it was the "most beautiful day" of his life.[24]

Such flattery had its desired effect and, convinced now of his future as emperor, Maximilian, always a dreamer, began to sketch out the infinite possibilities of his new empire. Franz Joseph was staying at nearby Venice, and the brothers celebrated the new year together, with Maximilian excitedly discussing his future kingdom. Franz Joseph agreed to lend the *Novara* to take his brother to Mexico. Until his arrival, Maximilian proposed, a regency would govern in his place. He would create a Mexican aristocracy, Maximilian explained, the title Duke of Veracruz especially appealing to him. These lengthy talks even covered who would make up the imperial household, Carlota's ladies-in-waiting, and the honours system Maximilian would introduce.

Having become emperor of Mexico in his mind, Maximilian decided to put an end to back channels and on January 2, 1862, wrote directly to Napoleon III. Just as the French emperor had seemingly brought order after the chaos of revolution in France, so too would Maximilian in Mexico. "I am, therefore," wrote Maximilian, "following in Your Majesty's footsteps in attaching my acceptance of the offer". Maximilian added the caveat that this was conditional on the "clearly expressed" wishes of the Mexican nation.[25] He did not even mention the other condition, British support as well as French, because Napoleon III had told him that it had been secured.

This was a lie.

3

FRENCH INVASION

The great director of mid-nineteenth-century British foreign policy, Henry John Temple, Lord Palmerston, had warned that the United States "will in Process of Time [*sic*] become Masters of the whole American Continent North and South". This was, he concluded, against British interests, but there seemed little that could be done to stop it. As Palmerston was now the British prime minister, Napoleon III was confident he could count on him to back a scheme designed to check US expansion. Outlining his monarchist conspiracy in a letter to be brought to Palmerston's attention, Napoleon III wrote that while the redress of "legitimate grievances" was the "ostensible purpose" of the joint French, British, and Spanish intervention in Mexico, it would be foolish to "tie one's hands in a manner to prevent a solution that would be in the interests of all".[1]

After seeing the letter, Palmerston agreed that a monarchy was preferable to a republic and that Maximilian would make a good sovereign; however, the British prime minister had his doubts. He questioned the popularity of monarchy in Mexico. Even with the support of the people, Palmerston reasoned, sustaining a monarchy across the Atlantic would require some twenty thousand European troops and many millions of pounds, neither of which Britain was willing to contribute. Once informed of the plan, Lord John Russell, the British foreign secretary, was even more sceptical, telling the French ambassador that while the British supported intervention to make Juárez repay foreign debts, they would have nothing to do with any attempt to overthrow the president and replace him with Maximilian. So adamant was the foreign secretary that he insisted on inserting into the Convention of London, the agreement that governed the joint intervention, a clause that bound Napoleon III's hands: the allies would not interfere in the internal politics of Mexico.

Given that Maximilian's acceptance was conditional on British support, Napoleon III's plan to reorder the Americas should have ended there. But Napoleon III simply ensured Maximilian never heard Palmerston's views. Instead, Napoleon III cheerfully explained to Richard Metternich that while Britain had initially been hostile, after seeing his letter Palmerston had supported the plan. If Maximilian accepted the crown, Napoleon III claimed, "then in twenty-four hours the thing is done".[2]

Signed on October 31, 1861, the Convention of London immediately became public knowledge, and Austrian diplomats asked awkward questions. Surely, the clause forbidding political interference in Mexico precluded an attempt to found a monarchy? Far from it, French politicians argued. In fact, they claimed, Britain was secretly in agreement, but could not put it in writing for fear of public opinion, parliamentary scrutiny, and opposition from the United States. So successful was this French disinformation that by the end of November, Metternich wrote to Rechberg, "Will the Mexican affair continue as well as it has begun? To hear the emperor talk we would be justified to believe it." Entirely unaware that he had been misled, the Austrian ambassador continued, "What is certain is that up to the present not a single fault has been committed."[3]

By the end of November 1861, six thousand Spanish, three thousand French, and eight hundred British troops were sailing to Mexico. Napoleon III gambled that Russell's nonintervention clause would be overridden by an additional one that the French emperor had

insisted on: commanders of the allied forces on the spot were authorised to execute any operations they deemed necessary in response to
local circumstances. As the French commander would work alongside Dubois de Saligny, a man who needed no encouragement to
fall out with anyone, it would be simple to engineer a rupture with
Juárez's government. Then, in response to whatever supposed outrage
Juárez was responsible for, the allies would march on Mexico City
and proclaim Maximilian emperor.

The commander in chief of the French forces, Admiral Jurien de
La Gravière, was issued secret instructions so that, unlike his British
and Spanish counterparts, he was aware of this plan. Napoleon III
stressed that upon European forces arriving in Mexico, one of two
things would happen. Ideally, the Mexicans "would immediately ac-
claim the Prince who will be named for them at the right time".
More likely, however, Juárez's forces "will try to perpetuate the state
of anarchy we wish to stop. In the first case, everything is settled,
but we must reflect on the second possibility."[4] In this eventuality,
Napoleon III told La Gravière privately before he set sail, French
troops must occupy the capital.

Napoleon III placed great emphasis on La Gravière fighting his
way to the capital because he had told Maximilian another lie. Far
from cheering crowds welcoming the allies, the French emperor
knew that popular support for monarchy was uncertain. Napoleon
III had offered Miguel Miramón an enormous sum of money if the
former president would go to Mexico with French troops, help overthrow Juárez, and proclaim Maximilian emperor. Miramón refused.
There was, he said, no monarchist party in Mexico.

As Miramón made clear, support for monarchy in Mexico was
far from guaranteed. Conservatives might rally behind Maximilian,
but they were scattered across the country and were not likely to
appear at Veracruz, the seat of Juárez's government during the civil
war and a liberal stronghold. As rumours circulated in Paris over the
practicality of the scheme, the previously sanguine Metternich began
to have doubts. "How many cannon shots will be required to bring

an emperor to Mexico, and how many will be required to keep him there? This is what I always ask myself."[5] He would soon have the opportunity to find out.

On January 9, 1862, French forces reached the port of Veracruz. Jurien de La Gravière was under no illusions. "I don't put any faith in the sympathies of the country", he wrote. To reach Mexico City, we must "wage war". "This isn't an expedition", he concluded. "It is a campaign". The admiral, though, was confident: "I have faith in three things, the bravery of our soldiers, the weakness of the Mexicans, and the wisdom of the emperor's plans".[6]

As they sailed towards land, the French soldiers' first sight of Mexico was the peak of Orizaba, 18,491 feet high, looming above the horizon, its top crowned with snow. Veracruz itself, gateway to the country, was less impressive. Approaching the town, a French officer, François Charles du Barail, remarked that "it appeared to us a black stain on a yellow backdrop".[7] Like many of the battle-hardened French expeditionary force, Barail was a veteran of the brutal colonial repression of Algeria. For these soldiers, Veracruz, surrounded by sand dunes, seemed like a piece of the Sahara stuck onto the coast of North America. But the French knew Algeria well; Mexico was a journey into the unknown. The army did not even have maps and had to borrow one from Napoleon III's personal collection.

Determined not to start a war with Britain, France, and Spain, Juárez allowed their combined forces to occupy Veracruz, but the question for the allied commanders was what to do next? True to form, Saligny wanted to immediately engineer a casus belli with Juárez. Knowing his demands would be refused, the French diplomat insisted Mexico pay France a $12 million indemnity. His allies, however, were in Mexico to discuss debt repayment, not settle spurious French claims. The Spanish commanding officer, Juan Prim y Prats, had been the last person Napoleon III wanted in charge. Ambitious, vain, and extravagant, Prim frequently clashed with Saligny. Worse still, Prim sympathised with Juárez. His wife's family even had ties to the Mexican government. The British representative Charles Wyke detested Saligny too and had no hesitation in rejecting his approach to negotiations. More to the point, though Wyke himself supported monarchy in Mexico, his orders prohibited British forces marching into the interior.

As the diplomats argued amongst themselves, the troops languished. Known to travellers as a charnel house for Europeans, Veracruz was so disease ridden that the British refused to even disembark their marines. The French were not so lucky. Crammed into what accommodation they could find, they found the heat suffocating, and locals—the men with flared trousers, serapes, and sombreros, the women dressed in ragged shawls or black mantillas—eyed the foreigners with hostility. Black-feathered vultures, known as *zopilotes*, which lined the streets and perched on the buildings, completed the port's "dismal and desolate appearance", as one French soldier noted. It reminded him "of a beautiful young woman who, ravaged by fever, has lost all her beauty".[8] Officers were kept busy filing reports, looking for suitable houses to garrison troops, and visiting hospitals to give comfort to the dying. The soldier had been right to fixate on disease. The first battles the French fought were against boredom, mosquitoes, and yellow fever—known in Mexico as *"vómito negro"* because internal bleeding turns the victim's vomit black. At the end of January, the expeditionary force reported 335 sick, more than 10 percent of the total.

As the crow flies, the journey from Veracruz to Mexico City is about 240 miles, but it was an arduous march from sea level to above 6,500 feet along bad roads and through difficult mountain passes. Without Spanish and British support, it would be suicidal for Jurien de La Gravière's small army to invade Mexico alone. But Prim and Wyke refused to support Saligny, and if the French stayed in Veracruz, then disease would destroy the expeditionary force.

Weeks of complex diplomacy between the allies and the Mexican government therefore followed, culminating in what was known as the Preliminaries of La Soledad. In return for allowing their troops to leave Veracruz's disease-ridden lowlands, the representatives of Britain, France, and Spain now agreed to acknowledge Juárez's government as legitimate before continuing negotiations. Desperate to move his troops inland, Jurien de La Gravière and a truculent Saligny signed the document on February 20. More than a month into the intervention, far from overthrowing the government and founding a monarchy, the allied forces had formally recognised Juárez as president of the Mexican republic.

WITH NEWS TAKING four to six weeks to reach Europe from Mexico, Napoleon III was oblivious to this lack of progress. He spoke as though the plan was an accomplished fact. Replying to Maximilian on January 14, 1862, Napoleon III began his letter, as he now would all his correspondence to the archduke, *"Monsieur mon frère"*. Along with fraternal sympathy, the salutation implied equality in rank, as if Maximilian were already emperor of Mexico. Napoleon III knew exactly how to flatter Maximilian, adding that the archduke was ideally suited for this "great and noble mission" because of his personal qualities combined with his illustrious ancestry. Never, Napoleon III continued, "will any task produce greater results. For it is a question of rescuing a whole continent from anarchy and misery; of setting an example of good government to the whole of America; and lastly raising the monarchist flag, based upon wise liberty and a sincere love of progress, in the face of dangerous utopias and bloody disorders."[9]

For all his confidence, Napoleon III realised that his initial expeditionary force was too small to accomplish what was required, and so in January he sent forty-five hundred more troops to Mexico under the command of General Charles Ferdinand Latrille, Comte de Lorencez. To rally local support, Napoleon III also wanted his own Mexican man on the spot, someone who could ensure that those in Mexico who backed the French intervention followed orders from Paris. For this task, the French emperor chose another exile, Juan Nepomuceno Almonte.

Born in 1803, Almonte was the son of a Mexican independence hero, José María Morelos, who had taken his family with him on military campaigns against the Spanish. His name, the story went, came from the times his mother would cry *"al montes"* (to the hills) when faced with superior Spanish forces. Before royalists executed Morelos in 1815, Almonte had been sent to New Orleans for safety. He returned to Mexico after independence, and his political journey took him from the company of radical liberals to the Conservative Party before establishing himself as a leading Mexican monarchist. A supporter of the conservative government during the civil war of 1858–1861, he was Miramón's diplomatic representative to France, but when Juárez took control of Mexico City in 1861 he was sacked. He remained in Paris, working with José Manuel Hidalgo y Esnaurrízar to promote monarchy, becoming a close confidant of Napoleon III.

Now, in January 1862, Napoleon III sent him to Miramar to hand-deliver a letter to Maximilian. The archduke should, the French emperor urged, appoint Almonte his representative in Mexico. Maximilian agreed and was thrown into excited action by the idea. Days of intense discussion between the pair followed, as Maximilian sketched out the detail of his imaginary empire to Almonte. Dusting off his plans for Lombardy-Venetia and drawing heavily on Napoleon III's example in France, Maximilian drafted a provisional liberal constitution. Ever the aristocrat, he decided that the old Spanish titles of nobility would be recognised, while Almonte was given authority to create barons, counts, and marquises. With these details settled, Almonte left for Mexico with the French reinforcements.

Napoleon III's selection of Almonte spoke volumes, too, of his views of some of the other candidates for the role. The French emperor did not trust José María Gutiérrez de Estrada or his allies, such as the exiled bishop of Puebla, Pelagio Antonio de Labastida y Dávalos. Indeed, despite having one of the most impressive address books in Europe, and not from want of trying, Gutiérrez de Estrada had never met Napoleon III. After pleading with Maximilian to get him an audience, the Mexican monarchist was finally granted an interview on January 16, 1862. Napoleon III and Eugenie had been underwhelmed. When asked what he thought of the Mexican, Napoleon III replied, "Nothing at all; he is a man who never stops talking". Eugenie was even more damning: "He is like a portrait that has been nailed to the wall for centuries and suddenly comes to life in the present". In Gutiérrez de Estrada, she thought she saw the ghost of Philip II, king of Spain from 1556 to 1598.[10] Hardly a revolutionary herself, Eugenie was shocked at the reactionary Mexican; Napoleon III refused to receive him again.

The emperor of the French believed that he represented progress, what he called the spirit of the century, a *juste milieu* between liberalism and conservatism. He drew on support from the Catholic Church but maintained, insofar as he interpreted them, the values of the French Revolution of 1789. Crucially, he supported freedom of worship and the nationalisation of church property, and he believed that the will of the people, directly expressed, should be the basis of government.

For his own ends, Napoleon III was using reactionaries like Gutiérrez de Estrada and Labastida, but the French emperor was at odds with their political views. For these Mexicans, liberalism was an impious philosophy that had ruined their country. They further argued that Catholicism must be the religion of the state to the exclusion of all others and that democracy was unworkable. Labastida reserved special disdain for 1789, fond, as he was, of delivering thunderous sermons on the evils of "revolution", meaning anything that deviated from the teachings of the Catholic Church. Not one for understatement, a typical polemic lambasted the "madness without precedent. The crimes without example" of liberal revolutions, which had left "Mexico, Catholic Mexico, noble and wealthy Mexico, plundered, scandalised, demoralised, persecuted, a place of evil, slave to the most bastard interests, prey to the most hateful, frenzied passions, weak, poor, miserable, consumed, affronted, ridiculed, despised, and hated by all the people on the face of the earth."[11]

As reports reached him of the impasse at Veracruz, Napoleon III had delayed writing to Maximilian. On March 7, 1862, he finally broke his silence: "I did not answer Your Imperial Highness before because I was waiting to receive news from Mexico before doing so", he explained. "That which has arrived", he continued, "is not very good because General Prim seems to be animated by personal ambition and has caused Admiral Jurien to take a number of rash steps." Napoleon III believed that "my reinforcements will alter the situation". Lacking any evidence, he claimed that the monarchist party in Mexico was making "remarkable progress" and that everything was in place for his plan to succeed.[12]

But then, on March 19, 1862, news of the Preliminaries of Soledad reached Napoleon III. When he heard, he was apoplectic, immediately sacking La Gravière and placing Lorencez in military command, while Saligny alone was to lead the political direction, working closely with Almonte. Privately, Napoleon III fumed that if he had wanted to negotiate so weakly, he would not have sent his military.

Still without information, but convinced that under Lorencez, Saligny, and Almonte his army must be marching on Mexico City, Napoleon III wrote to Maximilian on June 7, 1862, that the "news from Mexico is very good," as "we have at last emerged from the fumbling and ridiculous advances that General Prim was making to the Mexican government". Napoleon III predicted that "the next post will no doubt bring decisive news, for if the great city of Puebla declares for us, the odds are that the rest [of Mexico] will follow." Concluding, he wrote, "I am most anxious to know what has been going on for the last month, General Lorencez wrote me that he reckoned upon being in Mexico City on 25 May at the latest."[13]

WHILE THE ALLIES spent months fighting amongst themselves, Juárez prepared to resist. He ordered twenty-five thousand new guns to reequip the Mexican Army and appointed Ignacio Zaragoza to command the Army of the East, which would defend the inland approaches from Veracruz. Key points on the route to Mexico City were fortified, while Juárez rallied the people: "Mexicans! . . . I appeal to your patriotism . . . , put aside hatred and the enmity . . . and sacrificing your resources and your blood, unite behind the government and in defence of the greatest and most sacred cause for humanity: the defence of our country."[14] For those who remained unconvinced, Juárez decreed on January 25, 1862, that anyone caught helping the intervention would be court-martialled and executed.

On March 4, 1862, nearly two months after French forces landed in Mexico, General Lorencez arrived with reinforcements. Now the French army was roughly seventy-three hundred men. This was still half the number of US troops General Winfield Scott commanded when he successfully fought his way to Mexico City in 1847; however, the French expected local support. A week before, Almonte had reached Veracruz and began to rally Mexican conservatives around the French.

This astonished Wyke. Although he personally respected Almonte, the British diplomat pointed out in a letter to Jurien de La Gravière, the man was a known leader of the Conservative Party, which was openly at war with Juárez. Worse, some of the men now working with the French were notorious for atrocities committed during the civil war. Concluding his letter, Wyke wrote that he could not believe the French government would give protection to men he considered little better than bandits, especially the infamous Leonardo Márquez.

Forty-two years old in 1862, Márquez was a ruthless, battle-hardened soldier with the manic glint of the devout in his eyes. He had fought in the US-Mexican War, but gained notoriety for his violence during the civil war, earning the nickname "the butcher of Tacubaya" or, if you were a conservative, "the tiger of Tacubaya". He gained this sobriquet in April 1859 when he had defeated liberal forces marching on Mexico City at the nearby town of Tacubaya, thereby saving the conservative government. After the battle, Márquez executed prisoners and took part in a "universal butchery" of the wounded and noncombatants, including medical students who had aided the dying. According to the *Times*, "Prominent persons and others suspected of liberalism were lanced, shot and mutilated in the most horrible manner".[15] The conservative story was different: seventeen traitors who had helped the liberal army were taken prisoner and executed; Márquez was the saviour of Mexico City.

In Wyke's view, Márquez was "infamous" for what the diplomat considered a far more heinous crime than killing innocent Mexicans. He had stolen money from the British. Acting under orders from his bankrupt government, it was Márquez who broke into the British legation and requisitioned $660,000, destined for London. One of the most effective generals in Mexico, Márquez was also one of the most reactionary, with an absolute devotion to the Catholic Church and a visceral hatred for liberals, or "demagogues," as he called them. The hatred was mutual. Juárez had declared Márquez an outlaw and put a $10,000 bounty on his head.

Although he had yet to rendezvous with the French, Márquez still commanded enough armed men to look after himself, but other conservatives whom Juárez similarly deemed criminals sought asylum in the French camp. Two such men were conservative generals, Robles Pezuela and Antonio Taboada, but their problem was that to get to the French, who, under the terms of the agreement signed with Juárez, had moved inland to higher ground near Veracruz, they had to travel through territory controlled by Juárez's government. They made it to a village only a few miles from a French camp, but Juaristas—as those who supported Juárez were known—were hunting them. Fearful for their lives, Robles Pezuela and Antonio Taboada raced the last leg of their journey on horseback. As they were riding, a lasso encircled Robles, and a hundred cavalrymen appeared from behind a ravine where they had been hiding. Taboada, trusting in God, and, perhaps more reliably, his excellent horse, burst into a gallop, sabre in hand, and broke through the liberal troops. Although injured, he made it to the protection of the French.

Robles was less fortunate. He was taken as a prisoner to a nearby town. On learning of his capture, Zaragoza merely said, "Let him be shot". Robles, for his part, denied he was a traitor. He hoped that if he explained his reasons for joining the French, his life would be spared. He was convinced, he argued, that if Mexico continued as it had before, then "there is no possible salvation for our unfortunate country; it will return to barbarism, and its territory will be occupied by the people who covet it [that is, the United States]". Robles added that he had not even resolved to join the French intervention, but merely wanted to find out what their plan was before deciding anything. "That is my crime," he concluded. "If I deserve death for it, just is the order of Zaragoza".[16] He was executed.

Lest other powerful military allies and the likes of Márquez meet the same fate, the French decided to move farther inland to protect their allies. On April 9, the French finally broke with Britain and Spain. Ten days later, military operations began. It was a bold move. Juárez could field some sixty thousand, albeit spread across the country, whereas, after those sick or required for garrison duty were accounted for, Lorencez had only six thousand French troops.

So it was that this small French army found itself marching alone in Mexico's vastness, approaching the town of Puebla, the nation's second city and a key strategic point on the route to the capital. Zaragoza had had months to fortify and prepare for any attack, but Lorencez was not worried. As the French general wrote to the minister of war, "We have over the Mexicans such a superiority of race, of organisation, of discipline, of morality . . . that I beg Your Excellency to be good enough to inform the emperor that now at the head of 6,000 soldiers I am the master of Mexico". Monarchy, he was also convinced, "is the only government suitable to Mexico".[17]

After winning some skirmishes, the French marched into the valley of Puebla. Here, at an altitude of some sixty-five hundred feet, they found themselves in fertile farmland, dotted with wealthy haciendas and villages, beneath towering mountains. To the east was the snowcapped Mount Orizaba; to the west were the enormous peaks of Iztaccíhuatl and the volcano of Popocatépetl rising some ten thousand feet on the horizon. Despite occasional torrential rain, the mornings were beautiful and clear.

On May 4, 1862, a few miles from Puebla, at three in the afternoon, the expeditionary force occupied the small village of Amozoc. The streets were deserted, the houses shut up, and an eerie silence reigned, except for the occasional sound of dogs barking. In the distance, the French soldiers saw a group of indigenous Mexicans, their backs bent under the weight of their possessions, fleeing towards Puebla. The six thousand marched in, taking possession of the abandoned village. That evening the small army's spirits were high. They dined on a now familiar cuisine of tortillas and beans. Meanwhile, in a poorly furnished house situated on the side of the main square, Lorencez and his officers planned their tactics. Outnumbered two to one by Zaragoza and his twelve thousand men inside the city, the French general did not have time or numbers for a siege. He resolved to storm Puebla the next day.

Puebla was a typical Spanish colonial city, with straight streets and numerous churches and convents, which loomed over the skyline. Situated on high ground, two forts, Guadalupe and Loreto, guarded the approach to the city. Built by Franciscans in the sixteenth century, these former monasteries were now imposing fortifications. Lorencez believed that if his army took Guadalupe, it would so demoralise Zaragoza that he would surrender or flee.

On May 5, nervous defenders looked on at a terrifying sight not seen in the Americas for decades: a European army deploying in battle formation. This was all the more striking as the well-drilled French soldiers in their distinctive uniforms of bright-red trousers and blue tunics manoeuvred in perfect unison to the beating of drums. So audacious was Lorencez's plan that Zaragoza had not expected a frontal assault and had to rush men to reinforce the forts. Ominously for the Juarista infantry garrisoning Guadalupe, the French artillery positioned itself to bombard the fort. Constant return fire, however, meant that the French heavy guns could not get close enough to do serious damage. After more than an hour of ineffectual shot, Lorencez gave the order for the infantry to charge.

At one o'clock, wave after wave of French soldiers threw themselves at the fort and into the deadly hail of musket and artillery fire raining from the bell towers and cupolas of the former monastery. The few soldiers who made it to the walls found themselves exposed to a deadly cross fire from the nearby fort of Loreto as they tried to traverse a deep ditch in front of the fort of Guadalupe. Yards away from the muzzles of the Mexican cannons, one officer fired his revolver through an opening for the artillery, while another soldier planted the regimental flag to rally the attack. When the flag carrier fell under a torrent of bullets, a junior officer raced to pick up the flag and was similarly despatched. Next, a veteran grabbed the banner, held it aloft towards the fort, and screamed a battle cry before convulsing as bullets tore into him. Clutching the flag to his chest, he fell and rolled with it into the bottom of the ditch. After hours of attacks, a violent thunderstorm broke out, pelting the combatants with huge hailstones. In the deluge, the slopes leading up to the fort became so slippery that the French soldiers could hardly stand, mud and water mixing with the blood of their stricken comrades. Seeing that the situation was hopeless, Lorencez ordered retreat.

Marching for more than a week and a half through the now familiar but still punishing terrain, the French made it back to the safety of the nearby town of Orizaba. With 476 French soldiers killed or wounded, the defeat was as comprehensive as it was unexpected. The French had lost 10 percent of their entire force; the Mexicans suffered only 83 dead.

The defenders of Puebla had humiliated the victors of the Crimean and Italian wars. "Glory to Mexico", proclaimed Mexico City's leading newspaper. "Our soldiers, the defenders of liberty, independence and reform have triumphed over the best soldiers in the world". The liberals in the capital celebrated the news, raising more than $10,000 in two days to buy Zaragoza a commemorative sword to commemorate the victory—Juárez was first on the list, personally donating

$100. Another liberal newspaper contextualised the victory, writing that monarchy "fixed its desolate eyes on America, thinking of prolonging its death throes: seeing it as new prey with which it could restore its strength."[18] But at Puebla, republicanism had triumphed. The day went down in Mexican history as Cinco de Mayo.

STILL UNAWARE OF the defeat at Puebla, Eugenie wrote to Carlota a month afterwards on June 7, 1862. Free from the British and Spanish, she claimed, Mexicans now felt safe to declare themselves in favour of the intervention. Thus, "Almonte, who, but yesterday an exile, is today the dictator of the provinces through which we have just advanced. The next mail will probably bring news of the arrival [of the French army] in Mexico City."[19] Instead, the next mail brought news of the catastrophic French defeat.

Far from deterring the French emperor, the defeat at Puebla saw him commit more men and money, ordering some twenty-five thousand reinforcements to Mexico. A government minister captured the mood of Napoleon III's innermost circle in a speech to the national assembly, the Corps législatif. Should the French army retreat, he asked rhetorically, when French blood has been spilt? "No, our honour is engaged. . . . We say that the [war] is just, necessary, legitimate and that our soldiers know that you, the same as the emperor, surround them with your sympathies, that the whole country is behind them and that the flag of France will never cease to be the flag of right, of justice and of civilisation and liberty!"[20]

In his reports, the man representing this flag in Mexico, Saligny, was quick to blame Lorencez for the defeat. "A fearful, lazy, sluggish person, not to say dull," wrote the diplomat, "a weak character incapable of initiative and unable to suffer that of others; he never asks for advice and takes offence at that which is given to him." In case he was not getting his point across, Saligny added, "He is subject to frequent absentmindedness which can be taken at times for the outbursts of a drunken mind which render him unapproachable for several days."[21]

Aware that Saligny was furiously scribbling this kind of vitriol for consumption in Paris, Lorencez wasted no time in sending his own version of the events, exonerating himself. He had attacked Puebla head-on, he claimed, only because Saligny and Almonte had promised that the city would rise up against Zaragoza once the assault began. Saligny could now add another name to his long list of detractors, with Lorencez including in his report a less than flattering character sketch: "totally inept in his dealings; without any judgement, he has no other aptitude than the deplorable talent for writing lies; his lack of dignity and his drunkenness have placed him, in the opinion of the army, at a much lower rank than his official position has given him. From day to day, I see myself being compelled to arrest [him] and put him on board a ship [for France]."[22]

Completely disillusioned by the defeat, and what he saw as the incompetence of Saligny and Almonte, Lorencez's positive assessment of Maximilian's chances as emperor evaporated. The French general wrote to the minister of war in Paris that he was "convinced that no one here supports us". Not only that, but the Mexicans were "infatuated with liberal ideas" and would prefer annexation to the United States than monarchy imposed by France. "I have never met a single supporter of monarchy in Mexico", he concluded.[23]

This made no mark on Napoleon III, who pushed ahead with the scheme he had conjured in his smoke-filled study at Biarritz, except this time with more troops. The original plan had failed not because of Almonte or Saligny, nor out of lack of support for monarchy in Mexico, the French emperor maintained, but because of Lorencez's military blunders. Napoleon III, therefore, appointed his third commander of the Mexican expedition in less than a year, General Élie Frédéric Forey. His main qualities were blind loyalty to the emperor and lack of imagination, a combination that ensured he could be trusted to follow orders from Paris to the letter. And Napoleon III gave Forey an actual letter to follow: a detailed, step-by-step guide for regime change, culminating in the occupation of Mexico City.

Events had demonstrated that this outcome was easier to imagine in Paris than it was to create in Mexico. Even so, as a correspondent for the *Times* pointed out, Napoleon III was used to getting his way. "People generally agree that four times the force now in Mexico will be required before General Almonte's regeneration plans be realized; and the Emperor, who has already made war successfully in Europe, Africa and Asia, and who probably wishes to do the same in America, will be sure to send double the number if necessary."[24]

There would be little use winning this war without a monarch to install, though—and it was at this point that significant official doubts first presented themselves to Maximilian and Carlota. The first of Maximilian's conditions for accepting the throne—that the Mexican people proclaim him emperor—now seemed unlikely given the republican resistance at Puebla. Of more immediate concern was that news had reached Maximilian regarding his second demand, the support of Britain. Aware that the British government's view had been misrepresented, Lord Russell, the foreign secretary, wrote to Vienna, alerting the Austrian government to the deception. He added that monarchy in Mexico would therefore be reliant on French troops. If the French military withdrew, Maximilian would be driven out by Juárez's forces, or the United States.

Meanwhile, in Washington, President Lincoln had resolved to uphold the Monroe Doctrine. He authorised his secretary of state, William Seward, to instruct US representatives in Europe to make clear that setting up a monarchy in Mexico would have grave consequences, inevitably bringing the powers that sustained it into conflict with the United States. In a letter forwarded to Maximilian at Miramar, Seward also warned that the interests and sympathies of the United States would always be with "the safety, welfare and stability of the republican system of government" in Mexico.[25]

In the face of these developments, Rechberg and Metternich now counselled Maximilian to reject the Mexican crown, Metternich stressing that the French government had misled them. To make the decision easier, the diplomat offered to inform Napoleon III personally that Maximilian was no longer a candidate for the Mexican throne.

But having become emperor and empress of Mexico in their minds, Maximilian and Carlota were loath to end their involvement at this point. Instead, they tried to ascertain for themselves whether a monarchy in Mexico was viable. Carlota turned to her father for support. What they needed, she explained in a letter, was an impartial observer on Mexican affairs. Some months earlier, she continued, one of their private secretaries was poised to depart for Mexico, but, with magisterial understatement, she added, events took "another turn, the thing did not seem quite so pressing and we resolved to wait". This secretary was now known to all the conservative émigrés in Paris and to Almonte in Mexico. This was a problem because their news came from these men, all "excellent", but they were not representative of public opinion in a country as big as Mexico. "We are not, thank god, tied to this affair and whatever turn events take we can always retire," she added; however, "as the question does not lack a certain interest we cannot abandon it without having studied it in depth and for that the first condition is to be instructed of the state and opinion of the country."[26]

In pursuit of that, Maximilian and Carlota turned to the *Times*' Mexican correspondent Charles Bourdillon. He had many years' experience reporting from Mexico and had followed recent events closely, sending back regular articles. The *Times* had an unrivalled network of international intelligence, and Britain's preeminent global position ensured that the paper wielded enormous influence. This gave Bourdillon prestige and access. In Paris he discussed Mexico in person not only with Napoleon III, but also with his finance and foreign ministers; in London, he met with Palmerston. Bourdillon also procured an interview with Leopold I, who described the journalist as a man who perhaps knew Mexico better than the Mexicans themselves. It was not clear what criteria the Belgian king based this on, but, after Bourdillon visited Maximilian at Miramar in January 1863, the archduke was similarly impressed. Maximilian felt that Bourdillon was well informed on Mexican affairs; however, what struck him most was that an Englishman and Protestant and, Maximilian therefore reasoned, someone completely disinterested in Mexican affairs concluded that Mexico should be a monarchy. Bourdillon went as far as to say that Mexicans would welcome Maximilian as their saviour.

But Bourdillon was hardly the impartial observer he purported to be. Not only did he hate Juárez and his liberal supporters, but he also had a very low view of the Mexicans that needed saving. He denied that there existed political parties in Mexico, merely factions fighting over power. Furthermore, their military leaders were from "the dregs of the people", with no pretence of political principles, for self-interest "alone determines them in their choice of the faction they espouse". They frequently changed sides; most, he claimed, had been "bought or sold at least half a dozen times". As for Juárez, he was a despot in spite of his claims about liberty and constitutions. Dismissing more than half the population, Bourdillon also wrote that "Indians have never taken any interest in political questions". Even a cursory glance at the political leaders should have disabused Bourdillon of this view. After all, Juárez was an "Indian", as was the conservative general Tomás Mejía. Regardless, Bourdillon argued, there would be no serious resistance to Maximilian, since Mexicans were "like rats": they always abandoned a sinking ship.[27] Such were the views of the man who Leopold claimed knew Mexico better than Mexicans themselves. Thoroughly charmed by the Englishman, though, Maximilian hired him as a personal agent, sending him back to Mexico to report on events.

Leopold also recommended a Belgian diplomat, Kint von Roodenbeck. Personally trusted by the Belgian king, Kint von Roodenbeck had spent time in Mexico as an envoy. As with Bourdillon, his supposed knowledge on Mexico brought interviews with Napoleon III and Eugenie before the now de rigueur sojourn at Miramar. After spending time with him, Carlota was captivated. In a letter to her father, she wrote, "He is perhaps in this moment the man whose cooperation is the most important to the success of the Mexican question".[28] But Kint von Roodenbeck simply told Maximilian and Carlota what they wanted to hear, concluding one exchange by saying that while a monarchy in Mexico could be a "crown of thorns," it was also a "great and beautiful work".[29]

Far from trying to extricate himself, Maximilian's main concern after the defeat of Puebla was that Napoleon III would abandon the idea. Rather than renouncing the archduke's candidacy, Metternich was engaged to sound out if Napoleon III remained committed. After discussing Mexico with the emperor and Eugenie in Paris, the ambassador reported back to Miramar that Napoleon III had said that Maximilian could depend upon him entirely. Thus reassured, Maximilian claimed he was honour bound not to end his interest in the throne. So taken was Maximilian after the guarantees from the Tuileries and conversations with Bourdillon and Kint von Roodenbeck that he behaved as though he was already emperor. In response to rumours that as a condition of his support Napoleon III would annex the Mexican state of Sonora, Maximilian grandly declared, "Never, would I lend my hands to the mutilation" of Mexico."[30]

So it was that the advice of a Belgian diplomat and an English journalist were preferred to the warnings of Britain, the United States, and Austria's own foreign ministry, not to mention, of course, Juárez's government itself, which urged Maximilian to reject overtures from a faction defeated in civil war.

Indeed, Maximilian and Carlota had become so fixated on their Mexican empire that they turned down employment closer to home. In October 1862, the unpopular king of Greece, the Bavarian Otto von Wittelsbach, a cousin of Maximilian, had fled his adopted country after a coup d'état. With the throne vacant, Palmerston had asked Maximilian if he might be interested, a suggestion that Maximilian found deeply offensive. "I can only", he wrote, "explain to myself such a lack of tact on the part of the man at the head of the English cabinet [Palmerston] as is to be found in this almost offensive proposal by the embarrassment in which he has been placed by the repeated refusals of the throne of Greece." Maximilian was also all too aware that the crown had been "hawked unsuccessfully around to half a dozen princes". But even if it had not been, he still would have rejected it. "I am too well acquainted from personal observation with modern [Greece] and its present corrupt state not to have been convinced for a long time past that its crafty and morally degenerate people are incapable of offering a firm foundation for an independent state."[31]

Having travelled to Greece, Maximilian was convinced the country was ill-suited to monarchy; having never been to Mexico, he was sure it was royalist. In February 1863, therefore, Maximilian's secretary wrote to Hidalgo, the Mexican émigré close to the French court, to refute rumours about the Greek throne. The archduke was "too seriously concerned with the scheme of your country to allow himself to be diverted by other thoughts."[32] This commitment was about to be put to the test; French forces were once again before Puebla.

IN MEXICO THE new commanding officer of the French intervention, General Élie Frédéric Forey, was determined not to act precipitately, as Lorencez had done. Forey's preparations to take Puebla were meticulous, albeit painstakingly slow. Arriving at Veracruz on September 21, 1862, he did not reach Orizaba, where his troops were safe from the tropical diseases of Veracruz, for another month. To get there the French had to march through the semidesert lowlands, the *tierra caliente* (hot land), marked only by sun-scorched bushes and cactus plants. Forey's men suffered terribly. Some 200 were too sick to leave Veracruz. Of the 515 that did set out with him, only 192 reached their destination; 70 of them had to be carried on mules, 112 were seriously ill, and only 10 reported for active duty on October 21.

It did not help that much of the surrounding countryside was held by Juarista guerrilla forces. So many French couriers were intercepted that the army resorted to sending messages written on the inside of rolled cigarettes. The reinforcements arrived in waves, making the difficult journey to Orizaba in small groups. As they marched into the foothills, soldiers were wary of guerrilla bands covered behind thick trees. These Mexican irregular forces waited for the most favourable moment, peppered the French with bullets, and then disappeared into the wilderness. The Juaristas had plenty of target practice: moving tens of thousands of soldiers into countryside sixty-five hundred feet above sea level had taken months.

By December Forey finally felt he was ready to march on Puebla. Determined to give the French intervention a Mexican character, he gave a leading role to Márquez and his troops, which numbered about 1,300 infantry and 1,100 cavalry. These men, however, were in a desperate state, so starved of resources and money that they resorted to pillaging, which turned the local population hostile. The French soldiers looked down on their allies, describing them as bandits and ridiculing the way that Márquez's pious Catholic followers went into battle crying, "Long live religion!" The French soldiers said that, given a choice, they preferred Juárez's slogan of "Liberty and reform!" Charles du Barail, a French officer who worked closely with the Mexican allies, described them as a pitiable, ragged army, mostly on horseback, "poorly dressed, badly equipped, shabby in appearance and followed by a troop of women almost as numerous, who arrived at the camp and were responsible for their care, cleaning, cooking, grooming horses and brushing the clothes of their lords and masters, whose gruesome faces were surrounded by blue clouds of cigarette smoke."[33]

Forey's cautious nature combined with the logistical problems of moving his army meant that it was not until March 9, 1863, that the French occupied, for the second time, the small village of Amozoc. This time the attackers outnumbered the defenders. On March 17, nearly the entire French army, some 26,000 men, deployed before Puebla. Juárez had visited the town a few months before to rally the 20,000 or so who garrisoned it, handing out medals to veterans who had defeated the French and then inspecting the defences, now greatly strengthened. Confidence was high, with one liberal newspaper correspondent boasting that Puebla would become a graveyard for the invaders if they dared attack it.

Rather than a frontal assault, Forey decided on siege warfare. Trenches were dug around the city, which allowed the French to approach strongpoints without exposing themselves to the fire that had repulsed Lorencez's attack. Gradually, one by one, the forts were reduced to rubble by artillery or taken in ferocious hand-to-hand combat. In Mexico City, where Easter celebrations saw effigies of Napoleon III, Saligny, and Forey burned in the main square, Juárez received news that the defenders of Puebla could not hold out much longer. He sent reinforcements, but the French army cut off and defeated them. After two months, the commander of the defence of Puebla, General Jesús González Ortega, who had replaced Zaragoza after his death from typhus months earlier, explained to his troops that lack of food and ammunition meant that they could no longer fight. The next day, May 17, Ortega surrendered.

On May 19, 1863, more than a year after Lorencez had been defeated, the French army marched into Puebla to the sounds of its own trumpets, bugles, and drums. Forey headed the procession, but no one greeted the victors as they marched through streets littered with debris, nor were there curious faces at the windows of the damaged houses. As one French officer, Charles Blanchot, remarked, "We were marching into a dead city", and once the trumpets and drums stopped, a lugubrious silence reigned on the abandoned avenues. As they entered the main square, there was at least a crowd of onlookers. These were the most devoted of the cathedral's congregation, and a Te Deum, a celebratory Catholic religious service, was held in honour of the conquerors. When Forey left the cathedral, sound finally filled the square as French soldiers erupted into cries of "Vive l'empereur!" and "Vive le général Forey!"[34]

Seeing that reinforcements could not reach the capital, and that his troops could not defend it, Juárez made the momentous decision to abandon Mexico City. Over the next few days, a great exodus began, as the government archives, treasury, and all its remaining soldiers began the trek to the safety of San Luis Potosí, more than 260 miles northwest. Sara Yorke Stevenson, a US citizen, and later a famed Egyptologist and suffragist, was living in Mexico City at the time and described the scene: "We heard the dull, steady tramp of men marching. . . . [L]ooking out the window we saw the debris of the defeated Liberal army making its way through the city. A strange, weird sight they presented in the moonlight—these men whose sole equipment consisted of a musket and a cartridge-box slung over their white shirts."[35]

At three o'clock on May 31, Juárez formally closed the final session of Mexico's congress before making the long journey north. In a last editorial before ceasing publication, the liberal newspaper *El Monitor Republicano* captured the elegiac but defiant mood of Juaristas: "Our cause is just and holy, and we will never abandon it. Wherever fate takes us, our pen and our sword will always fight in defence of the nation and of liberty!"[36]

After Juárez's retreat, Forey ordered his most gifted general, Achille Bazaine, to occupy Mexico City. Bazaine's force took the route of the conquistadores to the Mexican capital, some 80 miles northwest. They had to navigate the mountain passes that cut through the volcanic range of peaks between the valleys of Puebla and Mexico City. Marching between high mountain walls that seemed to stretch endlessly skyward on either side of the narrow road, and trekking through glacially cold nights, the force emerged from the mountains just as dawn broke over the valley of Mexico below.

The view was magnificent, an immense arena closed off by an amphitheatre of mountains, the sun reflecting on the five great lakes that surrounded the capital. The French troops stopped there for an hour, staring at the vista below, lost in their reveries. Many turned their thoughts to Hernán Cortés, who some 344 years earlier had looked down from here before seizing the capital of the Aztec empire. Indeed, so potent was this historical moment that the comparison was made in a speech to the troops: "Our victorious eagles will enter the capital of the ancient empire of Moctezuma; instead of destroying, like Hernán Cortés, you are going to build; instead of reducing a people to slavery, you are going to free them."[37]

Bazaine quickly secured the city, which had already been abandoned by die-hard liberals, and prepared the reception for the triumphal entry of Forey's army into Mexico City. The French, finally, were welcomed as liberators. Under brilliant sunshine, at nine on the morning of June 10, the bells of the cathedral, churches, and convents drowned out the sound of French trumpets, bugles, and drums, as the French army marched towards the enormous central square of Mexico City. Almonte and Márquez were given prominent places in the procession, receiving loud cries of "Long live Mexico, France, religion, and peace".[38] It seemed as if the entire population, some one hundred and fifty thousand people, had come out to line the streets, while the balconies of the grand houses were filled with women—"almost all pretty," in low-cut ball gowns, remarked one French officer—who threw so many garlands of flowers at the feet of the French troops that the streets resembled a colourful dyed carpet as the petals were trampled under thousands of feet. Sara Yorke Stevenson, sixteen years old at the time and watching from a balcony, noticed that the soldiers "began to ogle us as only Frenchmen could".[39]

The route had been decorated with triumphal arches, the flags of Mexico and France flying side by side, some with portraits of Maximilian and Carlota hung from them. As the French approached the square, the doors of the cathedral were already open, and the plaza was lined with clergy in their ceremonial robes. Beaming with pride, Forey rode towards them—the vast presidential palace, former seat of Juárez's government, to his right—dismounted, and entered to attend the obligatory Te Deum. Afterwards, he reviewed the troops in the enormous square to loud cries of "Vive l'empereur!" and "Vive l'imperatrice!" As Forey later reported to Paris, "The entire population of this capital welcomed the army with a delirious enthusiasm. The soldiers of France were literally crushed under wreaths and bouquets".[40] In the evening, the streets were ablaze with illuminated decorations, with the revelries continuing into the early hours.

There followed several days of celebration, culminating with a ball for almost four thousand guests at the National Theatre, an immense neoclassical opera house. The stage was transformed into an artificial forest whose darkness contrasted with the brilliant light of the rest of the immense hall. The walls were decorated with flowers, mirrors, and military trophies from captured artillery, bombs, rifles, guns, swords, and drumsticks; candles were put into the mouths of cannons or tied to bayoneted rifles. At half past ten, Forey, the guest of honour, entered, wearing his uniform, and as the music for the first dance began, he, Almonte, and Saligny partnered with Mexico City's most illustrious women, sweeping across the dance floor. In the city outside, the French soldiers threw themselves into their own festivities, enjoying the pleasures of the capital.

The ball was a celebration of the political reorganisation that had been choreographed for the outcome Napoleon III intended. It was Saligny who directed this political theatre, appointing prominent members of the Conservative Party to positions of power. Key amongst these selections were the Junta Superior del Gobierno, composed of 35 men, set up by decree in June 1863. This body then nominated Almonte, Labastida, and an old general named Mariano Salas as a Regency Council exercising executive power. Next, the junta selected an assembly made up of 215 men, supposedly representing the will of the Mexican people, to vote on the form of government Mexico should adopt. The process was, of course, carefully stage-managed, with Forey reporting to Paris, and Almonte to Maximilian, that the assembly would vote in favour of monarchy before it did so.

The assembly announced its decision on July 11, 1863. To applause, cheers, and wild shouts of joy from spectators who packed the galleries, a statement was read out: Mexico would be an empire.

The hollow question of who should be emperor was soon answered too. Maximilian, because of his illustrious ancestry as much as his personal qualities, was called to reign over Mexico. The statement made clear that the original plan of Mexican independence, so beloved by Gutiérrez de Estrada, had finally been realised after forty years of struggle. The assembly made sure that votes of thanks were given to the principal architects of this new regime, first and foremost Napoleon III, but Saligny, Gutiérrez de Estrada, and Hidalgo got their due, and even the supposedly impartial Kint von Roodenbeck made it onto the list. A year and a half after French forces first landed, the Second Mexican Empire was proclaimed (Iturbide's had been the first).

Proclaiming it was one thing, but, as Barail noted, "while we danced and flirted in Mexico City, in the rest of the country we had a little less fun".[41] Juárez had retreated, not surrendered. Now, he was regrouping his forces and directing a remorseless guerrilla campaign against the French, who occupied only a thin line of strategic points from Veracruz to the capital. The empire was but precariously established, especially as its would-be emperor remained in Europe, yet to definitively accept his crown.

4

THE MEXICAN CROWN

On October 3, 1863, two years after the idea of monarchy had first been discussed with Maximilian, eleven Mexicans, including José María Gutiérrez de Estrada and José Manuel Hidalgo y Esnaurrízar, travelled the short distance from Trieste to Miramar to formally offer him the crown. Always with an eye for ceremony, Maximilian had arranged for their carriages to be greeted by rows of servants dressed in striking black uniforms with silver embroidery. At the castle's main entrance, Maximilian had stationed halberdiers, men chosen for their colossal height, their long and thick beards offset with three-cornered hats, silver chevrons, and white feathers, armed with long metal pikes, decorated with crimson velvet, and wearing thin white gloves. Recalling the Habsburgs' medieval past, the reception was a carefully composed statement to the Mexicans that they were dealing with a European dynasty with centuries of power behind it.

When the clock struck midday, the doors of the castle were opened. The Mexicans walked through to a lavishly furnished room, where portraits of Maximilian and Carlota's family hung. There Maximilian waited, dressed in a tailcoat and wearing the Order of the Golden Fleece, a Habsburg honour introduced in the fifteenth century. Once the Mexicans were in position, Gutiérrez de Estrada stepped forward. In white tie and black gloves, he then read the speech he held awkwardly in his hands. This was the moment he had dreamt of for twenty-three years.

Drawing upon his considerable talent for flattery, he implored Maximilian to accept the crown and rescue Mexico from the republican abyss into which it had sunk after independence. He assured his audience that he would not dwell on the misfortunes everyone knew Mexico had suffered. He then dwelt, at some length, on this subject before arguing that only Maximilian could save Mexico.

Maximilian's reply was more succinct, and circumspect. He was flattered that the Mexicans had turned to the Habsburgs, the family of Charles V. Restoring Mexico under a constitutional monarchy was a noble task; however, Maximilian reiterated the conditions stated nearly two years earlier: the empire must be guaranteed by France and Britain, and a popular vote must proclaim him sovereign. With French troops occupying less than half of Mexico and the British government resolved not to enter into any agreement with Maximilian, these conditions were impossible to fulfil. Given this set of facts, it was fitting that the ceremony concluded with celebrations on board Maximilian's yacht, *La Fantasia*. As they watched fireworks light the high white walls of Miramar in red, green, and white—the colours of the Mexican flag—the Mexicans still had no idea if, let alone when, Maximilian would come to reign over them.

Whatever misgivings they had, however, had been eased earlier when they had been formally introduced to Carlota, whose intelligence, piety, and nobility deeply impressed them. At dinner, Carlota had shone in a regal rose dress with a crown of matching flowers, adorned with diamonds. The food and service were elaborate, while an orchestra played sequences from the most fashionable operas of the day. The whole affair had the desired effect; despite stopping short of definitive acceptance, the Mexicans left convinced of the majesty of Maximilian and Carlota.

Yet Maximilian and Carlota were less convinced about the Mexicans. Carlota was as shocked as Napoleon III and Eugenie had been about Gutiérrez de Estrada's political views. She described him as a *cangrejo* (literally a crab), which in Mexico was a liberal pejorative term for a conservative. Warming to the crustacean theme, she went further and called him a "retrograde crayfish". She pardoned his faults because of his age, the time he had spent away from Mexico, and the role he had played in creating the Mexican throne, but she believed that nostalgia made him pine for Spanish rule in Mexico, not caring that the world had moved on.[1] For his part, Maximilian also deemed most of the deputation reactionaries at odds with his more liberal views.

After departing Miramar, the Mexicans went to Paris, where political differences were even more apparent. They presented an official vote of thanks to Napoleon III, placed in a silver box wrapped in the tricolour ribbon of the Mexican flag, but the subsequent dinner was less pleasant than the one at Miramar. At the palace of Saint-Cloud, Eugenie insisted to her guests that the Mexican empire must heal the wounds of civil war and reconcile the parties, just as, she claimed, had happened in France after 1848. Gutiérrez de Estrada was horrified. How could this happen, he asked, when the revolutions of Mexico were so much worse than those in Europe? One ought not, Eugenie replied, "surround oneself with old pictures and portraits—I mean, to live in a world which no longer exists." This was exactly the world Gutiérrez de Estrada wanted to live in. He shot back that there were no old pictures in Mexico. There had been no Middle Ages, and the institutions of Spanish colonialism, especially the church, were as relevant now as ever. In an attempt to placate the empress, he concluded by saying that Mexico should have "a dictatorship on the pattern of that established in France."

This was a mistake. Despite the coup d'état of 1851, Napoleon III and Eugenie did not believe they ruled a dictatorship. "Yes," the empress angrily replied, "but a dictatorship which should bring liberty".[2] Gutiérrez de Estrada, losing all reserve, retorted that the problem in

Mexico was that they had too much liberty. Hidalgo, also at the dinner, came to the aid of the empress and suggested political coop- eration with Mexican moderates, which then led to the two émigrés arguing while the empress listened on, smiling. After all, with thirty thousand troops in Mexico, Napoleon III could do what he wanted. As long as his army was there, he would not support Gutiérrez de Estrada's reactionary ideas.

Despite tensions between them, Napoleon III and the Mexican conservatives still had to work together and persuade Maximilian to drop his insistence on a British alliance. Yet Franz Joseph had pressured Maximilian to maintain this condition before accepting the Mexican throne. After reading his brother's reply to Gutiérrez de Estrada, he telegraphed Maximilian. "You cannot", he warned, "place yourself in a state of dependence on France alone".[3]

Napoleon III, Mexican conservatives, and the personal con- nections of Maximilian and Carlota with Queen Victoria were all brought to bear in one last attempt to win British support. This combination cajoled the British prime minister, Lord Palmerston, into meeting with Francisco de Paula Arrangoiz Berzábal, a former Mexican finance minister who had won the confidence of Maximil- ian and spoke good English. Arrangoiz was briefed by Maximilian at Miramar before travelling to Paris to speak with the French foreign minister. Taking a circuitous route to London, he went via Brussels, where Carlota had been visiting Leopold I. She gave him a letter from her father, which Arrangoiz was to present to Palmerston.

Unimpressed, after the meeting Palmerston merely mentioned to his foreign secretary, Lord John Russell, that a Mexican with an unpronounceable name had come to speak with him, but British policy would not change. Given that the archduke was making British support a condition of acceptance, Russell wanted to inform Maximilian categorically that the government would never give it. Palmerston stopped him, arguing that a monarchy tied to Europe and challenging the United States was in their interest, especially when it came at no cost to the British government.

For Maximilian and Carlota, this ambiguous attitude gave them hope; it allowed them to concoct an argument for proceeding without British support. Even if Britain did not enter into a formal treaty before they went to Mexico, they felt sure that Palmerston would recognise their government once they were there. Maximilian had bought into the geopolitical rationale that lay behind the Mexican empire, writing that "unceasingly menaced by the American spirit of conquest [Britain] is bound to realise in the end that her own interests demand that she should forward a work which tends to set limits to the encroachments of her ambitious neighbours."[4]

That the American Civil War had turned into a long struggle further convinced Maximilian that British support was less important than it had been two years earlier, in 1861, when the condition had first been formulated. Then Maximilian feared that the United States, hostile to monarchy and hungry for more land, would invade the Mexican empire after a quick victory over the Confederacy. By 1863 the outlook was different—at least to Maximilian. He had begun corresponding with Confederates, who assured him that the South would win. James Williams, a Confederate agent in Europe, contacted Maximilian, writing that "the final triumph of the Confederate cause is an event which may be delayed, but cannot be prevented." As for a Mexican kingdom, Williams believed that, should it succeed, "Your Imperial Highness will have founded what is destined to be one of the great empires of the world." Such flattery, and wishful thinking, saw Williams added to Miramar's ever-lengthening list of invitees. Maximilian was even in communication with Rose O'Neal Greenhow, a notorious Confederate spy, who assured him of the South's support. Maximilian replied, thanking her and praising the "fortitude and patriotism which so greatly distinguish the American ladies".[5]

With the Confederacy still fighting the Union, Maximilian began to rationalise away the need for British support. As he wrote to Napoleon III, the French army alone was enough to deter the United States from any hostile action. Naturally, Napoleon III agreed. "The

United States are well aware", he wrote, that the Mexican empire is "the work of France [and] they cannot attack it without making enemies of us at once."[6] Thus reassured, Maximilian's solution to the insoluble problem of British support was to drop it as a requirement.

Explaining this decision to Franz Joseph via Johann Bernhard von Rechberg, who must have felt as though a large part of his remit as foreign minister was negotiating between archdukes, Maximilian now claimed, somewhat unconvincingly, that when in 1861 he had insisted on obtaining a guarantee from Britain, he had in fact meant that *once his empire was founded*, he would work to secure an alliance afterwards. No doubt aware that his reasoning was not the firmest, he added, "It seems to me that it is neither prudent to aim at the unattainable, nor honest to hold out to [Napoleon III] the prospect of acceptance under conditions which one has recognised to be chimerical".[7]

Still, he also asked his brother for help to avoid complete dependence on Napoleon III. Might Franz Joseph not enter into an alliance with France, guaranteeing the Mexican empire? Franz Joseph pleaded interests of state, arguing, rather pointedly given Maximilian's position as commander in chief, that Austria's navy lacked the power to undertake expeditions across the Atlantic and therefore would not be able to defend Mexico.

Franz Joseph now saw the Mexican affair as impractical and wanted nothing to do with it officially. He had been further put out by a bizarre request from Maximilian that their youngest brother, Ludwig Viktor, marry one of the two daughters of Dom Pedro II, emperor of Brazil. Given that Dom Pedro II had no heirs, such a marriage might found yet another Habsburg dynasty in Latin America. Maximilian let his imagination get the better of him. He dreamt of Habsburg rule one day extending over much of North, Central, and South America. He therefore went to see his younger brother, a homosexual and cross-dresser with a reputation as a libertine, to persuade him of the merits of marriage.

The meeting did not go well. Maximilian wrote to Franz Joseph that Ludwig Viktor was "anything but pleased with the idea". Maximilian had managed to extract a promise that Ludwig Viktor would obey a direct order from Franz Joseph. Such an order, argued Maximilian, was exactly what his younger brother needed. As Maximilian wrote to Rechberg, "All who know my brother well must desire that he should be removed from the aimless existence which he has led hitherto in the atmosphere of Vienna". Tough love was required. "I am convinced that under the strong and judicious, though cold and possibly selfish governance of the Emperor of Brazil, his character might be given a healthful direction".[8] This was hardly an endorsement for a future father-in-law, and Franz Joseph balked at ordering one brother into an unwanted marriage merely in pursuit of another brother's hubristic fantasy.

Franz Joseph's grave reservations about the Mexican crown were shared by his mother as well. The flight of her nephew King Otto of Greece had terrified Sophie, and she wrote to Maximilian that a similar fate might await him in Mexico, but with more disastrous consequences. Maximilian hated confrontation and left it to his wife to allay Sophie's concerns in a long letter. As for Greece, Carlota wrote unsympathetically, which "seems above all to have alarmed you", there could be no comparison. Mexico was a former Habsburg territory, whereas Bavaria, where Otto was from, had no connection to Greece.

Sophie was also worried, not unreasonably, that Maximilian would be seen as a foreign ruler imposed by French bayonets and thus unable to win over Mexican nationalists. Far from it, Carlota argued. Maximilian had been acclaimed monarch by the Assembly of Notables, and this would soon be ratified in a national election. Somewhat contradicting herself, Carlota then went on to cite examples of successful foreign intervention in recent history, notably Belgium. Returning to the point of nationalism, if Sophie believed that Benito Juárez represented the Mexican nation—a man who she claimed betrayed his country to the United States while oppressing the Catholic faith—then nationality was nothing more than an "empty simulacrum".

Having gotten slightly lost on this tangent, Carlota pulled the letter back triumphantly to seven—she numbered them—arguments that supposedly destroyed the comparison with Greece. Key amongst these was that in Greece, the royal family had to adopt a "schismatic religion" (Greek Orthodox), whereas Maximilian and Carlota's work in Mexico was to save the Catholic Church from the attacks of revolutionaries. Furthermore, Greeks, she believed, were beyond redemption, whereas the "Spanish" and the "Indian races" in Mexico retained admirable qualities, despite what she referred to as years of debasement in republican anarchy. Returning to foreign intervention, Carlota then pointed out that after the 1848 revolutions, order had been restored in the Austrian Empire only with the help of the Russian army. This was a low blow, as Sophie still keenly felt the shame of 1848. In response to the concern that the French troops would not be enough to support them in Mexico, Carlota argued that the love of the people, which would be won by wise government and Maximilian's charisma, was more important. Without that, no amount of bayonets would ever suffice.

Concluding what Carlota described as an "interminable letter", she stressed that whatever the difficulties of ruling Mexico, Maximilian's wisdom and grace would overcome them. She ended with a final appeal to emotion: "I would even say," Carlota wrote, "that your behaviour does not seem like you at all. I pray you will not cause Max further grief because he already has so many sacrifices to make, ties to break and friends to leave in order to fulfil this difficult but worthy mission."[9]

Convinced of Maximilian's greatness, Carlota was determined that he become emperor of Mexico and she empress. Writing to her grandmother, she further outlined her reasons. Mexico was a beautiful kingdom that would give Maximilian purpose, whereas if he stayed in Austria he would be nothing but a glorified janitor at Miramar who occasionally travelled. Carlota also wanted action. "I have too little known life not to desire something to love and to strive for". She could not bear to do nothing. "I need to act". Moreover, Carlota saw God's providential hand in her imperial future. She had consulted her priest, who confirmed that the Mexican crown was a holy mission. Concluding the letter, written on the anniversary of her mother's death, she wrote that "we lost an angel on this earth in order to have a protector in heaven and this angel herself would have encouraged us in this work so worthy of her approval".[10] With her dead mother taking care of spiritual matters, Carlota had her father for political advice. "Shall I go to Mexico?" she asked. "It is your duty", Leopold replied. Carlota also placed enormous, uncritical faith in the genius of Napoleon III, who she believed was the only man with the power and resources as well as the disinterest to undertake a work of such grandeur as regenerating Mexico.[11]

By December 1863, then, Maximilian had rationalised away the obstacles to becoming emperor of Mexico and was ignoring the warnings of his Habsburg family. But there was still the issue of popular proclamation. Here Napoleon III stepped in. He assured his protégé that elections and assemblies could wait. "Allow me to lay great stress upon one point: a country torn apart by anarchy cannot be regenerated by parliamentary liberty. What is needed in Mexico is a liberal dictatorship." The *Times*, he pointed out, published a "very remarkable article" arguing this exact same point: establish order, and liberty will follow.[12]

The *Times* article was hardly neutral political journalism, written, as it was, by Charles Bourdillon. Maximilian's agent had also written directly to the archduke, putting things more bluntly than Napoleon III: constitutional government in Mexico would be like "placing a razor in the hands of a lunatic. . . . [H]e will in all probability cut his throat".[13] Although Napoleon III still hoped to organise some kind of ratification of Maximilian's nomination, what most convinced the archduke that a Mexican empire was possible was not any expression of Mexico's national will, but the fact that the French army was pushing Juárez back to the northern borders of Mexico.

IT WAS NOT Élie Frédéric Forey who was leading this charge. Once Mexico City was taken, everyone expected a campaign to consolidate French power, but Forey proved as dilatory as ever. Instead, he made himself comfortable in the capital and, under the influence of Dubois de Saligny, turned Mexico's administration over to members of the Conservative Party. They wielded their power vindictively, confiscating the property of Juaristas and reimposing the authority of the Catholic Church. Several laws were passed, including one specifying a fifty-dollar fine, or fifty days' imprisonment, for anyone who worked on a Sunday without first hearing mass and getting permission from a priest. This was so unpopular that it had to be repealed; however, it did not augur well for Maximilian's plan to reconcile the factions in Mexico that the first acts of his Regency were distinctly theocratic.

Annoyed at the lack of military progress and at reactionary direction, Napoleon III disguised a sacking as a promotion. He elevated Forey to the highest rank in the French army, a marshal of France, but in the letter accompanying the news, the emperor explained that the minutiae of government was beneath such an illustrious rank; Forey must leave Mexico. The newly appointed marshal followed this order at his customary speed, first organising another ball to celebrate his new rank. Portly, with a ruddy complexion, Forey reached a nadir of humiliation when the chair he was resting on after dancing collapsed under his weight. He was helped to his feet as onlookers tried to hide their amusement.

Achille Bazaine, Forey's replacement, was a striking contrast. He had been instrumental at the siege of Puebla, commanded the respect of his men, and spoke fluent Spanish. Fifty-two years old in 1863, Bazaine had spent his adult life in the army and was the embodiment of the professional soldier. Having worked his way up from the lowest rank, he too would receive the French army's highest military honour when he was named a marshal of France in 1864. He had served in the French Foreign Legion in Algeria and Spain as well as with distinction in the Crimean War. As the numerous bullet and shrapnel wounds he had received over the years attested, one of which scarred his face, he led from the front. Now he found himself at the head of a French army that was a well-equipped, disciplined, and ruthless fighting force, one whose soldiers had learned their trade in the bloodiest conflicts of the mid-nineteenth century.

Bazaine, however, was as yet unable to unleash this force against the Juaristas. Forey refused to leave, and because he was senior in rank, Bazaine was unable to issue any orders. Forey eventually departed on October 4, but there remained the stymieing presence of Saligny. In Paris he was seen as too close to the conservatives and had also been recalled. Saligny was not the kind of man to let orders get in the way of his own interests, though, and he dallied in the capital while finalising lucrative business deals as well as arranging to marry into a wealthy Mexican family. Saligny, despite several increasingly angry letters from the French foreign minister, held on for six months after his reassignment until December 1863, when his wedding took place, blessed by the archbishop of Mexico. Saligny finally returned to France greatly enriched and thus with the distinction of being the only person to prosper from the undertaking thus far.

With Saligny and Forey gone, Bazaine was free to put his plans into action. Civil government still had to be nominally conducted through the Regency, meaning that Bazaine spent much of his time writing letters—194 of them between October 1, 1863, and March 10, 1864—to Juan Nepomuceno Almonte with "recommendations". As Napoleon III made clear to Bazaine, it was imperative to maintain the Regency "as a way of avoiding the idea that I might want to keep Mexico"; nonetheless, in reality Bazaine had "the duty of controlling everything and deciding on everything". The key was to "pacify and organise Mexico by appealing to the men of goodwill and avoiding being reactionary."[14]

This put Bazaine in conflict with the man who blessed Saligny's marriage, Pelagio Antonio de Labastida y Dávalos, now archbishop of Mexico. The Regency Council was made up of Almonte, Mariano Salas (a former general and twice interim president), and Labastida. Although an important politician in his day, Salas was happy to defer to Almonte, who in turn worked, albeit at times reluctantly, in accordance with French wishes. Labastida, on the other hand, saw in these wishes the same sins that Juárez's liberals had committed. For him, the crucial issue was the forced sale of church property under liberals nearly a decade earlier. For many conservatives, the whole point of supporting a foreign invasion and then backing a monarchy was to roll back what they saw as Juárez's impious reforms. Now in power, Labastida expected exactly that.

But Napoleon III had other ideas. Despite Forey's lackadaisical approach to orders from Paris, at the French emperor's insistence he had issued a proclamation on June 12, 1863, that called on Mexicans to put the civil war behind them. Instead, moderate citizens from all sides should unite together to form one party—the Bonapartist dream in France. To facilitate this universal harmony, Forey confirmed that those who had bought church property under Juárez's reforms would keep it. After all, the nationalisation of church property in France had been one of the foundations of the revolution of 1789.

What was now uncontroversial in France, however, remained radical in Mexico. For conservatives, all evil could be traced to the French Revolution, the ideas of which had ruined their beloved Mexico. In their view, the French Revolution was nothing more than the incoherent expression of atheists; philosophes like Voltaire, Rousseau, and Diderot were not heroes of the Enlightenment, but enemies of Christianity. Moreover, in giving power to ordinary people who were in no way intelligent enough to use it, the 1789 revolution had unleashed a tiger that ripped apart a beautifully ordered, hierarchical, and pious world constructed over centuries, leaving behind only blood, violence, and instability. In the memorable words of one of the conservatives' preferred philosophers, Joseph de Maistre, the revolution was "the universal law of violent destruction. . . . The entire earth, continually steeped in blood, is only an immense altar on which every living thing must be immolated without end, without restraint, without respite until the consummation of the world, until the extinction of evil, until the death of death."[15]

A showdown between the ideas of 1789, as Napoleon III referred to them, and Labastida's political thought, which significantly predated this, was inevitable. At their first meeting in October 1863, relations between Bazaine and Labastida got off to an inauspicious start. The French general made it clear that the sale of church property would never be overturned; the archbishop made it equally apparent that he would never accept anything less. The next day, Labastida called a special meeting of the Regency Council, which Bazaine was asked to attend. Here the archbishop reiterated his position, adding that he would accept nothing unless the pope sanctioned it first. Then, turning to speak directly to Bazaine, he said superciliously, "If your army was well received on its arrival in the capital, it was the work of the clergy. And if you do not support [the church], if you do not go along with it, bring another 15,000 men because your friends of today. . ." At this point Labastida trailed off, leaving the sentence unfinished, merely making a gesture that Bazaine interpreted as indicating the French could no longer count on their current allies.[16]

Bazaine and his French bureaucrats were unmoved. They explained that the empire would be run in line with the ideas of the 1789 French Revolution—what Napoleon III called the "spirit of the century". The austere clergyman paused and then, with withering disdain, replied to the French that to look for European solutions to Mexican problems was a "chimera". "The revolution", he continued, "here has sacrificed everything to greed". Concluding what must have felt like a sermon, he said, "As regards to the century, we are part of the current one, but only chronologically; Mexico shares nothing more with this century than the date, that is all."[17]

Days later, a furious Bazaine demonstrated the material power of the French army over abstract theology. In full uniform, he marched into a meeting of the Regency Council with soldiers flanking him and stated plainly that French policy over church property would not be altered. Labastida then refused to attend further meetings of the Regency, hoping to paralyse the government. This impasse lasted until November 17, when Bazaine forced Almonte and Salas to decree that Labastida was no longer a member of the council. Labastida protested, but he was left with no choice but to withdraw.

With Labastida temporarily neutralised, Bazaine could focus on discovering the will of the nation. Napoleon III had instructed Bazaine to have the "election of Maximilian ratified by the greatest possible number of Mexicans". This was essential because, as the emperor well knew, "the hasty nomination already made has the grave fault from the European point of view that it does not seem to be the legitimate desire of the country."[18] How best to manifest that desire was left to Bazaine's discretion. In practice, this meant that whenever possible, Mexicans under the control of the Franco-Mexican army would sign a petition declaring their allegiance to the empire. Yet even organising this proved impossible in many areas where French authority was thin on the ground. In the end, it was decided that the plebiscite on the empire would largely amount to stating that the areas under nominal French control had declared themselves for it. The people in each area would be counted and then the numbers sent back to Paris as proof that Maximilian had been called by the Mexican people.

The problem in October 1863, though, was that even on these somewhat shaky democratic foundations, the so-called vote would be close. The Regency governed only the corridor of land from Veracruz to Mexico City and the immediate countryside around the capital. Thus, before the benefits of imperial rule could be explained to the electorate, it was first necessary to conquer their constituencies.

In Bazaine the intervention had found the dynamism it required after more than two years of questionable leadership and little progress. His strategy was to roll up liberal forces by fanning out from Mexico City and occupying the main cities, forcing Juárez to abandon his new capital at San Luis Potosí. As soon as Forey left in

October, the plan was put into action. Two columns of French soldiers marched northwards. Leonardo Márquez commanded a Mexican army on the left flank, while another local army was on the right under the command of Tomás Mejía, who had recently declared his allegiance to the empire.

Like Márquez, Mejía was deeply religious, but whereas Márquez was a creole, Mejía was an Otomí, an indigenous people from the Sierra Gorda range near Querétaro. A cavalry officer in the US-Mexican War, during the civil war Mejía fought for the conservatives, recruiting a fiercely loyal force from his home region. Refusing to surrender even after Juárez had taken Mexico City in 1861, Mejía held out with around fifteen hundred soldiers in the mountains. The government sent an army of seven thousand to defeat him; however, Mejía soon routed these seemingly overwhelming numbers. Even the French, who tended to dismiss the military skills of their allies, held Mejía in high esteem. Barail had no time for Márquez, but he described Mejía as "a first-rate general, loved and respected by his soldiers, of proven courage, . . . conscientious, loyal, faithful to his word, a slave to his duty and a patriot to his very soul".[19] Now he was one of the empire's best generals, leading the charge against Juárez and his beleaguered forces.

In November, Mejía occupied Querétaro, an important town about 130 miles northwest of Mexico City. A conservative stronghold, and close to Mejía's home region, the troops were welcomed as liberators and met with delirious enthusiasm. A religious procession followed, as eight hundred women holding candles walked through the streets while onlookers cheered and waved. Similar scenes played out as conservative supporters came out to cheer the rapid advances of the Franco-Mexican army. Bazaine's reports back to Europe were, therefore, a list of towns taken and tremendous distances covered— Mexico was conquered more with their legs than their swords, as one soldier noted.

On the map, this advance was impressive, but "in reality", noted Barail, "we were only masters of the space we occupied."[20] Guerrilla forces controlled much of the countryside, and the French had enough troops to garrison only the most important towns. Juárez could still count on some twenty thousand soldiers, albeit dispersed throughout the vastness of Mexico. His strategy was simple: trade space for time. With the tide of war turning against the Confederates north of the border, Juárez hoped that US support for his cause would soon yield men, money, and munitions.

An added difficulty for the French was finding moderate local allies who might help them win hearts and minds, showing that the intervention was not merely the conservatives reigniting the civil war with foreign help. In one town, Bazaine could find no one willing to take over the administration and had to appoint an illiterate conservative guerrilla named Chavez. It was not, however, his lack of learning that most worried the French. After Chavez's irregulars had been involved in a skirmish with Juaristas, a French officer asked how the enemy wounded were being treated. Chavez replied that his treatment consisted of beheading them. Violent acts were commonplace on both sides, of course, but while Napoleon III and Maximilian might extol their liberal virtues, there seemed little hope of reconciling the parties in Mexico with men like Chavez governing in the name of the Regency Council.

Despite these problems, the military performance of the Mexican allies was promising. Though he had initially refused to support the intervention, the dashing young former president Miguel Miramón had been persuaded in July 1863 to return to Mexico, pledge allegiance to the empire, and lead a battalion of local soldiers. With Miramón, Mejía, and Márquez, the intervention had an effective, and ruthless, fighting force to work with, which had the political expedient of giving the campaign a Mexican face, albeit a conservative one unlikely to endear many liberals to the imperial cause.

As the intervention advanced, Márquez was given the task of garrisoning the old colonial town of Morelia. With a population of some twenty-five thousand, Morelia was the capital of the state of Michoacán, its roughly half-million people key to the "vote" if it could be brought under Regency control. With the French army far from Morelia, General José López Uraga, a Morelia local who was a veteran of the US-Mexican War and had lost a leg in the civil war fighting conservatives, saw an opportunity to humiliate the imperial cause. On December 17, 1863, Uraga, with twelve thousand men under his command, launched an attack well supported by artillery against Márquez's thirty-five hundred or so defenders. Márquez had fortified the town, with a perimeter around the main square the last point of defence. As the liberals advanced, conservatives desperately rang the cathedral's bells, Márquez reminding his outnumbered troops that they were engaged in a holy war.

The *imperialistas*, as supporters of Maximilian were known, managed to hold the liberals at bay overnight, but the attack resumed the next morning. As Uraga's men advanced, vicious street fighting ensued as the imperialistas fell back, until all they controlled was the perimeter around the town's main square. In the melee, Márquez was shot in the face and badly wounded, but his troops rallied. Again the attack was resisted, bloodily and triumphantly. Only forty-five of Márquez's men lay dead, compared to nearly six hundred of Uraga's, with many more taken prisoner. More important, it was an enormous blow to the prestige of the republican forces, who had been defeated not by the French, but by their own countrymen. So proud was Márquez of this victory that he sent a long account, maps, and tables detailing the numbers involved to Maximilian in Europe.

A few days after Márquez defeated Uraga at Morelia, Mejía advanced on San Luis Potosí, the seat of Juárez's government. Once again, Juárez was forced to flee, this time another 280 miles or so north to the state of Coahuila. This put Juárez closer to the US border than Mexico City. Increasingly disillusioned, many liberals now began to desert the president's cause. Some of his most loyal lieutenants petitioned Juárez to resign.

He refused. On January 20, 1864, Juárez instead wrote to his critics, arguing that as the people had entrusted the nation to him, he would leave his post only if they voted him out or if he was thrown out by the French and "their traitorous" allies. Until then, Juárez resolved to do everything to "help the country in defence of its independence, its institutions and its dignity". It was true, he admitted, "that the situation is unfavourable for us now," but "making war in whatever way possible against the enemy is the only means of salvation".[21]

At this stage, the man proving most effective at waging war in whatever way possible was Juárez's implacable enemy, Archbishop Labastida. At the end of December, Mexico City's citizens had awoken to find a letter decrying the tyranny of the Regency government pasted to buildings and pushed beneath doors. This was, however, not Juarista propaganda, but the work of anonymous clergymen. The letter claimed the intervention was working against the religious beliefs of the country and threatened those who refused to return former church property with excommunication. Charles Louis Camille Neigre, the French general left in charge of Mexico City, suspected Labastida and wrote to him on January 16, 1864. Neigre bluntly stated that the French army was reluctant to use violence, but would resort to any means necessary to repress the enemies of Mexico, even if they were priests.

Labastida's reply was unrepentant. Not only did the intervention, he claimed, make the church subject to the same outrageous laws as under Juárez, but the French also more bitterly persecuted the clergy than ever before. Thus, Labastida, who only months earlier had opened Maximilian's private chapel at Miramar with a celebratory mass, now claimed that he preferred Juárez's government to the Regency. As many French officers began to complain, it seemed the worst enemies of the intervention were those who supported monarchy.

Once again, though, the showdown between church and the state came to a swift end. Every Sunday in Mexico City, the archbishop gave a mass for the French army. While the dispute raged, though, he insisted that the doors of the cathedral would remain closed. Hearing this, the French general sent an aide-de-camp to Labastida's palace with the message that if the doors of the cathedral were not open the following Sunday morning, then they would be blown apart. The mass was due to begin at 8:00 a.m. At 7:30 a.m. the doors remained closed. Neigre reportedly ordered the artillery to deploy in the enormous main square, muzzles pointed at the cathedral. Shortly afterwards, the doors opened, and Neigre, in full military uniform, took his usual seat for mass.

In reports to Maximilian, these tensions were played down. Instead, he read about Bazaine's campaign, of Márquez's spectacular victory, Mejía's rapid advances. On a map, it looked stunning. All this, Bourdillon wrote to Maximilian, confirmed that monarchy was popular in Mexico. Juárez was all but defeated, Almonte assured Maximilian. It was, therefore, time for him to leave Europe and reign as emperor in Mexico.

Buoyed by these reports, in January 1864 Maximilian wrote to Napoleon III that the advance of the French army meant that soon the majority of the Mexican nation would declare its support for the empire. Maximilian now got down to one of his preferred activities, planning his residences, instructing his secretary to write to Almonte, asking him to prepare the National Palace. Then, towards the end of the month, Maximilian sent his cook, groom, and architect to Mexico under conditions of great secrecy.

Alarming rumours had reached Maximilian that the silverware used by Mexico's former presidents might not be up to the standard required of an emperor. He was right to be worried, for in February 1864 Almonte regrettably informed him that it would be necessary to buy a new table service for forty people. The presidential cutlery had disappeared. Almonte would do his best and get the finest he could in Mexico, but he feared, ultimately, it would be necessary to replace even that. In the end, Napoleon III stepped in, giving Maximilian and Carlota a silver-plated table service as well as a dining table.

With such pressing details settled, on March 5, 1864, Maximilian and Carlota arrived in Paris. Napoleon III and Eugenie welcomed them as fellow emperors and empresses, laying on dazzling receptions, dinners, and parties. Carlota, insisting on speaking in Spanish with Eugenie, radiated excited confidence. Maximilian, by contrast, seemed to have aged. He was weighed down by the enormity of the undertaking, not least the ongoing discussions over the French military alliance and details of a loan to cover the bankrupt Mexican treasury. For these discussions, Napoleon III had used his machinery of state to ensure France got favourable terms, whereas Maximilian, having alienated the Austrian Foreign Ministry and much of his family, depended on the advice of his father-in-law, Leopold, and Belgian diplomat Kint von Roodenbeck.

This one-sided negotiation, known as the Treaty of Miramar, placed onerous obligations on Maximilian's empire. He agreed to pay the entire cost of the intervention from January 1862 to July 1, 1864, which the French calculated at 270 million francs, plus 3 percent interest. After this, Mexico would have to pay for the privilege of its occupation at 1,000 francs per man per year to keep the French army across the Atlantic. The intervention had been precipitated because Juárez's government could not honour Mexico's international debt, yet in Mexico Maximilian must meet his monthly payments because otherwise he would be in breach of the treaty and Napoleon III could withdraw his troops. A loan was raised to cover immediate expenses, but it also piled further debt on Maximilian's would-be government. Worse, most of the money never reached Mexico. It remained in France, an advance on what Maximilian had agreed to pay for his kingdom.

In short, to avoid the costs falling on the French treasury, Napoleon III leveraged the conquest of Mexico and outsourced its administration. As Richard Metternich noted, the burdens of the treaty and loan were "enormous", and Mexican "finances will have to be very well regulated if the weight of these monstrous demands is not to prove crushing." Napoleon III, however, wrote to Maximilian on March 18, 1864, to assuage any doubts. "You may be sure", wrote the French emperor, "that my support will not fail you."[22]

After Paris, Maximilian and Carlota travelled to England. Here they dined with Leopold I, who was also visiting, and saw Carlota's cousin Queen Victoria. "They are going to Mexico, which I cannot understand", recorded the queen in her journal. She was not the only one. Marie Amélie, Carlota's grandmother and a former queen of France now exiled in England, warned her granddaughter, "They will murder you!"[23] Carlota was unmoved. Maximilian, however, could not contain his emotion, leading a six-year-old girl who witnessed the scene to remark incredulously that it was normally women who cried.

Becoming emperor had gone from a pleasant reverie to an imminent reality, and the enormity of the task was daunting for Maximilian. What upset him the most, however, was a memorandum his brother had handed him before leaving for Paris. Fearful that the throne might pass to Maximilian or his descendants and thereby put Austria in the absurd position of being ruled from Mexico, Franz Joseph had suddenly demanded his younger brother renounce his rights of inheritance, and those of any children he might have, to the Habsburg throne before he left Europe. With his entire identity wrapped up in the ancient lineage of his family, Maximilian was devastated.

Once back in the Austrian capital, a magnificent dinner attended by the highest echelons of Viennese society was held in honour of Maximilian and Carlota. Carlota, emboldened that she would soon be of equal status to her sister-in-law Sisi as a fellow empress, ostentatiously wore a diamond and emerald tiara specifically designed for her new rank. But the next day, Austria's foreign minister, Rechberg, gave Maximilian the document to sign renouncing his inheritance. Maximilian refused.

"My dear brother", Franz Joseph wrote when he heard, "according to the information I have received, you are disposed to accept the throne of Mexico. . . . I find myself compelled as Supreme Head of the House of Austria", he continued, "to notify you that I can grant my consent to this grave and momentous act of state only on the condition" that Maximilian abandon "you and your heirs' rights of succession."[24]

Seething with anger, Maximilian replied the same day, complaining that renouncing his rights in Austria had never been raised in more than two years, and only cursorily before he had left for Paris two weeks prior. He had now drawn up a treaty, agreed to a loan, and "pledged my word of honour, which is respected throughout all Europe, to a population of nine million people which had appealed to me, trusting in a better future and in the hope of seeing an end of the civil war which had been raging for generations past; I did so at a time when I was unaware of any such condition as you have now imposed on me".[25]

As tempers frayed, Maximilian and Carlota left Vienna for Miramar. Franz Joseph sent a cousin after them to insist on Maximilian's signature. Maximilian would not yield. Instead, he turned the tables, posing a question: Should he inform the Mexican deputation and the French government that the reason he could not accept the throne was because of his brother's demands? Fearing the reaction in Paris, now Franz Joseph took the extraordinary step of informing the French ambassador to Austria that he needed Napoleon III's help resolving this family argument. The French emperor must persuade Maximilian to sign the document, or he could not go to Mexico. After spending hundreds of millions of francs, risking tens of thousands of lives, and promising the French people that all would be resolved through the reign of Maximilian in Mexico, Napoleon III was astounded to hear that all of his plans hung in the balance.

At two on the morning of March 28, Metternich was awoken at home by one of Napoleon III's aides-de-camp. He carried a letter from Eugenie. She referred to the disagreement as a "family matter of no importance" when compared with "the confusion" into which the "whole world" would be thrown. She signed off the letter, "Believe me, yours, in a most justifiable temper".[26]

That same morning, Metternich rushed to the Tuileries for an interview with Napoleon III and Eugenie. Napoleon III felt personally betrayed. Two weeks before, he had agreed to all the details in person with Maximilian, who had initialled the treaty between Mexico and France prior to signing it as emperor of Mexico. As Metternich tried to explain the situation about inheritance, Napoleon III interrupted, "But the archduke must have known that beforehand." The French emperor then made it clear that Maximilian's decision would seriously affect relations with France and all but threatened war. Metternich reported back to Rechberg, both once again in their familiar, if unhappy, roles as family counsellors, that it was essential the matter be resolved "in the interest of our own peace". Whether he was referring to Austria's or his own is unclear. This "deadly quarrel", he added, was "so undignified that it makes me groan".[27]

Still the same day, Napoleon III wrote to Maximilian. Desperate to forestall any immediate decision, he telegrammed as well: "I implore your Imperial Highness to arrive at no decision contrary to our engagements before receiving my letter". He sent the letter with a trusted adviser, General Charles de Frossard, who was to convey it in person. The letter read, "I am writing to Your Highness under the influence of strong emotion". The treaty, the loan, the assurances given to Mexico—all of these, argued Napoleon III, were engagements Maximilian was no longer free to break. "What, indeed, would you think of me," asked the emperor rhetorically, "if, once Your Imperial Majesty had arrived in Mexico, I were to say that I can no longer fulfil the conditions to which I have set my signature?" Knowing the weight Maximilian placed on honour, the French emperor told Frossard to remind the archduke of the promises made in Paris.

On the day that Napoleon III was doing everything to persuade Maximilian to change his mind, Carlota penned a letter to Eugenie renouncing the Mexican throne on her husband's behalf. Heaven deprived us of the happiness of taking the Mexican throne, she wrote, but Maximilian's honour would not allow him to accept his brother's conditions. The next day, therefore, he would explain to the Mexican deputation he could no longer become emperor.

Napoleon III's telegram arrived just before Maximilian was to inform the Mexicans. "Reception of deputation adjourned", Maximilian telegrammed Paris. He added that he would go to "the utmost limits of what personal honour will allow" in order to find a solution.[28] Carlota's letter was never sent.

Two days later, Frossard arrived at Miramar and handed over Napoleon III's letter. Maximilian was deeply moved, saying that the French emperor was not only a friend but also like a father. His honour, however, was engaged as an archduke and as a husband. He could not accept the Mexican crown. When Frossard replied that Maximilian's honour was also engaged with the French emperor, France, and the entire world, Carlota pointed out that it was they who were doing Napoleon III a great service in going to Mexico. "Your Highness will recognise that the services are at least mutual", Frossard pointedly replied.[29]

The French general made daily visits to Miramar and spent much time with Carlota. He found her determined to be empress of Mexico, but profoundly frustrated at the humiliation that Franz Joseph had forced on her husband. Nonetheless, while Maximilian focussed on Europe, Carlota looked to their position in Mexico and urged compromise.

Maximilian, therefore, tried to negotiate with Franz Joseph, asking him to amend his demands: the archduke should be allowed to keep his financial interests in Europe, and a secret clause should be added—if Maximilian abdicated or was deposed as Mexican emperor, then he could return to Austria and enjoy the same rights that he had when he left. Franz Joseph relented on the finances; he insisted on the renunciation.

This was not enough for Maximilian. Refusing to speak in person with his brother, he now sent Carlota to Vienna to plead his case. Resolved to be empress of Mexico, Carlota argued with her brother-in-law for more than three hours. Unimpressed with Franz Joseph's intellect, she felt his arguments made no sense. Still, Franz Joseph would give no concessions. While in Vienna she received advice from her father, whom Napoleon III had cajoled into trying to re-solve this impasse. Leopold telegrammed Carlota, "It is now almost impossible to break with the Mexicans. . . . We must attempt to find a middle way."[30]

Yet with Franz Joseph intractable, there was no middle way: Max-imilian must back down or give up the Mexican throne. Without Carlota, he had fallen into a depression, resorting to writing poetry to pass the time, but when she returned her tenacity steeled him. That, and the considerable pressure Napoleon III had brought to bear, convinced Maximilian on April 8, 1864, after more than a week of mental torture, vacillation, and despair, to finally accept the crown. A much-relieved Napoleon III telegrammed Maximilian, "You can rely upon my friendship and support."[31]

On April 9, Franz Joseph came to Miramar. There the brothers shut themselves up in the castle's opulent library, arguing amidst the busts Maximilian had installed of Homer, Dante, Goethe, and Shakespeare. With the room overlooking the Adriatic, the brothers spent hours in heated discussion, their loud and emotional voices heard throughout the castle. When they eventually emerged, they were both exhausted, but a weary Maximilian had signed away his Habsburg inheritance. Franz Joseph then left, Maximilian escorting him to the station. Just as the emperor was about to board the train, the normally cold, reserved Franz Joseph suddenly turned round, strode up to his brother, and exclaimed "Max!" before tearfully em-bracing him.

The next day, April 10, 1864, the Mexican deputation, patiently waiting in Europe after offering Maximilian the crown more than six months earlier, returned to Miramar. Drained and anxious, Maxi-milian welcomed them in the state reception room of the castle. With Carlota close behind him, Maximilian nervously stood over a small table and thumbed through a document that listed all the Mexican towns that had supposedly declared in his favour. Then Gutiérrez de Estrada gave another long, sonorous speech extolling Maximilian's virtues and thanking him for accepting the crown. After this, his voice unsteady with emotion, Maximilian read a statement he had prepared in Spanish. When he finished, the crowded room broke out into cries of "Long live Emperor Maximilian! Long live Empress Carlota!" The thunder of cannons sounded across the bay, as warships saluted the Mexican imperial flag now raised over Miramar.

For all the solemnity of the occasion, this cannot have been how Maximilian I—as Mexico's new emperor now styled himself—had imagined this moment. For almost three years the prospect had mesmerised him, but now the difficulty of the task that lay ahead overwhelmed him. After Maximilian signed numerous documents, the Treaty of Miramar, the details for a loan, plans for volunteer legions to be raised in Austria and Belgium, his doctor found the new emperor collapsed, head down and arms outstretched on the table. Suffering from nervous exhaustion, Maximilian had fallen into a depression that would not lift for days. That evening he tried to attend a banquet in his honour, but, pale, quiet, and exhausted, he soon withdrew, leaving Carlota to represent him. Becoming an empress had the opposite effect on the young princess; she was energised and radiant, confidently receiving the numerous guests presented to her.

Maximilian and Carlota had planned to leave for Mexico the next day, but Maximilian's mental state made it impossible. Carlota even had to compose a letter of thanks to Napoleon III, which Maximilian signed as though it were his own. As he convalesced, telegrams of congratulation poured in at the last moment, Maximilian's parents writing, "Farewell. Our blessing—Papa's and mine—our prayers and our tears accompany you. . . . Farewell for the last time on your native soil, where alas we may see you no more. We bless you again and again from our deeply sorrowing hearts".[32]

Finally, on April 14, Maximilian felt well enough to depart. The people of Trieste lined the gardens and jetty of Miramar to wave farewell. The mayor read an address, and, once again, Maximilian burst into tears. He tried to control his emotions as he was rowed out to his beloved ship, the *Novara*, which was to be escorted by a French frigate to Veracruz. Carlota, in contrast, beamed with pleasure and pride as she saw the Mexican imperial standard. One of Carlota's ladies-in-waiting noticed that as soon as Maximilian boarded the *Novara*, he sequestered himself in his cabin to hide his uncontrollable despair.

Maximilian could not stay there for long. Four days later, the ships pulled into Civitavecchia, the port for Rome. Here they saw the Roman ruins, attended extravagant dinners, and, most important, visited the Vatican. Carlota went to Saint Peter's tomb and was overwhelmed with religious wonder, crying out, "My god, I believe!"[33] At an audience with Pope Pius IX, Maximilian and Carlota received his blessing, but all difficult discussion of church property in Mexico was avoided. It was instead agreed that a papal nuncio, as the Vatican termed their diplomats, would follow them in a few months to arrange a concordat regulating church-state relations.

After Rome, the *Novara* stopped off at Gibraltar, and then the party made its way on to Madeira, before making the Atlantic crossing. Carlota suffered from seasickness, spending much of the time in her cabin preparing for her new life, studying maps of Mexico, reading books on its politics and history, and improving her Spanish. Meanwhile, Maximilian discussed the future with Mexican politicians travelling on board; his main focus, though, was composing a book of etiquette for his court, modelling it on the rigid and centuries-old traditions of the Habsburgs and on that ultimate incarnation of absolute monarchy, Louis XIV and his *Étiquette de la cour royale*. The detail it contained was obsessive. Palace guards, it stipulated, must be at least six feet tall. Every official occasion that the imperial couple would preside over was painstakingly arranged, down to the exact position of each participant in relation to the emperor based on a hierarchical system that included more than two hundred ranks. At what point, and to whom, Maximilian would hand his hat and Carlota her handkerchief was also covered.

After forty-four days travelling, the coast of Mexico came into view. Maximilian went up on deck, his face imperturbable as he scanned the horizons of his new empire.

5

EMPEROR AND EMPRESS

As the *Novara* sailed towards land on May 28, 1864, Maximilian and Carlota saw their new kingdom for the first time. Clouds obscured the peak of Orizaba, but against a backdrop of distant mountains black vultures circled over the ramshackle town of Veracruz. To their left as the imperial couple approached the port, they passed the Isla de Sacrificios, where, more than three hundred years earlier, Hernán Cortés's conquistadores had seen dismembered bodies piled on top of bloodstained stone altars. The name was still apt, for the island was now covered with crosses marking the graves of French soldiers who had died creating Maximilian and Carlota's kingdom. The wreck of a French ship on a nearby reef added to the sense of dilapidation and decay that overwhelmed those on board the *Novara*, which, under a scalding tropical sun, anchored at two that afternoon.

As the thunder of 101 cannons firing across the bay resounded from a nearby fort, announcing their arrival, Maximilian and Carlota anxiously scanned the docks and saw that the port was nearly deserted. Endemic yellow fever made Veracruz a dangerous place to stay, and Juan Nepomuceno Almonte, who was meant to greet the imperial couple, was waiting in safety nearby for news of the

Novara. The news had not come in time. As he desperately rushed to the port, panicked officials and curious onlookers milled about on the docks.

The first person to welcome Maximilian and Carlota to Mexico was a Frenchman, the commander of the French navy at Veracruz. He did not wait for Almonte's arrival, and as soon as the admiral stepped on board the *Novara*, he harangued Maximilian in front of his entourage for anchoring in the most contagious part of the port. Maximilian had ordered the *Novara* to set itself apart from the French fleet with the optimistic hope of symbolically distancing his arrival from the foreign intervention; however, according to the admiral, sailors had contracted yellow fever after spending just one night at the *Novara*'s mooring. He then told the astonished passengers that guerrilla bands were lying in wait outside Veracruz to capture Maximilian and Carlota and that the commander in chief of the French forces, Achille Bazaine, was too busy to personally escort them to Mexico City.

Almonte finally reached Veracruz later that evening, rounding up the relevant dignitaries before being ferried out to receive Maximilian and Carlota. Formal speeches were read and pleasantries exchanged, but it was now late and Maximilian and Carlota decided to stay aboard the *Novara* and enter Veracruz at five the next morning. Too nervous to sleep, they wrote letters to family in Europe. Carlota, trying to reassure her worried grandmother, wrote that it was a mistake to call the Americas the "New World" because all that was lacking was "the telegraph and a little civilisation, which, I hope, will come to link it to what we call the Old".[1] At four thirty, mass was heard on board the ship, and then the imperial couple was rowed towards land in the twilight darkness. Carlota's confident letter belied the anxiety she felt, slipping into her kingdom at dawn, worried about the reception she would receive from her new subjects.

She was right to be worried. In the early hours of May 29, cannon fire again disturbed the bay, shocking the *veracruzanos*, who, violently awoken at an inhospitable hour, preferred to stay in bed rather than line the streets to cheer their new monarchs. Crowds would have been unlikely at any time of day, for Veracruz had been the seat of Benito Juárez's constitutional government during the three-year civil war. Most *veracruzanos* were liberals and looked on with hostility as the Conservative Party, backed by French troops, overturned the legitimate republican government of Mexico and replaced it with a European monarchy.

The imperial couple thus made a sombre procession in an open carriage through disconcertingly empty streets. Above them, the morning's first vultures rose into the air. Maximilian and Carlota passed unfinished triumphal arches designed to celebrate their arrival; strong winds the night before had blown down the scaffolding, which now lay littered on the ground. So chilling were her first impressions of Mexico that they nearly reduced Carlota to tears.

The imperial couple reached the town's railway station, where a train awaited, beginning the journey to the Mexican capital. Hastily built to transport battle-hardened French troops, not royalty, the rickety line made its way through the semidesert lowlands of the state of Veracruz only as far as a small village some seventy miles from the port. The rest of the journey had to be completed by carriage—or, rather, many carriages, for the large party Maximilian had brought with him numbered eighty people, including servants, cooks, and even a famed Austrian conductor to lead the emperor's personal orchestra. The group also contained numerous aristocrats, who were to set up Maximilian's court in Mexico City, accompanied by Carlota's coterie, including her ladies-in-waiting. Only once these passengers had disembarked from the train could the five hundred pieces of luggage be transferred into carriages and coaches. This caravan presented an extraordinary sight: the elite of Habsburg society dressed in the finest European fashions, driven towards the capital by local muleteers clothed in leather jackets, goatskin trousers, and wide gold-trimmed sombreros.

The route followed precarious roads, passing mountains and volcanoes, which required drivers to navigate valleys or ravines with sheer drops on either side. If the driver managed to negotiate these obstacles, there was always the danger of bandits or, worse, Juaristas. As Carlota wrote, "We passed through many most-suspicious look-ing spots, where several thousand partisans lay concealed. I confess on the first day of our journey . . . I should not have been surprised if Juárez himself had appeared with some hundreds of guerrillas."

The journey was not a comfortable one. Although Maximilian and Carlota kept reassuring their Mexican escorts that they did not mind, the empress confessed that "as a matter of fact it was beyond all words and we needed all our youth and good humour to get off without cramp or a broken rib".[2] Maximilian limited himself to the diplomatic comment that the journey would never be effaced from their memory, and that while it had afforded them the opportunity to see the beauty and riches of his country, it had also shown them the appalling state of the roads.

Yet once out of the coastal lowlands, the trek to the capital finally became the expected triumphant procession. Almonte and Bazaine had prepared detailed plans for the couple's reception at the major towns on the route, and at every stop local officials welcomed their new monarchs. They attended mass, were feted at banquets, and watched firework displays. Locals lined the streets to cheer them, while thousands of indigenous Mexicans lit the road with flaming torches at night.

Much of what they saw was alien to Maximilian and Carlota. Even the most godforsaken, poverty-stricken villages in the Austrian Empire had more in common with the imperial court at Vienna than some of the remote Mexican villages that the imperial couple passed through. Maximilian was a talented linguist, speaking some ten languages; however, nothing could have been more alien to him than being addressed in Nahuatl, the language of the Aztecs, when indigenous leaders greeted him.

In one village, Maximilian and Carlota invited these leaders to eat with them. As a newspaper noted, this presented a fascinating spectacle, as the young sovereigns used to dining with the most illustrious company of the Old World ate at the same table as indigenous Mexicans in traditional dress. Maximilian and Carlota were also given their first taste of Mexican food, trying *mole de guajolote*, turkey in a spicy sauce, and tortillas with chili washed down with *pulque*, a local Mexican drink the colour of milk made from the sap of the agave plant—a meal they could not finish because the food was too spicy.

On June 5, nine days after their first glimpse of Mexico, Maximilian and Carlota reached more familiar surroundings at Puebla. The empress compared the neighbouring countryside, enclosed by mountains, to northern Italy, while Puebla's regular streets, churches, and government buildings seemed European to Maximilian and Carlota. Cheering crowds saluted them as the imperial couple drove through the city towards the cathedral under triumphal arches—finished this time—adorned with Mexican, French, Austrian, and Belgian flags. Celebrations here were particularly magnificent because June 7 was the empress's birthday, and that evening the most characteristic event of European aristocratic court life, a ball, was held in her honour. There Carlota appeared in a simple white silk dress, with a crown of emeralds and diamonds as well as a magnificent diamond necklace and bracelets, no *mole de guajolote* or *pulque* in sight.

Moving on from Puebla, the imperial caravan pressed towards the capital. On June 11 the royal couple made a pilgrimage to the Basilica of Our Lady of Guadalupe, about six miles north of Mexico City, near where legend, and the Catholic Church, has it that in 1531 the Virgin Mary made her first appearance in the New World to an Aztec convert. This was Mexico's most sacred site. The capital's elite went to meet their new rulers, filling two hundred carriages with young women from the most distinguished families of Mexico, escorted by five hundred gentlemen on horseback. The next day, after celebrating mass in the church, Maximilian and Carlota arrived at their new seat of power.

They were not disappointed; Mexico City was an imperial capital par excellence. Time, war, and revolutions had faded some of the grandeur, but the city retained the magnificence constructed over the previous three hundred years as the wealthy epicentre of Spanish North America. With its wide paved streets, innumerable beautiful churches and mystical convents, renowned opera houses and theatres, shops with goods from across the world, and vast government buildings, the architectural splendour of Mexico City still rivalled all but a handful of European cities. In short, the empire's capital lent itself to an imperial procession.

And the reception for Maximilian and Carlota's arrival was spectacular, eclipsing the entry of the French army one year previously. The streets and plazas were packed. The balconies were full of spectators, all shouting, "Viva el Emperador! Viva la Emperatriz!" The ubiquitous triumphal arches marked the route of the procession, while the houses were decorated with flowers and flags. Mexican lancers, renamed the imperial guard, led the parade, whilst behind them rode a squadron of French Chasseurs d'Afrique in their striking uniforms of red trousers and blue tunics. Travelling in an open carriage, Maximilian and Carlota beamed as their new subjects cheered them. Their final destination was the Gothic cathedral, built on the old Aztec Templo Mayor, site of countless human sacrifices. The main square was filled with thousands of people. Deeply impressed by their reception, they now made their way through the crowds to attend a Te Deum presided over by Archbishop Labastida, with all the solemnity the occasion demanded.

After days of celebration, the pomp and ceremony concluded on June 19 with another ball. Fearful of the national stereotype that Latin Americans are never on time, the punctilious Austrian in Maximilian had insisted that his new subjects be at the theatre where it was held at half past eight. In a rare display of Mexican promptness, one newspaper reported, everyone was assembled at the appointed hour. Within, candlelit chandeliers dazzled in mirror-lined walls, and a glass patio had been adorned with plants and flowers, Venetian lamps hidden in the foliage. Fine biscuits, ices, and liqueurs were piled on tables as refreshments for some three thousand guests.

At nine thirty, the new rulers arrived to the cheers of an enthusiastic crowd outside the theatre before proceeding inside to sit on thrones erected especially for the occasion. The couple had made sure they looked the part: the emperor was dressed in black and wearing a medal of the Grand Master of the Order of Guadalupe, an honours system Maximilian had created; the empress wore a dress of pink silk with English lace and her crown of diamonds.

Republicans criticised the pageantry that marked the progress of Maximilian and Carlota to Mexico City. It was expensive and contrasted with Juárez's austere republican government. However, it was a carefully orchestrated publicity campaign, and, despite the underwhelming arrival at Veracruz, the journey proved a triumph. The imperial couple's stage-managed entries into the main cities demonstrated the splendour, wealth, and power of monarchy, but more crucially projected the impression, real or otherwise, of popular support. Everything—the balls and banquets, the processions and triumphal arches, the meetings with indigenous leaders, the Te Deums, the pilgrimage to the holy site of Guadalupe—had been choreographed to reassure the elites, fete the people, and present the monarchs as the defenders of Catholicism and the champions of Mexico's indigenous population.

Maximilian set out to establish a modern, popular monarchy that married tradition with ideas of democracy closer to those of Juárez than to the caricature of aristocratic European courts. This was to be a regime that relied not on divine authority propped up by a propertied class alone but on the support of the nation. Charles Bourdillon, still in Mexico as the *Times*' correspondent and Maximilian's agent, stretched journalistic license when he reported that the "lower classes" frequently said, "These are true Princes! How unlike those wretched Presidents, who could never move out unless by an escort of soldiers to ride down those who came in their way!"[3] But this was the impression that Maximilian wanted to project, an image he hoped would bridge the contradiction between Mexican nationalism and European dynastic rule.

Old habits die hard, though, and Maximilian insisted on the strict code of etiquette he had written on the voyage from Europe. Contemporaries ridiculed him for this. In so doing, they missed a serious point. Maximilian, Napoleon III, and those who supported the empire were not, as some alleged, trying to implant an Old World kingdom in the New. Nor were they trying to establish a reactionary regime modelled on some romanticised notion of a colonial past; they were trying to create a world that had never existed. This world had to be constructed in the realm of ideas as well as on the ground; to this end, the image the imperial couple and their court projected was crucial.

The rigid court discipline did have teething problems. When the leading women of Mexico were presented for the first time to the empress, one, the wife of the regent Mariano Salas, went to embrace Carlota. A common greeting in Mexico, known as an *abrazo*, this level of intimacy was horrifying to Carlota, who drew herself to her full height and stepped back with tears of indignation in her eyes. Compounding the offence, Señora Salas then offered Carlota a cigarette by way of apology before bursting into tears herself. Carlota politely declined to smoke on the grounds of health, and smoking in public amongst women in high society soon disappeared. Other trends inspired by the empress were less successful: women tried to imitate her elegant fashion by wearing the fine Parisian bonnets she favoured, but what was the height of sophistication in the Old World became a source of ridicule in the New; Mexicans wore them back to front. In one town thousands of women came to greet Carlota, who reviewed them graciously and seriously, occasionally stopping to talk to her new subjects; however, afterwards she began to laugh until tears streamed down her face, so ridiculous did she find their outfits.

Cultural differences aside, the Mexican Empire began well. In league with Almonte and Bazaine, Maximilian and Carlota had proved adept at projecting an image of popular royal power. Moreover, the receptions at Orizaba, Puebla, and, above all, Mexico City convinced Carlota that "according to all I have seen, a monarchy is feasible in this country and responds to the unanimous needs of the people". The empire, however, was a fragile edifice built on the foundations of a republic. As the empress wrote, "It remains an enormous experiment, for we have to struggle against the wilderness, distance, the roads, and the most utter chaos".[4]

CHAOS THERE WAS. On arrival at Veracruz, Maximilian had issued a proclamation: "Mexicans!" it began. "You have desired my presence! Your noble nation, by a willing majority, has elected me to watch over your destinies! I gladly submit to this call." Maximilian's statement was sincere. He believed, because the Mexican émigrés and Napoleon III had told him so, that there was popular support for his kingdom in Mexico. After all, in March, the French diplomatic envoy in Mexico had written to Paris to inform the foreign minister that 5,498,587 Mexicans out of a total population of 8,629,982 supported the empire, but these suspiciously exact numbers amounted to little more than an estimate of the population under nominal Franco-Mexican control. Barail noted the Mexicans would have elected the "devil . . . if we had presented [his] candidature at the point of our sabres and bayonets."[5]

The truth was that Maximilian may have held the title emperor of Mexico, but this was recognised only in the country's central states; in the others, a president still governed. Despite the success of Bazaine's campaign, Juárez held Nuevo León, Coahuila, Tamaulipas, and Chihuahua in the north; Sinaloa, Colima, and Guerrero on the west coast; and Oaxaca, Tabasco, and Chiapas in the south. Even in states nominally under imperial control, such as Veracruz, Michoacán, and Puebla, Juaristas kept up incessant guerrilla warfare, and outside of the main towns Maximilian's authority existed only on paper.

Juárez had set up his latest capital in Monterrey, Nuevo León, a state that bordered the Rio Grande, the river that marks the US-Mexican border in the northeast. From there, he directed republican opposition; after numerous setbacks, he had perhaps no more than fifteen thousand soldiers thinly spread across various fronts. Facing them, Maximilian had some thirty thousand French as well as roughly twenty thousand Mexican troops. Yet these soldiers would need to end Juárez's regular and guerrilla resistance in a country of nearly 760,000 square miles. To further complicate this task, Maximilian inherited the problems all Mexican governments had faced: a weak state and perilous finances.

To win over Juaristas, Maximilian immediately adopted a liberal manifesto, although the fact that it had been written by a French journalist who had been in Mexico for only two weeks hardly reassured Mexican nationalists. *Le Programme de l'Empire* was published on the day Maximilian arrived at Veracruz, a small pamphlet that served as an ambitious blueprint for a new empire based on the middle way Napoleon III had ploughed in France. Previously, argued the manifesto, the word *empire* had been associated with absolute government, but Napoleon III had made an intimate alliance between the modern principles of progress and democracy, on the one hand, and conservatism and stability, on the other. The Mexican Empire was to be underwritten by reconciliation after the rancour of civil war; through the organisation of a stable government supported by the law, religion, and the nation; and by economic progress and democracy. Under this heady mixture, Maximilian would repeat Napoleon III's supposed success in France, and Mexico would one day be richer and more powerful than the United States.

Maximilian dreamt of his realm as a modern empire of iron and steel, embracing technology. The emperor fantasised of connecting his extensive territories with telegraph lines and railways, while steamships crossed the Atlantic carrying the manufactured goods of a newly industrialised and liberal nation that would rival the great powers of the age. Yet although Maximilian and Carlota ridiculed the antiquated beliefs of their conservative allies in private, they were not yet strong enough to break publicly with the men who had done so much to bring them to power. As a result, important points of policy, especially involving church property, remained unresolved.

In the meantime, two issues required the emperor's immediate attention. First, he had to form a government and win over liberals loyal to Juárez. Second, he needed to organise Mexico's finances. This latter was crucial given the Treaty of Miramar's arduous obligations. Maximilian's government had to pay for the foreign army protecting it, but in 1864 the Mexican treasury did not receive enough revenue to meet such an expenditure on top of the costs of governing the country. This cost was temporarily covered through the loan Maximilian had agreed to before he left for Mexico; however, it was only a stopgap, which considerably added to Mexico's long-term debt. It was imperative that the Mexican treasury balance its budget, for if Maximilian was unable to pay France, he would be in breach of the treaty and Napoleon III would have the right to withdraw the French army. Thus, financial reforms—regular budgets, cuts in expenditure, and new taxes—were urgent. But instead of taking any of these measures, Maximilian did what governments keen on giving the impression of activity have done throughout the ages: he established commissions to report back to him.

Meanwhile, Maximilian seemed more concerned with perfecting his imperial residences than reorganising the nation's finances. The National Palace in Mexico City, good enough for presidents, was apparently not suitable for royalty. This austere, grey two-story building dominates the eastern side of the Zócalo, adjacent to the cathedral, and measures more than 210 yards in length. Inside its warren-like, endless corridors and cavernous rooms, Maximilian felt like a solitary nun in a convent, forced to sleep on a billiards table to avoid the plague of rats and bedbugs, which infested the palace. After only eight nights, Maximilian and Carlota abandoned it for Chapultepec Castle, three miles outside the city centre.

Constructed in the late eighteenth century as the residence of Spanish viceroys, Chapultepec had been built on a sacred Aztec site, in a forest of gigantic trees that stretched upwards of 200 feet. Perched atop a hill, the views from the palace were magnificent, overlooking the valley of Mexico, with the volcanoes Popocatépetl and

Iztaccíhuatl commanding the horizon. The castle, though, was in a state of disrepair, another casualty of the US-Mexican War. So, in a move that hardly boded well for future financial austerity, Maximilian spent enormous sums restoring his new home, summoning his preferred gardeners and architects across the Atlantic. He furnished it at great expense with rich crimson silk tapestries from Europe and magnificent chandeliers from Venice, while candelabras illuminated the large white vases and statues that adorned the main staircase. Maximilian allowed himself to be distracted from the pressing affairs of state and delved into the minutiae of the refurbishment. He even handpicked all the furniture, as well as the fine, delicate china and crystal, which were shipped from Europe and then carried in mule trains from Veracruz to the capital.

At Chapultepec, the imperial couple settled into their new routine. Maximilian was industrious, rising at four to look over state papers, working until about seven, before going riding. Then he had a generous breakfast with Carlota and a few secretaries. Afterwards, Maximilian was driven to the National Palace, where he held cabinet meetings, attended ceremonies, and conducted other government business. Leopold I, Maximilian's father-in-law, always insisted on communicating with all staff through written memo. In Mexico, Maximilian adopted the same practice because he could not stand to be interrupted. Even the empress was permitted to see Maximilian only at his invitation or mealtimes. As per his childhood routine, Maximilian was in bed by eight, one of his maxims being that eight hours of sleep was essential for health and long life.

Carlota brought her own European entourage, although she soon appointed some Mexican women as ladies-in-waiting. This small army trailed in her wake, accompanying her on walks, to the theatre, and to mass. As part of her routine, Carlota held regular soirées on Mondays to entertain diplomats, military officers, friends, and other supporters. These were formal white-tie occasions, with the best cuisine and no expense spared. Oysters, vol-au-vents, salmon tartare, quail, and truffles were frequently on the menu, washed down with numerous wines and—one advantage of heading a regime backed by France—the finest champagnes. The imperial wine cellar was reported to run through several hundred bottles a month. As entertainment, orchestras would play Strauss, Verdi, or Schubert.

Court life was a novelty to the citizens of a former republic, and aristocratic fever broke out amongst the upper echelons of Mexican society, all eager to secure a position at court. So many now pored over their family histories in an attempt to prove they were descended from Spanish nobility that Maximilian commented it was a shame Chapultepec did not have a parchment factory because it would make him rich. For Juaristas, however, Maximilian's court life embodied the decadence of European monarchy. There never was, nor could there ever be, one liberal writer argued, a proper aristocracy in Mexico, and Maximilian should have been embarrassed by Mexicans who pretended to be nobles. More damaging from a propaganda point of view, Maximilian's court was profligate: he was assigned $125,000 a month; the salary of a Mexican president had been $30,000 a year.

Maximilian, though, did not relish the more extravagant side of court life, shunning balls and banquets because they jeopardised his precious eight hours' sleep. "The so-called entertainments of Europe," he boasted to his younger brother, "such as evening receptions, the gossip of tea parties, etc., etc., of hideous memory, are quite unknown here, and we shall take great care not to introduce them."[6] Unfortunately for Maximilian, they were known, just not yet organised. Once they were, Maximilian often left them to Carlota, who enjoyed basking in their imperial splendour. As one of her ladies-in-waiting commented, Carlota had a childlike joy in showing herself at great state occasions to the people when she could wear her crown and gold embroidered robe with a long and highly adorned red-velvet train hanging from her shoulders.

Maximilian could not escape every court event, and after those dinners he had to attend, he liked to challenge his guests to games of billiards, where he made fun of his Mexican ministers in German, assuming they would not understand. If his guests lost they were forced to crawl under the table as a forfeit, but if Maximilian lost a servant would do so for him. Maximilian had a lewd sense of humour and loved to gossip the morning after a social event. Speaking to his Mexican private secretary, José Luis Blasio, Maximilian commented that one of his court officials had twelve children and so clearly made excellent use of his time, toiling patriotically to increase the population of the empire. That official, the emperor added, ought to be exempted from his duties so that his time might be used more agreeably and profitably for the nation. On another occasion, after Blasio fell asleep in a carriage, his head inadvertently resting on the shoulder of a beautiful woman travelling next to him, Maximilian joked that even if his eyes were shut Blasio had never been more wide awake. Less amusingly, the emperor refused his secretary permission to marry because he did not want him like a "rabbit" with "ten children and then farewell to work, to judgement", and to getting up at four.[7]

Once in Mexico, Maximilian spent less time with Carlota, which affected their private life. To the outside world and to close family, Maximilian and Carlota projected the image of the perfect royal couple. In letters to her grandmother, Carlota stressed that she was happy and united in all things, political or otherwise, with Maximilian. In Europe this had been true, although Carlota never shared Maximilian's reservations over Mexico. The couple's personal correspondence is touching, with Carlota beginning her letters with a variation on "dearly beloved treasure" and Maximilian with "beloved angel". But Carlota, only twenty-four years old at the start of their rule, became especially lonely when Maximilian travelled within Mexico. On his first trip away from the capital in August 1864, left alone at Chapultepec, she wrote to Maximilian that she was sick and time passed painfully while she remained "mummified in this swampy palace"—it was the rainy season, and there were frequent storms in Mexico City.[8]

Another problem was that Maximilian's eye began to wander. Something of a ladies' man in his youth, and now only thirty-two years old, he was enchanted by Mexican women. This shocked Blasio, who asked how this could be when Maximilian was married to one of the most attractive women in the world. "Answer me frankly, amigo," replied the emperor. "Each day you have all sorts of fine food at the imperial table, but now and then don't you enjoy a meal of hot Mexican food, washed down with the white liquor of the country?"[9] Moreover, Maximilian and Carlota never slept in the same room, maintaining separate quarters at Chapultepec. Even when travelling together, after local dignitaries had left, Maximilian would angrily order servants to find another room in which to set up a camp bed rather than sleep in the one prepared for himself and the empress. Later, Maximilian maintained another imperial residence at Cuernavaca, a town about fifty miles south of Mexico City, where he spent much of his time. Rumours circulated that he did so for affairs other than those of state, including with the daughter of his Mexican gardener.

Having set up his residence and court, in July Maximilian finally turned his attention to the government of the empire. Maximilian's determination to rule above faction, turning liberals and conservatives into imperialistas, created a number of converts. He appointed moderate liberals to cabinet positions, most notably José Fernando Ramírez as foreign minister. This was significant because Ramírez had opposed the French intervention, as well as the establishment of the monarchy, and had pointedly refused to decorate his house to welcome the imperial couple into the capital; a conservative described him as "one of the reddest republicans".[10] This was hyperbole, but moderates like Ramírez were exactly the kind of men whom Maximilian needed to consolidate his empire.

There were, however, considerable missteps. To the irritation of his Mexican supporters, the emperor embedded his European coterie at the core of his new empire. His Hungarian secretary wielded enormous influence, as did a Belgian, Félix Eloin, who was appointed head of Maximilian's imperial civil cabinet. The Mexicans especially despised Eloin, a former mining engineer, not only because he was a Protestant who spoke no Spanish, but also because he insisted that all government business pass through him before reaching Maximilian. This meant documents had to be laboriously translated into French before they could be read by Eloin, who not only knew nothing of Mexico, but had no previous experience of running a country any-where. In the words of one Mexican critic, this private cabinet was "a polyglot, a sort of Tower of Babel, composed of French, Belgians, Hungarians and I do not know what other nationalities", which did much to impede the good governance of the empire.[11]

Still, Maximilian's magnetism combined with his striking ap-pearance helped him win over many sceptics. His private secretary, Blasio, described Maximilian as "arrogant, majestic and slender", but with a gentle expression, adding that his voluminous blond beard, parted in the middle, gave him such an aspect of majesty that it was impossible not to be captivated.[12] As emperor, Maximilian was generous, retaining the leniency that had marked his governorship of Lombardy-Venetia and frequently pardoning enemies whom his sup-porters urged him to execute. This frustrated Bazaine, who believed that a firmer hand was required to "pacify" Mexico. Maximilian, however, was determined to be loved, not feared, and still carried his twenty-seven aphorisms for good conduct. Now, in Mexico, "We forget the shadows of the past" became a favourite, a maxim aimed at reconciling Mexico's divided political factions.

The campaign to win over the empire's enemies bore fruit in the summer of 1864. That August, Santiago Vidaurri, a fiercely indepen-dent liberal leader, betrayed Juárez, writing to Maximilian that he recognised him as emperor. Vidaurri became an invaluable member of Maximilian's inner circle and one of the most determined impe-rialistas. Similarly, another of Juárez's best generals, the one-legged José López Uraga, whom Márquez had defeated at Morelia, limped over to the empire, becoming another trusted confidant. Maximilian courted these men with determination, meeting with them and convincing them to fight for the imperial cause. Once won over, Carlota charmed them over dinner. Republicans like these, Carlota wrote to her grandmother, rallied to the empire because the government worked ceaselessly for the well-being of the nation. "The work is difficult," she continued, "but feasible with perseverance and courage, and neither are lacking on our part."[13]

The rapid advance of the Franco-Mexican army in 1864 did much to persuade those who had abandoned Juárez they had made the right decision. In fact, the problem for Bazaine was not winning battles so much as it was finding republican forces to win them against. Juárez's generals continued to avoid open conflict, retreating in order to overextend French lines of communication, aiming to tire the French with marches across the punishing terrain of a country four times larger than France. Thus, much of the campaign in the summer of 1864 saw French troops again occupy important towns unopposed. Monterrey was taken on August 26. Juárez, with a few supporters in old carriages and behind them a wagon carrying the nation's archives, fled farther into Mexico's northern desert, this time to Chihuahua, but not before he sent his family to the United States for safety.

Matamoros, on the Rio Grande, was the last important Gulf of Mexico port in liberal hands. When it finally fell on September 26, Mejía led his troops jubilantly through the streets, drums beating and flags flying. Here the two wars on the North American continent collided. Months earlier, Confederates had retaken Brownsville, the US town directly across the river. A few days after Mejía occupied Matamoros, grey-coat soldiers rushed across to congratulate the imperialistas on their victory, while nearby Union troops eyed suspiciously the arrival of the French navy in the Gulf of Mexico.

Starved of resources, with his supporters deserting him in droves, and fleeing the advancing French, Juárez now looked less like the legitimate president than the defeated leader of a lost cause.

MAXIMILIAN FOCUSSED ON these positives in correspondence to his family. Everywhere he went, he claimed, he was received with enthusiasm, and the endless, exciting possibilities of the New World were immeasurably superior to the insufferable, stifling Old. Nonetheless, Maximilian was aware that his empire was not the arcadia that he depicted. One person he could not mislead was Napoleon III, who received exhaustive reports from, amongst others, Bazaine, which detailed the financial, political, and military state of Mexico. These told the French emperor that a return on his considerable investment was in danger; nothing had been done to reform the Mexican treasury. Addressing this must, Napoleon III urged, be Maximilian's immediate priority.

On August 9, Maximilian assured the French emperor that it was: "The financial question in Mexico is too vital not to be the object of my unremitting attention."[14] The next day, however, he set out on a tour of his kingdom that would last nearly three months. These trips would become such a regular feature that his opponents labelled him a royal tourist. And it was a strange way to prove that finances were the object of his unremitting attention because, as French reports to Napoleon III noted, Maximilian's absence from the capital led to paralysis in government.

The idea of the tour, Maximilian maintained, was to get to know his kingdom and its people so as to identify and then address their problems; however, the journey coincided with the rainy season, which made already bad and lawless roads almost impassable. Undeterred, while urgent questions remained unresolved in Mexico City, Maximilian set out with a large entourage and larger military escort. As with the journey from Veracruz, the tour was stage-managed: troops secured routes from a distance, and only a small number would accompany the emperor into towns, giving the impression the area was safer than it was.

Maximilian's tour also coincided with the anniversary of Mexican independence—or at least one of the anniversaries. Nothing demonstrated the chasm that divided Mexico more than the charged debate between liberals and conservatives over which date to celebrate. The liberals dated independence back to the first insurrectionary movement against the Spanish. That had been led by a priest, Miguel Hidalgo y Costilla, who on September 16, 1810, had launched the Grito de Dolores, literally the "Cry of Dolores", after the town in which Hidalgo had made a historic speech urging his parishioners to rebel against the Spanish.

For conservatives, however, Hidalgo was the embodiment of the French Revolution, unleashing the mob and encouraging the murder of creoles. They argued that Hidalgo's supporters had embarked upon a bloodthirsty rampage against the white race, culminating in the massacre of more than three hundred men, women, and children who had sought refuge from Hidalgo's advancing army in a granary. Hidalgo's men set the building on fire, slaughtering those who did not burn to death.

For conservatives, to celebrate Hidalgo was to celebrate murder. Instead, they marked September 27, 1821, when former royalist officer Agustín de Iturbide entered Mexico City after declaring independence. The liberals, on the other hand, saw Iturbide as a traitor turned tyrant after he crowned himself emperor; to the horror of conservatives, the liberals of the early republic had executed him by firing squad in 1824. In short, the conservatives accused liberals of celebrating a priest who preached genocide and of having executed the Mexican equivalent of George Washington, while the liberals claimed that conservatives revered a despot, whilst themselves honouring a revolutionary priest who preached equality and justice. More than forty years later, these events continued to divide Mexicans, who could not even agree on what day to celebrate independence.

Maximilian remained blissfully unaware of this debate. He had to ask his advisers who the heroes of Mexican independence were, and, in keeping with his antipathy for the conservatives, he adopted the liberal interpretation, decreeing that the two celebrations would be combined, but, crucially, on September 16. To celebrate, Maximilian visited the town of Dolores, where he planned to emulate Hidalgo, giving a speech from the house where the first cry for independence had gone up. When he entered the town, Maximilian must have felt every bit the Mexican hero: crowds cheered him, and fireworks burst in the sky. He even dined with Hidalgo's grandson (the divine right of kings was not the only Catholic doctrine that this revolutionary priest had challenged), and, swept up in the moment, Maximilian wrote to Carlota that Juárez was "finished".[15]

Yet if Maximilian was hopeful about the future of his empire, he was less enamoured at the prospect of delivering his Independence Day speech. He was not a confident public speaker; he worried that people would laugh at him and was extremely nervous as he climbed to the second floor of the house and onto the balcony. Looking out, he saw the square packed with officials, French soldiers, and imperialista Mexican troops, all of whom listened to the speech in respectful silence before bursting into loud applause and the now de rigueur cries of "Viva el Emperador!" As a relieved Maximilian wrote, "It went off well, thank god, and the enthusiasm was indescribable".[16]

For others, though, it was describable: "I assure you", wrote one witness, "that never have we seen one of these occasions in which there has been so little enthusiasm." It was a "ridiculous and shocking spectacle [to see] a foreign army celebrating the anniversary of independence, it cannot but inspire a profound disgust." The contradictions of the French army cheering an Austrian emperor on the anniversary of Mexican independence were lost on Maximilian. The ironies did not end there, for, as a Habsburg, Maximilian was a descendant of Emperor Charles V, in whose name Cortés had first conquered Mexico, enslaving its people under the harsh rule of Spanish colonialism. Thus, not only was a French army cheering a foreign prince, but this prince was reenacting the very moment when Mexicans first challenged the Spanish empire, which Maximilian's own ancestor had imposed. Maximilian also used the speech to demonstrate his liberal credentials. He wrote to Carlota that it contained new ideas that would frighten conservatives. And in this he was correct, with one of their leaders describing it as "imprudent, untrue,

[and] offensive . . . to the ancestors of Maximilian, to the reigning family of Spain, to the Conservative party".[17]

The reactions illustrated the enormous difficulties that Maximilian faced. As Napoleon III had seemingly done in France, Maximilian hoped to find a *juste milieu* between radical liberals and reactionary conservatives, but years of civil war had so polarised Mexicans that the centre was a lonely place. Although men like Juárez and Labastida held antithetical worldviews, they unquestionably believed in their visions for Mexico. Maximilian seemed blind or indifferent to the fact that in making his liberal credentials clear, he was alienating his traditional supporters. While the emperor could boast some high-profile converts to the imperial cause, the conservatives argued that he would never win die-hard nationalist republicans—men like Juárez—over to a foreign monarchy and that first he must crush his enemies before magnanimously pardoning any who survived.

In part, Maximilian's tour was intended to placate Mexican nationalism by showing the emperor as a Mexican ruler rather than a European aristocrat. To that end, the emperor appeared before his subjects in traditional Mexican clothing, presenting an astonishing spectacle as he rode into each town. He wore trousers with silver buttons down each side, a white vest, and a jacket off set with a red cravat and sombrero. To add to the effect, he rode a black horse with a Mexican *charro*, or cowboy, saddle. Compared to the traditional English saddle, these were enormous, ornately decorated leather seats designed for riding horses long hours over rough terrain. The *charro*'s most distinctive feature was a large horn or pommel at the front, which allows the rider to hold on with one hand, freeing the other for lassoing or shooting. But in Mexico to dress like this was a political statement. The emperor's choice of clothes, especially the red cravat, was associated with radical republicans. For conservatives, this was not the attire of royalty. When they had invited a Habsburg to rule over them, they had not expected him to dress as a revolutionary cowboy.

It was in this costume that Maximilian entered, in October 1864, the former liberal stronghold of Morelia, capital of Michoacán state and scene of Márquez's stand against Uraga. Despite ruthless "pacification", this region was not secure. Nonetheless, large crowds came out to see the emperor—a dangerous mix of those who supported the empire and those merely curious to see the face of a Habsburg. In Morelia people wanted to discover what the difference was between an emperor and an ordinary man. The cry went up that Maximilian looked just like a local Prussian businessman, Victor Backhaussen, and as the news filtered around the town, more and more people joined the crowd to see if the rumour was true.

But all this was lost on Maximilian. As he wrote to Carlota, "In all my life I have never experienced anything like the reception, it was not enthusiasm, but something more, the people no longer shouted but bellowed", the volume of these shouts perhaps rendering the comparisons to Backhaussen inaudible. The day concluded with a party to which more than five hundred women were invited, some of them, according to Maximilian, very beautiful. They flooded his room and shouted excitedly at him for a quarter of an hour, after which they all wanted the dreaded *abrazo*, which Maximilian claimed, to his wife at least, he protested against strongly. This enthusiasm continued throughout the tour: Maximilian was met with large crowds wherever he went. As Blasio noted, though, this meant that it was impossible for him to realise that "he was detested and regarded as a usurper and an adventurer in places where he was not known."[18]

Had he been allowed to travel farther from Mexico City, Maximilian would have seen appalling sights. One French soldier, for instance, described how his troops marched past a line of naked corpses hanging from trees. The harsh sun had dried out the bodies, presenting a horrific, macabre sight. Nearby, a freshly dug grave had been marked with a cross, with the message "Death to the French" emblazoned across it. When a soldier tried to remove the cross, an enormous explosion rang out: the grave had been booby-trapped. Musket fire then rained down on the French as guerrillas lying in ambush began their assault. A few days later, the same troops came across the body of one of their number who had gone missing, hanging upside down by his leg from a tree. His naked corpse was riddled with bullets and stab wounds, and his heart had been torn out of his chest.

Atrocities were committed on both sides. Juárez had declared that all Mexicans who aided the French were traitors and would be executed if captured. For Bazaine, the conflict was "a war to the death, a war without quarter, which is engaged in today between barbarism and civilization. It is necessary for both sides to kill or be killed."[19] To help with this goal, a division of the French Foreign Legion, the Contre-Guérillas Françaises, was formed with the special purpose of bringing "civilisation" to Mexico.

The commander of this new unit, Colonel Charles du Pin, had, like Bazaine, a long record of service in the French army, notably in Algeria and Crimea. Unlike Bazaine, however, du Pin was not what might be termed an honourable soldier. One member of the French Foreign Legion said that du Pin had all the vices possible, with the exception of drunkenness. This made him ideally qualified to lead the Contre-Guérillas, where he cut a remarkable figure: dressed in an enormous silver braided sombrero, the red jacket of his former regiment always worn open with a white shirt underneath, and medals hanging on the left side of his chest. He finished off the look with white pleated trousers, contrasting with his knee-high black leather boots and spurs. He wore a pistol nonchalantly harnessed through his belt, carried a sabre, and had a cigar permanently fixed in the corner of his mouth.

Du Pin's tactics were vicious. When a female guerrilla refused to give up information on the whereabouts of her fellow fighters, the Contre-Guérillas suspended a rope from the ceiling, placed a watch on the table, and told the prisoner that if she did not talk within five minutes, she would be hanged. She said nothing, and when the five minutes were up the soldiers slowly lowered the noose around her neck until, trembling, she made a confession. She was lucky, for male guerrilla fighters regularly had information beaten out of them before they were executed. The only way to defeat irregular forces, who blended into the local populace, du Pin believed, was to terrify Mexicans into giving up their compatriots. Torture, executions, and cruelty were his preferred means, and he burned villages on the slightest provocation. As he admitted in a letter to his niece, he had waged an "atrocious war". "If I were Mexican," he wrote, "what hatred I would have for these French, and how much I would make them suffer."[20]

Whatever tactics the French employed, they did not have enough troops to occupy all of a country the size of Mexico. As one soldier noted, the French army's job resembled the tapestry of Penelope: what it did one day unravelled the next because the Mexican army was unable to conserve the points the French had conquered. As another officer complained, the French army "spent itself gloriously in the immensity of space"; its troops "traversing Mexico resembled a ship gliding through the water, leaving behind it no traces of its voyage."[21] Territory was temporarily occupied, but without the numbers to garrison every town and village, civilian imperialistas were soon attacked by guerrillas, who moved in once the French army had left. Maximilian was shielded from all this on his journey around the safer parts of his kingdom, although in Mexico City Carlota worried that guerrillas might launch a surprise attack on Chapultepec.

THE EMPEROR FINALLY returned to his capital on October 30, almost three months after he had left. Here he received increasingly concerned letters from Napoleon III, who had read alarming reports from Bazaine and French diplomats about Maximilian's inactivity. In a letter of November 16, 1864, the French emperor sent a thinly veiled admonishment: it was time to settle the questions "which concern the actual organisation of Mexico as speedily as possible". Maximilian must impose his will on the country and put an "end to uncertainty with regard to some highly important points." The most critical was financial. Even though a second loan was being organised, it was crucial, Napoleon III implored, that the Mexican treasury be reformed.

Having himself built an empire on the ashes of a republic, Napoleon III offered advice that he hoped would address Maximilian's indecisiveness. "In labouring to found a new empire it is impossible to arrive at perfection all at once", but the mark of a good sovereign was in making choices where the advantages outweighed the disadvantages. Presenting a united front, Eugenie wrote separately to Carlota that the "main question is the financial one". A month later, Eugenie again pressed Carlota for news on whether any decisions had been made on financial reorganisation. They were pleased in Paris, she wrote dismissively, to hear that Maximilian's tour of his kingdom had been a success, but they were "impatiently waiting for news of his return so as to see what financial measures" were to be taken.[22]

Stung by the none too subtle tone of the letters arriving from Paris, Maximilian finally responded to these accusations from Paris on December 27, 1864. Laying the blame firmly on the French, he wrote that he had hoped that Bazaine and the Regency would have "cleared the way" and taken "preparatory measures" to settle "the great questions of reform and reorganisation of the country" before he arrived in Mexico. However, "everything remained to be done". He insisted that he was now resolving all the issues that confronted his regime. Why Maximilian had not begun all this six months ago upon his arrival, Napoleon III may well have wondered, but it appeared that the Mexican emperor was at last taking matters firmly in hand.

It was crucial that he do so because he was confronted with two further challenges. First, the papal nuncio arrived in December 1864. Maximilian needed to organise a concordat with the pope to settle the religious questions that had ripped Mexico apart since the 1850s. The most critical issue remained whether Maximilian would ratify the laws liberals had passed confiscating and then selling church lands. If Maximilian accepted this, he would permanently alienate his conservative allies, but if he restored the land to the church he would lose any hope of reconciling liberals to the empire. His only chance of avoiding isolation from at least one of the most powerful factions in Mexican politics was to persuade the nuncio that the pope must endorse the confiscation of church land. Papal blessing would force conservatives to support the policy, while confirmation of one of their flagship reforms would please liberals.

The second issue was the US threat. While the fate of the Union hung in the balance during the American Civil War, Lincoln and Seward had been cautious not to take any action that might upset France and precipitate European intervention. But in 1864 the House of Representatives felt confident enough of defeating the Confederates to turn its attention farther south. So it was that on April 4, US congressmen had passed a resolution declaring that "the United States are unwilling, by silence, to leave the nations of the world under the impression that they are indifferent spectators of the deplorable events now transpiring in the Republic of Mexico." The Union, continued the text, would not allow "a monarchical government, erected on the ruins of any republican government in America, under the auspices of any European power."[23]

How Maximilian dealt with the spiritual power of the Catholic Church and the material might of Washington in the coming year would go a long way towards answering the question of whether the Mexican empire was merely an ephemeral dream.

6

LIBERAL EMPIRE

In December 1864 the Swedish envoy to Mexico, making his way from Veracruz to the capital, watched as a team of thirty mules dragged a delicate and ornate carriage through a morass of mud. Desperately scrambling for purchase, the beasts nearly drowned in the viscous swamp that in places passed for a road to Mexico City. Inside the carriage was the titular archbishop of Damascus, and papal nuncio to Mexico, Francesco Meglia.

Given the significance of his guest, Maximilian ensured his arrival in the capital was in stark contrast to his perilous journey. Personally devising the etiquette for Meglia's welcome, Maximilian was so proud of the programme—thirty-seven steps in all—that he sent a copy to Napoleon III. This covered every detail, from how many carriages for the procession to the palace, to which doors would be opened when the nuncio arrived and the number of footmen in attendance. Much to the chagrin of the Swedish diplomat, Meglia got six horses, escorting carriages, and an honour guard for his reception, whereas the Swede had only a four-horse carriage and no escort or guard. The nuncio was given precedence because, unlike the Swede, Meglia had it in his power to end decades of bitter religious conflict.

Hoping to win over Juaristas, Maximilian wanted a church-state settlement that incorporated many of Juárez's earlier reforms and demonstrated the empire's dedication to the cause of progress, liberalism, and modern civilization. It was, therefore, unfortunate that on the day after Meglia arrived in Mexico City, Pope Pius IX denounced "progress, liberalism and modern civilization" as contrary to the ideas of the Catholic Church, in what became known as the Syllabus of Errors.[1] Part of a papal encyclical, the Syllabus listed eighty false doctrines considered anathema, including freedom of worship, which was branded a pestilence more deadly than any other.

Although the publication of the Syllabus the day after Meglia's arrival was coincidence, the nuncio carried instructions from the pope reflecting its message. Juárez's laws should be reversed, Catholicism must be the state religion to the exclusion of all others, and nationalised church property had to be returned. Shocked at Meglia's intransigence, Maximilian offered a liberal counterproposal, but the nuncio, in conference with Labastida, refused to consider it. There would be no negotiation, Maximilian was informed. The nuncio had come to dictate terms.

Carlota was appalled. She saw her mission in Mexico as holy work, restoring Catholicism to its rightful place. In Europe she assumed this meant supporting the church; however, after six months, she had come to the conclusion that it needed urgent reform. The scandals of the Mexican clergy, she wrote to her grandmother, were so outrageous as to prove the truth of their holy religion, because if Catholicism were not divine, then it would have disappeared long ago in Mexico. Carlota hated Labastida and believed that the archbishop wanted church property returned only so he could live in even greater luxury while parish priests starved. Upon seeing a programme for a public event that the archbishop was to attend with his "venerable" council, she crossed out the word *venerable*, remarking that nothing was venerable in Mexico, least of all the high clergy. The news that Meglia was in agreement with the Mexican archbishop left

Carlota incredulous. She told Bazaine they should throw the nuncio out the window.

After his terms were rejected out of hand, Maximilian was furious. He informed his ministers that if the nuncio refused to negotiate, then a decree would be issued confirming all of Juárez's laws. As ever, Maximilian avoided personal confrontation, instead sending Carlota on December 23 to issue the ultimatum to Meglia. Unmoved, he brushed aside her arguments "like dust" and "seemed quite at home in the void which he created around him and in his utter denial of all the light." Just as Labastida had threatened Bazaine a year earlier, Meglia told Carlota that it was the clergy who had created the empire and its survival remained contingent on their support. "Monsignore, whatever happens", she warned the nuncio as she left, "we are not responsible for the consequences; we have done everything to prevent what will now happen, but if the Church will not help us, we shall serve her against her will."[2]

The consequences were that on December 27, Maximilian decreed freedom of worship, confirmed the sale of church property, and accepted most of Juárez's reforms. Labastida shook with anger when he heard the news. Hoping to be delivered from these evils, he explained in writing to Maximilian, the church had supported the empire, but, Labastida now threatened, the difficulties facing the emperor would increase dramatically because the clergy could not back an ungodly regime.

This was no idle threat. As Carlota wrote to Eugenie in January, "Every passion is let loose", and behind it all she saw Labastida, "whose bad Italian I know so well that I can recognise it in every line". More seriously, "It is said that the era of *pronunciamientos* [revolts against the government] is not at an end, that it is perhaps only beginning." Previously sanguine over the empire's prospects, Carlota now felt that since Meglia had arrived, Mexico had been in crisis. "I have come to ask myself", she wrote to Eugenie, "whether, if the difficulties continue to increase at this rate, there is any human possibility of emerging from them."[3]

The atmosphere in Mexico City was febrile. The wife of one of Maximilian's officials wrote, "The disorder is still great!" The clergy "are rabid", and, worse, "they are conspiring, a general has escaped Mexico City and is six leagues from here with a thousand men, our guards are doubled. Nobody rides into the city from here without a revolver, there will be more robberies and murders than ever." Guerrillas continued to harass the route from Veracruz to Mexico City, but the author was more afraid of the clergy than the Juaristas. "They say a couple of bishops will have to be hanged", she concluded.[4]

So seriously did Maximilian take the threat of revolt that he felt he could no longer rely on the loyalty of Miguel Miramón and Leonardo Márquez. He sent them overseas, Miramón to Berlin to study Prussian military tactics and Márquez as a diplomat to the Ottoman Empire. Court gossip was that Maximilian had deliberately sent the fanatically devout Márquez to a Muslim country. Maximilian then went even further, disbanding much of his small Mexican army because he feared its loyalty was to conservatives rather than himself. Napoleon III warned against this move, but Carlota defended the decision to Eugenie, arguing that the imperial army was more of a danger than the guerrillas. This soon became a moot point; suddenly without income, many of these fighters joined Juarista forces.

Many conservatives now simply refused to serve the empire. The Mexican whose name Lord Palmerston had trouble pronouncing, Francisco de Paula Berzábal Arrangoiz, had been (annoyingly for Palmerston, one presumes) appointed Mexican envoy to Britain. Upon hearing of Maximilian's policy towards the church, he resigned. In a letter of protest, he attacked Maximilian, claiming that the emperor had "broken all his promises". Arrangoiz was particularly annoyed at Carlota, believing, correctly, that she hated Mexico's high clergy. "An issue as serious, as transcendental as that of the Church," ranted the reactionary Arrangoiz, "was not the business of a woman."[5]

Maximilian then broke with the man who had done the most to bring the empire into existence. Upon hearing of Maximilian's liberal policy, José María Gutiérrez de Estrada, who had chosen to stay in Europe, wrote an eighty-four-page letter admonishing the emperor, explaining that Mexico was Catholic and conservative and should be ruled as such. This was too much for Maximilian. He replied that the pious Catholicism that the conservatives had told him so much about was a myth: the Mexican clergy did not understand their own religion. Maximilian had visited regions whose people had never seen their bishop, where adults were not baptised, and where knowledge of the holy sacraments was altogether absent. In his reply, Maximilian made a point he might have given weight to earlier: Gutiérrez de Estrada had not been in Mexico for twenty-five years and could have but little accurate knowledge of the country.

WHILE THE RISKS of alienating his conservative allies were grave, Maximilian was now free to govern as the benevolent liberal monarch that he had always dreamt of becoming. He passed some of the most progressive laws anywhere in the world. In addition to outlawing corporal punishment and regulating child labour, decrees provided for such unheard-of things as lunch breaks, limits to working hours, and days off. Moreover, debt peonage—a system wherein hacienda owners forced tenants to pay debts through labour—was abolished. Large landowners and factory owners also had to provide free schools and, in some cases, access to water and shelter for their workers.

As one former Juarista who joined the empire noted, Maximilian's reforms proved his "intention to preserve and develop the progressive liberal ideas prevailing in the country." The emperor had "become Mexican", and the empire, therefore, had a glorious future. On the anniversary of Mexican independence in 1865, Maximilian emphasised this commitment to his adopted country. Reviewing his troops in the great central square of Mexico City, he declared, "My heart, my soul, my work, my loyal efforts belong to you and our beloved nation. Nothing in this world could make me waver in my duty, every drop of my blood is now Mexican." He might die, continued Maximilian, "but I will die at the foot of our glorious flag".[6]

He was also keen to give his empire cultural lustre, creating the Imperial Academy of Sciences and Literature. At its inauguration in July 1865, he told his audience that Mexico's traditions could proudly be shown to the world, listing the pyramids of Teotihuacán, the ruins of Uxmal, and the Aztec calendar. All this reflected the dawning of "a triumphant era of science and art in this country". Moreover, he claimed, this "genius" and its "miraculous works" were more advanced in many respects than anything in Europe at the time.[7] Maximilian delighted in these contrasts, frequently depicting the New World as emancipated and democratic in contrast to moribund and conservative Europe. He revelled in his liberal policies, which he believed made him a "sort of anti-Christ" to his "devout and reactionary" family in Vienna. Free from their shackles, he felt he could finally "contribute a few drops of oil to the great lamp of enlightenment".[8]

Maximilian's celebration of Mexico's indigenous culture also contained a radical message for his new subjects. Mexico's creole elite, liberal and conservative, often denigrated the indigenous past as barbaric; Maximilian embraced it as part of modern Mexico. Indeed, he increasingly felt that his empire should rest on Mexico's majority indigenous population. Liberal land reforms in the 1850s had not only stripped the church of its property, but also declared communal village landholdings illegal, breaking them up for private sale. Maximilian restored rights to shared landownership for indigenous villages. Mexico's indigenous population was diverse, with numerous different languages, groups, and interests. Many were opposed to the empire; some, however, including notably Tomás Mejía, had long supported the conservative alliance with the church, and Maximilian's decision to return land provided a powerful incentive for others to back the empire. To stress his sympathy with the indigenous peoples, Maximilian had government decrees published in Nahuatl, the language of the Aztecs, for the first time in independent Mexico. He also met indigenous leaders, providing a striking contrast when they came dressed in traditional clothing to talk with the Habsburg emperor of Mexico in his aristocratic finery. For her part, Carlota had appointed an indigenous woman as a lady-in-waiting. As always, though, Maximilian's attempts to please some alienated others, with many contemporaries accusing the imperial couple of "Indiomania".

So confident was Maximilian of winning people over to his liberal empire that he had even envisaged working with Juárez, perhaps as prime minister. Maximilian's secretary wrote to a confidant of the president, suggesting a personal interview. Maximilian, the letter continued, wanted to bring peace and stability to Mexico: "A frankly loyal effort on the part of the principal politicians of the liberal party, and especially with him who has been until now the legitimate head of the country [that is, Juárez], and whose political sentiments the archduke has never failed to appreciate, would aid definitively in bringing about this end."[9] Naive, trusting, and arrogant, Maximilian could not understand why a man who had dedicated his life to fighting the church, the Conservative Party, and then the French intervention would not work with an empire sustained by all three. Carlota was more realistic. Although the most fervent republicans, she claimed, were "fascinated" with Maximilian's personality, he should not count on them. Monarchy was incompatible with their worldview. Moreover, she added, Juárez would always be more democratic than Maximilian and, crucially, more Mexican.[10]

But as Maximilian dreamed, others were growing aware of an enormous problem: most of Maximilian's new laws were never enforced. The emperor was at his happiest when overseeing a paper empire, but his state was much greater in his imagination than in reality. The emperor was increasingly ridiculed for the gap between theory and practice. Although Mexico had never had a navy to speak of, as a former sailor Maximilian was determined to develop one. He appointed a French officer to oversee the project. The officer's house was on a road in Mexico City that frequently flooded. His fellow officers bought a toy flotilla, decked it out in miniature Mexican flags, and sailed it down the street, much to the amusement of onlookers.

In part, the inertia at the heart of the empire was a result of its labyrinthine structure. Imperialistas complained that contradictory instructions were often issued, the French received their orders direct from Paris, Mexican ministers issued their own directives, and still others came from Maximilian's private cabinet. Bazaine especially despised the man who headed this latter institution, Félix Eloin, characterising the Belgian as unreliable, open to bribery, and best avoided. To make matters worse, Maximilian continued to take long tours around his new domain, frequently leaving matters of state languishing.

While Maximilian travelled, Carlota ruled, remaining in Mexico City as regent, a role that afforded her the kind of action she had craved in Europe. "Activity suits us," she wrote to her grandmother. "We were too young to do nothing". When Maximilian chaired cabinet meetings, his ministers spent hours debating many issues but deciding little; Carlota, by contrast, would study the problems in detail and then present her own conclusions to the cabinet. Ministers were too astonished or polite to contradict her, and thus she rarely had a policy rejected. "Today we had a council of ministers and lasted almost three hours, and I covered myself in glory", she wrote to Maximilian. "You can be confident in me", she told him. "I would even appear at the head of the army if the situation demanded it." She was, though, unimpressed with most of her politicians. "Beware of advocates!" she warned, the phrase in English. "They are a sickness in modern society".[11] For Carlota, there was much talk but too little done.

While the abyss between policy and action widened, the imperial couple continued to apply a thick veneer of pomp and power. Key to this were regular and immense balls at the National Palace, where the former residence of Mexico's presidents was transformed into the height of aristocratic luxury, as guests hurried through the vast, candlelit complex to see Carlota's entry. At one ball, she appeared promptly and imperiously at 9:00 p.m., wearing a blue brocade dress with a long train, diamond necklace, and bracelets. Presented to guests, she approached with grace and pride, conversing with ease in Spanish, French, German, English, or Italian. Before the ball began, she sat on a throne overlooking the dance floor. For the first dance, she choose José Fernando Ramírez, Maximilian's elderly foreign minister, a poor dancer, but Carlota laughed off his ineptness, and the old politician beamed with joy. Afterwards, she returned to her throne, with the eyes of some thousand guests fixed on her as the orchestra played Richard Strauss, Joseph Lanner, and Joseph Labitzky.

In these moments, the empire seemed at the apotheosis of its power. French and Austrian veterans, many of whom had fought each other in 1859, mingled with inexperienced Belgian officers, Hungarian hussars, and Polish Lancers, while Old World diplomats—one young British attaché singled out to dance with Carlota—darted around the rooms. Europeans mixed with imperial Mexican politicians and officials alongside the wealthiest families of the country amongst candelabras lighting tables overflowing with the finery of French cuisine. In the early hours of the morning, Carlota's departure was taken as the cue to leave. Guests filed out into the great square, the cathedral towering to their right, the silk ball gowns and military uniforms contrasting with the simple clothes of indigenous market girls unloading their street wares in the dawn light.

Notably absent from all this was the emperor. Maximilian avoided these occasions whenever he could, but he characterised those balls he did attend as great successes. Writing to his brother, he noted that the "the loveliest women" in Mexico took part in the dances. He was also pleased with the quality of the imperial wine cellars and kitchens, especially as more foreign diplomats arrived at court. If they had to have "boring receptions and dinners," at least the envoys drank and dined so well that "as a rule after dinner they can only mumble inarticulate sounds". Maximilian's irritation at having to entertain was offset by his delight with the publication of his court etiquette that governed these occasions—"a thick printed book, a gigantic piece of work". It was, in the emperor's view, the most "finished piece of work that has ever been done" in this genre.[12]

Those bound by the etiquette, however, found it less enjoyable. "I have to say, we were not having a wild amount of fun", wrote

Bazaine's aide-de-camp Charles Blanchot. He found the rules stifling, the severe reserve, "often haughty", of the imperial couple preventing anyone from enjoying themselves. The people who were obliged to attend were, he added, extremely bored.[13] Sara Yorke Stevenson agreed, describing Carlota's Monday receptions as dull, formal affairs in a badly lit hall.

One notable victim of Maximilian's protocol was the British representative in Mexico. As friends of Queen Victoria, Maximilian and Carlota were delighted when her government recognised the empire. The diplomat sent from Britain, Peter Campbell Scarlett, was a sixty-year-old widower who brought his son and daughter. This caused a minor crisis, as Maximilian's etiquette prohibited unmarried women from attending state concerts. Rather than offend his daughter, Scarlett sent back the invitations to one without reply. Upon hearing of this affront, Maximilian flew into a rage, threatening to write to Queen Victoria to demand the diplomat's recall. Eventually, realpolitik prevailed, and Scarlett reported back to London that he and his daughter were invited to see a play at the palace. The incident, though, was a further reminder of Maximilian's erratic approach to leadership and priorities, especially as he himself had identified winning Britain over to the empire as a key policy.

In fact, Maximilian disliked diplomats and left entertaining them to Carlota. She spent a day with Scarlett and his family outside the capital at a nearby beauty spot. Near a waterfall and surrounded by volcanoes, this was one of Carlota's favourite places. She made sure to spend a long time in conversation with the British diplomat, who told her how Maximilian's declaration of freedom of worship was admired in Britain. Maximilian was "much more liberal than his ministers", Scarlett told Carlota, and offered the counsel of a good Victorian imperialist: "One must force civilisation on the country".[14]

It was France rather than Britain that Maximilian and Carlota needed to impress, however. A new French envoy to Mexico, Alphonse Dano, had arrived in May 1865. Maximilian described him as amiable—although he "does not seem to me a great genius".[15] Whether he was or not, his first task would be to produce a comprehensive report on the empire, and Maximilian understood his importance, writing to Carlota that they must charm him. Carlota duly entertained Dano upon his arrival in the capital, successfully giving him the impression that despite earlier worries over the clergy, she was now optimistic. Dano proved her equal in dissimulation. Less sanguine about the future of the empire, he reassured the foreign minister in Paris that he would never show his true feelings. He characterised Maximilian and Carlota as extremely sensitive to criticism, adding that they listened to counsel only on the condition that it was given to them with the greatest care.

Regardless of the charm offensive, Napoleon III received numerous critical reports. Dano observed the lack of political implementation and book-balancing at the heart of the regime, reporting to Paris that *government* was too grandiose a word for Maximilian's administration. "Nothing serious is done", the diplomat wrote. "Decrees are published every day, but none of them are executed."[16] Maximilian and Carlota nevertheless remained convinced that the French emperor would never abandon them. Carlota reassured Maximilian that "if at any time you come to doubt Napoleon in your low moments you can be convinced that he has a heart that beats nobly for us and that, after his son and those friends who helped him to power, we are those who he loves the most because we have sacrificed something and he knows the value of it".[17]

Napoleon III, however, was more concerned with what he had sacrificed, the value of which his finance and war ministers could tell him precisely in francs and dead soldiers. With Maximilian's treasury still in arrears, a new loan had been raised in Paris to cover Maximilian's immediate expenditure for 1865, but the money must be used wisely, warned the French emperor. It would not be possible to secure another. Tired of waiting, that summer Napoleon III sent one of his closest financial advisers, Jacques Langlais, to reform the Mexican treasury. Unhelpfully for the Mexican budget, though, Langlais could be induced to go only on an enormous salary of $150,000 a year.

The truth was Napoleon III was rapidly losing faith in Maximilian. In August 1865, the French foreign minister made this point clear. "The lustre of a court, academic solemnities and the spread of compulsory education are the lights of the most advanced civilisation", wrote the French minister, and "we would applaud these intentions and acts more willingly if we were able to observe at the same time the effects of [Maximilian's] government on the social, political, administrative, financial and military reorganisation of a country, where, despite our efforts and our sacrifices, everything remains in crisis." A government "born under [the French] flag, and defended by [French] arms," seemed determined in its political direction to "make every day the task of sustaining it more onerous [for France]." "I cannot understand," Napoleon III wrote to Maximilian, "by what fatality it always happens that the most essential measures are always adjourned or opposed".[18]

It was unfortunate that when Napoleon III wrote this letter, Maximilian was on another royal tour. Travelling with his foreign minister, José Fernando Ramírez, a prodigious gourmand, Maximilian seemed oblivious to the mounting criticism, his most pressing concern sampling Mexico's culinary delicacies. One exquisite lunch consisted of mussels, prawns, and tropical fish. So splendid was the feast before him that Ramírez was, apparently, moved to tears, the amount he ate scaring Maximilian. This gastronomic tour backfired. The seafood had to be brought up from the coast, and soon Maximilian and Ramírez were suffering from food poisoning. With the French now exasperated and having angered conservatives over the church, one diplomat's gastronomical turn of phrase was pointedly fitting: "To eat a priest for breakfast and a Frenchman for dinner, when one has been called to the throne by the clergy, and must rely upon France for sole support, may be regarded as a dangerous policy".[19]

The Marriage of Maximilian and Charlotte, 1857, by Cesare Dell'Acqua.
Credit: Su concessione del Ministero per i Beni e le Attività Culturali, Museo Storico
e il Parco del Castello di Miramare

*Portrait of the Archduchess
Charlotte in Brianza Costume*,
1857, by Jean François Portaels.
Credit: Su concessione del Ministero
per i Beni e le Attività Culturali,
Museo Storico e il Parco del Castello
di Miramare, photo credit @
fabrice_gallina

Maximilian (standing center, hand on hip) with his three brothers, Karl Ludwig (standing far left), Franz Joseph (sitting), and Ludwig Viktor (standing, far right).
Credit: Library of Congress Prints and Photographs Division, Washington, D.C.

Elisabeth of Austria Arrives at Miramare, 1865, by Cesare Dell'Acqua. Maximilian and Franz Joseph are just about to disembark, while Carlota greets Elisabeth, Franz Joseph's wife. Miramar can be seen in the background. This visit took place in 1861.
Credit: Su concessione del Ministero per i Beni e le Attività Culturali, Museo Storico e il Parco del Castello di Miramare

Maximilian and Charlotte Depart for Mexico, 1866, by Cesare Dell'Acqua.
On April 14, 1864, Maximilian and Carlota leave Miramar for Mexico via
Rome. Maximilian was in tears; Carlota proud and confident.
Credit: Su concessione del Ministero per i Beni e le Attività Culturali, Museo Storico e il
Parco del Castello di Miramare

Portrait of Maximilian, Emperor of Mexico, 1865, by Santiago Rebull.
Credit: Su concessione del Ministero per i Beni e le Attività Culturali, Museo Storico e il Parco del Castello di Miramare

Benito Juárez, president of Mexico from 1858 to 1872.
Credit: Library of Congress Prints and Photographs Division, Washington, D.C.

Miguel Miramón, led the Conservative Party in the War of Reform against Juárez and then fought for Maximilian. Credit: Library of Congress Prints and Photographs Division, Washington, D.C.

Tomás Mejía, one of Maximilian's best generals and most loyal supporters. Credit: Library of Congress Prints and Photographs Division, Washington, D.C.

The 'infamous' Leonardo Márquez, another of Maximilian's generals. Credit: Library of Congress Prints and Photographs Division, Washington, D.C.

Maximilian's firing squad.
Credit: The Metropolitan Museum of Art, New York, Gilman
Collection, Museum Purchase, 2005

Maximilian's embalmed corpse. The body remained for months in Mexico City before it was sent back to Austria.
Credit: The Metropolitan Museum of Art, New York, Purchase, The Horace W. Goldsmith Foundation Gift, through Joyce and Robert Menschel, 1989

The Execution of Maximilian, by Édouard Manet.
Credit: Copyright: bpk / Kunsthalle Mannheim / Kathrin Schwab

Military matters were also increasing tensions between Maximilian and the French. Juárez remained undefeated, and the French army continued to undertake costly military campaigns charged to the Mexican treasury. Maximilian interpreted this as profligacy. Mexican general Porfirio Díaz, who had escaped French captivity after the May 1863 defeat at Puebla, rallied republican forces in Oaxaca. In January 1865, Bazaine took command and put the city under siege. Lacking munitions, Díaz had ordered the church bells of the town and surrounding villages melted down and turned into shells. As one French soldier noted, these were a rather beautiful bronze, but they proved ineffective as artillery, often failing to explode. By contrast, the French bombardment was relentless. Lasting for five days, when it ended ruins, rubble, and corpses lined the formerly grand streets of Oaxaca. The French army then deployed to assault the city; however, Díaz surrendered and, along with some four thousand Mexicans, was again taken prisoner. While Bazaine had triumphed militarily, Maximilian complained to Napoleon III that his victory came at a cost of some $2 million. Bazaine, he said, was plunging the empire into ruinous expenditure.

A power struggle now took hold. It annoyed Maximilian that, although emperor, he did not control his armed forces. Maximilian shied away from confrontation and relied on Carlota's correspondence with Eugenie as his informal channel to attack a marshal of France. Here she made clear what she thought needed to be done. "In order to civilize this country", she wrote to the French empress, "one must be absolute master of it. . . . [O]ne must be able to make one's power effective every day through large battalions". What was required was more French troops and garrisons throughout the empire. Without these, guerrillas picked off towns and villages after the French left them. Concluding what amounted to a memorandum on military strategy, the young empress added, "I believe that by displaying great activity and energy in this direction . . . solid results would be achieved at small cost. . . . Anybody having at their disposal such a fine army who was prepared to use it conscientiously would pacify Mexico in less time than the ablest military commander who neglected to pay attention to it."[20] The implication was twofold: whatever Bazaine's abilities, he was pursuing the wrong strategy and moreover lacked "energy" in what he was doing. True or not, Carlota should have realised that the military advice of a twenty-four-year-old was not going to be taken seriously in Paris. Bazaine, Eugenie disdainfully made clear, retained the full confidence of Napoleon III.

For her part, Carlota had fallen in with a clique of French generals below Bazaine. She invited them to her Monday soirées, which ended with dancing—quadrilles followed by a galop, a fast-paced country dance popular in France. No doubt aided by the champagne, fine wines, and raucous choruses of the Marseillaise, "somebody always ends by falling down".[21] The granddaughter of a French king, Carlota was able to charm these French officers in a way Maximilian never could. She was "as majestic as beautiful, as gracious as distinguished, as attractive as kind," wrote one particularly smitten French officer after dinner at the palace. He added that if Carlota could have made a tour of her empire, she would have conquered it better than any army. For Auguste Henri Brincourt, a brigadier general, Carlota was "a woman of great sense, perfectly capable of directing matters." Sadly, he lamented, "she does not wear the trousers . . . in politics!"[22] But as they dined, drank, and then waltzed with Carlota, these French generals criticised their commanding officer's military strategy.

Soon, the imperial couple's contempt for Bazaine was an open secret in Mexico, and the French general felt it keenly because he had just gotten married. At the end of 1863 while on campaign, news had reached him that his wife of fifteen years had died. He was distraught, but a year later, at a ball in Mexico City, a young Mexican woman who was waltzing by stopped to repair a tear in her dress. "Who is this?" Bazaine asked his entourage. "It is extraordinary how much she reminds me of my wife"—a statement that soon became redundant because within a year he married her.[23]

Her name was Josefa Peña, and she was, according to Carlota, pretty, with infinite grace and magnificent black hair. She was also only seventeen years old. Even by the standards of the nineteenth century, the age gap was scandalous. Maximilian wrote to his brother, "In spite of his fifty-four years, the marshal is perfectly infatuated; may this hazardous conjugal happiness agree with him." Maximilian was, of course, not looking forward to the wedding. "We have, alas, another great state entertainment at the palace", he lamented.[24] At the wedding, Maximilian accompanied the bride, and Carlota took the arm of Bazaine. This show of unity between the French army and the Mexican empire, however, belied the reality. Behind his back, Carlota spread rumours that Bazaine's martial spirit had been blunted by marital bliss, while Maximilian complained that not only was the French general exhausted, but his military decisions were incompetent.

Instead of intriguing against the French army, Maximilian should have been organising his own. Having sent away his two best generals—Miramón and Márquez—and demobilised most of his Mexican forces, Maximilian now depended on the Austrian and Belgian volunteers who had arrived in Mexico. By January 1865, there were roughly 1,300 Belgians and some 6,000 soldiers in the Austrian Legion, made up of people from throughout Habsburg lands. Adding to the cosmopolitan nature, or confusion, of Maximilian's army were 450 Egyptians, whom the French had secured from their North African ally.

Maximilian placed especial hope on the volunteers from Habsburg lands who had come to Mexico to fight on his behalf. Swearing an oath of allegiance directly to Maximilian, the officers formed an intensely loyal cadre around the emperor, but added to the administrative confusion. Given control over certain regions, they frequently clashed, sometimes violently, with the French army, whose authority they resented. Maximilian, however, enjoyed the company of these officers, who reminded the emperor of his homeland. On one occasion, Maximilian went to see the troops at night as they sang Austrian and Venetian songs so beautifully that he admitted to Carlota what he never would to his friends and family. He was homesick. He had cried as he listened to the songs, but "luckily", he wrote, "it was dark and nobody could see."[25]

While the Austrians tended to be veterans of Habsburg wars, the Belgians were young men with little or no military experience. Ordered to the state of Michoacán, they were to take part in a campaign to sweep the region of guerrillas. Two columns of French, Mexican, and Belgian troops fanned out from the state capital, Morelia, but, as usual, could not find the enemy. Around 300 Belgians had been left to garrison the nearby town of Tacambaro, protecting the flank as the columns advanced. Having evaded the main force, 2,000 guerrillas surrounded the town.

Under the command of Major Constant Tydgadt, the Belgians had turned the small church at the centre of the town into a fort. In the early hours of April 11, the guerrillas launched a surprise attack. Outnumbered, the Belgians made numerous sorties to push back the attackers at bayonet point. The guerrillas then set fire to the church, and the wooden roof soon collapsed. The remaining Belgians retreated into an inner room, desperately maintaining musket fire to hold back the Juaristas. This one-sided conflict was brought to an end after a four-hour siege. The mortally wounded Tydgadt surrendered; 187 soldiers were taken prisoner, while 27 died. Devastated at the news, Carlota lay awake all night thinking about the deaths of her countrymen. For his part, Maximilian added the event to his list of grievances against Bazaine, whom he blamed.

Stung by the numerous accusations against him, Bazaine resolved to make a significant military statement, planning to occupy Chihuahua City in the far north of Mexico, where Juárez had made his capital. The French would either capture the president in the process or force him to flee across the border. Maximilian had been urging this for some time. He believed that if Juárez left Mexico, he would renounce his claim to be president and the United States would then recognise the empire. General Brincourt, a favourite of Carlota's, started at the beginning of July with 2,500 men on a journey of some 370 miles across the harsh terrain of northern Mexico, much of it desert. This, Brincourt was confident, would be "without doubt the last military act" of the intervention.[26]

On August 15, the birthday of the original emperor Napoleon Bonaparte, Brincourt marched into Chihuahua. "I am writing to you comfortably seated on the presidential armchair of citizen Juárez", Brincourt boasted in a letter. "Yesterday we made our triumphant entry in this capital in order to celebrate the birthday of the emperor and the end of the Mexican war". In his reports, the French general included a rumour that Juárez had left Mexico. Along the way, rumour was retold as fact. When this reached Mexico City, Maximilian was elated. "Mexicans! The cause sustained with so much courage and consistency by Benito Juárez", the emperor triumphantly decreed to his subjects, "has degenerated into faction and remains abandoned by the fact of the exit of its chief from the nation."[27]

But Juárez had merely relocated to a small town on the US-Mexican border called El Paso del Norte, better known today as Ciudad Juárez. Here he issued his own defiant proclamation: the Mexican people "will never cease in the struggle everywhere against the invader and will end infallibly in triumph in the defence of its independence and republican institutions."[28] El Paso del Norte was only 55 miles north of Chihuahua, a few days' march; however, Brincourt could not advance. Events across the border made Bazaine fearful that French troops might clash with US soldiers, and he ordered Brincourt to go no farther.

As MAXIMILIAN AND Napoleon III both knew, the great obstacle to the Mexican empire was the United States. In March 1865, Napoleon III had comforted Maximilian with the analysis that the American Civil War would last a long time yet. By the time this letter reached Mexico, the Confederate armies had surrendered. The Mexican empire was a monumental gamble, dependent upon the conflict north of the border. Weakened by years of fighting, or perhaps divided in two, the United States would recognise the Mexican empire, ending Juárez's lifeline.

At enormous cost, however, the Union had emerged from the conflict not only victorious but more powerful than ever, with a veteran army larger than at any point in previous US history. Moreover, bellicose Union generals, now popular war heroes, notably Ulysses S. Grant, were keen to use this army to uphold the Monroe Doctrine and US supremacy in the Americas. For men like Grant, Maximilian's empire represented a nightmarish mix of papal conspiracy and monarchical European power that, in league with the Confederacy, challenged republican democracy. If war were necessary to end Maximilian's rule, reasoned Grant, then so be it.

Throughout the American Civil War, Lincoln and Seward had been a restraining influence, combining a strategy of nonintervention while refusing to recognise Maximilian's government; however, Lincoln's assassination less than a week after the end of the war jeopardised this position. There was wild speculation that the new president, Andrew Johnson, would bow to pressure from his generals and invade Mexico.

As was so often the case when major news broke, Maximilian was away touring his kingdom as word of the Confederate defeat reached Mexico City. The news electrified the capital, emboldening the empire's enemies. Carlota, acting as regent, was, therefore, rather ungracious when she heard of Lincoln's murder, seemingly unaware that he had been a calming influence on US policy towards the empire. "Here the mood is excellent since the death of Lincoln, the head of demagoguery in America; it is as if the reds [Juaristas] are struck by lightning and they attribute it to your good fortune". Carlota loathed the United States, her piety fusing with her burgeoning Mexican nationalism. She saw Mexico's neighbour as a nation bereft of religion, principles, and liberty. The Civil War was a consequence of this degradation, she argued: "Soon a million men will have perished, immolated in a holocaust to their improvidence and evil passions."[29] She believed that the United States was intent on further expansion at Mexico's expense and would replace Catholicism with Protestantism. Stopping this, she felt, was a holy war. Still, she was pragmatic, and, hoping Lincoln's death would lead to Johnson recognising the empire, she wrote letters of condolence to Lincoln's wife and the new president.

In the following weeks, imperialistas scanned the US press for any sign of Johnson's plan. Early indications were encouraging, Seward continued his policy of neutrality, and Maximilian could not understand why the secretary of state persisted in not recognising his government. Traditionally, Washington diplomatically acknowledged whatever regime held the capital. With Juárez wandering the northern deserts, this was indisputably Maximilian. Besides, as Maximilian argued to friends, what difference did it make in Washington whether Mexico had a president or an emperor, especially when that emperor believed in liberalism and progress? Convinced of the righteousness of his cause, Maximilian sent diplomats to Washington to seek recognition from the US government, but their months spent in the capital proved futile. The secretary of state refused to abandon Juárez in favour of the "so-called" emperor and his "so-called" empire, terms that were used in any official US correspondence to describe Maximilian or his regime.

Nonetheless, as the stasis of neutrality prevailed, imperial fears of US invasion gradually receded. Maximilian even began to see the South's surrender as an opportunity. He hoped to attract veteran Confederate soldiers to form militias to fight Juárez's guerrillas. To organise these mercenaries, he appointed several former Confederates to important positions. Chief amongst them was a former naval officer and scientist, Matthew Fontaine Maury, who was named head of astronomy, counsellor of state, and imperial commissioner for colonisation, adding yet another nationality to the cabinet. To encourage migrants, an English-language newspaper, the *Mexican Times*, was set up with government support. The paper's self-declared remit was "immigration and progress", although strangely much of it was given over to poetry—including in the first edition, for the benefit of exiled readers, "Home, Sweet Home!" by John Howard Payne. The adverts for "Virginia Chewing Tobacco" and the "National Bar Room—conducted in the American style" and "prepared to satisfy the most fastidious taste in the art of mixing liquors"—perhaps better reflected the interests of its readership.[30]

Meaningful US support, however, flowed not to the empire, but to Juárez. To support republicanism in the Americas, Seward did not believe war was necessary; all that was required was time to arm and supply Juárez's forces. By April 1865, Juárez had only a few thousand poorly equipped fighters facing off against the French. He could not effectively resupply his armies because during the American Civil War there had been an embargo on the export of weapons from the North. Johnson revoked the ban in May 1865, and military equipment soon flooded across the border. One businessman alone provided Juárez's forces with 5,020 Enfield rifles, 1,000 pistols, and 6 artillery pieces, with 20,400 rounds of ammunition, as well as 1,308 pairs of underwear and 813 frying pans.

It was not only supplies that poured over the US border, but also men and money. Juárez had his own secret agents, some in the US military, who helped lubricate this support. Lew Wallace, future author of *Ben-Hur* but at this time a Union officer, was in direct contact with Juárez's generals, while Mexicans with varying degrees of success—and in some cases varying degrees of fraud—raised loans for the near-bankrupt republican cause. A dizzying number of pro-Juárez clubs provided another source of revenue, while so many US veterans swelled Juarista ranks that an elite corps called the American Legion of Honour was created for them. Although Brincourt's capture of Chihuahua in August 1865 saw Maximilian's empire at its greatest territorial extent and Juárez precariously holding out on the northern border, the liberals were finally able to finance, recruit, and equip their depleted forces with help from across the Rio Grande.

Witnessing this transformation firsthand was Tomás Mejía. For some time, he had been stationed at Matamoros. On the other side of the Rio Grande was Brownsville, founded in 1848, the epitome of a Wild West frontier town, where merchants got rich smuggling goods into Mexico. Now it was a refuge for Juaristas working to bring down the empire. In the summer of 1865, restaurants and smoke-filled saloons were filled with liberal exiles, adventurers, and Union officers. And there were plenty of those officers, for veteran Union soldiers were organised into the "Army of Observation", some fifty thousand US troops sent to occupy the former Confederate state of Texas, but also to keep an eye on Mexico. From across the river, Mejía watched on helplessly as US officials turned a blind eye when rifles and artillery discarded after the Civil War ended up in Juarista hands.

To keep up imperial morale, Mejía had a band play every week in the main plaza, and a grand ball was hosted to celebrate Mejía's birthday. Despite beleaguered finances, the empire could still throw a party. Ernst Pitner, an officer in the Austrian Legion, had been sent there with three hundred men to bolster Mejía's garrison. Pitner recalled how the town gave them a magnificent banquet, three thousand elegantly served places in an open square. Every man had a bottle of claret, masses of English beer, and champagne, which helped wash down stewed fruits, pies, and ham. Despite this luxury, the position was perilous. The imperialistas were strong enough to hold only the town. Elsewhere, guerrillas attacked Mejía's men before slipping across the border to the safety of US territory.

It was the US buildup of troops that worried Napoleon III. As soon as he learned of it, he ordered Bazaine to withdraw French soldiers southwards and prepare for a US invasion. Not only had this order prevented Brincourt's march on Juárez at El Paso del Norte, but now only Mexican troops guarded Matamoros. Without the protection of the French army, and fearful of the "almost direct support" the United States gave to the "dissidents", Mejía painted a bleak future for this outpost of Maximilian's empire. "No matter how violent my situation may become", Mejía maintained, "I am resolved to die in this town before abandoning it".[31]

He got his chance to prove this in October 1865, when a liberal army arrived before the gates of Matamoros and presented Mejía with an ultimatum to surrender within two hours. Outnumbered, Mejía coolly replied that the liberals need not wait so long before beginning their assault. Juaristas, including numerous Americans, attacked at dawn the next day, fanning out towards the fortifications in the dim early-morning light. Despite fierce imperialista resistance, the liberals kept coming and seized a fort defending the town.

At that moment, an imperial gunboat joined the fight and unleashed a deadly barrage into the liberals holding the fort. As the iron and lead cut down the Juaristas, Mejía, at the head of five hundred cavalry, crashed into them, pushing the enemy back. Another imperial gunboat now joined the fray; steaming down the Rio Grande, it was constantly fired on from the US side—liberal forces knew that the imperialistas had orders not to return fire across the border, lest it gave occasion for a bellicose US response. This second gunboat blunted the attack. After a costly siege, the liberals realised that Matamoros could not be taken without enormous losses, and they melted into the surrounding countryside as suddenly as they had appeared.

As Mejía clung on in the northeast, the French, desperate to impose control before they were pulled farther back into the interior, waged a savage war in the northwest under General Armand Alexandre de Castagny. As part of this campaign, a small group of French soldiers garrisoned a village called Veranos. On the night of their arrival, their mules were stolen by Mexican guerrillas, meaning the company was now unable to leave with their equipment. The next day, the stranded French amused themselves by drinking the local firewater. At seven in the evening, Juaristas surrounded the church and houses that the enemy soldiers had fortified. After a four-hour siege, during which the guerrillas set fire to the church, the French surrendered.

A few, though, had managed to break through the Mexican lines, reach safety, and call for reinforcements. Determined to exact revenge, the French relief force arrived at the still smouldering village the next morning. On the ground were the corpses of eighteen of their soldiers, some unrecognisable after pigs had eaten their faces, some still alive, though mortally wounded. Almost as soon as they had buried their comrades, mounted guerrillas, waiting in ambush, launched another attack, killing more French soldiers, before disappearing into the surrounding countryside.

Furious, General Castagny, who had accompanied his troops, ordered the village razed to the ground. The population had long since fled, but Juaristas claimed the French killed the one woman who remained. Whatever the truth of that, Veranos was far from the only village French soldiers burned in Mexico, and events there resulted in bloody retribution. Any Mexican found bearing arms was immediately shot. This was a conflict without truce or mercy, remarked one French soldier, whilst another admitted how the army devastated and burned the state as payback. The guerrilla reprisals were just as vicious, with patrolling French soldiers often stumbling across stragglers from their ranks hanging from trees.

Far from condemning French brutality, Bazaine argued that the war needed to be prosecuted even more pitilessly. Bazaine felt that Mexico needed to be pacified with a firmer hand than the lenient Maximilian had thus far allowed, pressuring the emperor into signing what became known as the Black Decree on October 3, 1865. In Maximilian's name, the following went out to all imperial forces: "The troops under your orders will take no prisoners. Every individual, of whatever rank, taken with arms in his hands, shall be put to death. In future let there be no exchange of prisoners. Let our soldiers understand that they can not surrender to such men. This is a death-struggle. On both sides it is only a question of killing or of being killed."[32]

MAXIMILIAN HAD ONLY reluctantly agreed to the Black Decree; he still hoped to win over his subjects with more traditional means. To that end, he planned another elaborate royal progress, this time to the distant war-torn state of Yucatán, in the far southeast of Mexico, but first he resolved to secure his dynasty. How he went about this astonished even his most devoted followers.

Rumours abounded as to why Maximilian and Carlota had no children—some claimed it was because Maximilian had picked up a venereal disease in the brothels of Venice or perhaps in Brazil. Whatever the reason, it was part of why Carlota sought a political role. Given her active participation in government, Carlota frequently had to defend herself from accusations of ambition, even from her family. She wrote to her grandmother that it seemed natural that a married woman without children shared her husband's work, while the only ambition she had was to do good and to fulfil the role of Maximilian's wife. "It is true that this woman is me", but the regal public persona was not a reflection of her true personality, or so she claimed.[33]

Nevertheless, as Maximilian well knew from his Habsburg upbringing, an emperor must have heirs. With none of his own, and to widespread bewilderment, Maximilian adopted the grandsons of the first emperor of Mexico, Agustín de Iturbide. Salvador, the eldest, was a teenager and living in Paris, where he remained. The second grandson, another Agustín, was only two and half years old and lived in Mexico. His mother, Alicia Iturbide, born Alice Green, was an American. The penurious Iturbide family pressured her into giving up her son when Maximilian promised them $150,000. Under duress, Alice signed the contract on September 9 and abandoned her child one week later. Leaving some of his favourite toys behind, she set off with the rest of the family for Veracruz.

She got only as far as Puebla before the pain of separation became too much, and she returned, distraught, to the capital. There she secured an audience with Bazaine, who promised to pass on a letter imploring Maximilian to renounce the contract. She apologised for reneging on the deal, but "a grief which has no bounds, a feeling the most intense known of humanity, have guided my steps in search of a son who is the charm of my existence." Pleading with Maximilian, she continued, "No longer to see my child! To separate myself from him perhaps forever! To abandon him when he most needs my care! There is no agony compared to this sad thought. Your Majesty cannot insist on a separation which puts in danger my existence".[34]

The response came two days later when a member of Maximilian's household guard appeared at Alice's apartment. The emperor and empress wanted to see her, he explained, and a carriage was waiting outside. Full of hope, Alice climbed into the carriage, but as the journey continued she noticed the driver missed the turn for the National Palace in the city centre. Alice then assumed they were going to Chapultepec, but when they passed the street for the castle it became clear that she was being forcibly deported. The carriage took her to a stagecoach, into which she was bundled, screaming in protest, and then driven all the way to Puebla, where she was reunited with her husband and told that they must leave Mexico on the next steamer from Veracruz. This was at least better than her husband's recommendation: that she should be locked up in a lunatic asylum. As soon as she reached the United States, Alice met with Seward in Washington, explaining the situation and asking that he intercede on her behalf with the French government.

Maximilian's subjects viewed the adoption with bemusement, but the French envoy, Dano, was incredulous at this "unexplained and inexplicable" decision, "as inopportune as puerile", as he put it in his report to Paris. Dano's reaction was matched by the acute embarrassment the French foreign minister felt when the US representative to France, John Bigelow, asked him to intervene in what amounted to a royal kidnapping case. Despite somehow managing to unite Paris and Washington behind the mother who pleaded the abduction of her child, Maximilian refused to listen. Explaining himself to Napoleon III, Maximilian wrote, "The young prince's mother, a half-crazy American, was suddenly recalled to Mexico, which she had left quite contently, and the two uncles, a pair of drunkards, have been incited to go to Paris and Vienna to stir up trouble and make my government look ridiculous."[35]

For many, though, Maximilian did not need help to make his government look ridiculous. By the end of 1865, the emperor was under so much pressure that he had to abandon his trip to Yucatán. Instead, he sent Carlota in his place. The empress set out in November 1865 with a large entourage, including the now much-travelled Ramírez, the still much-hated Eloin, many ladies-in-waiting, and an army of servants, as well as an actual army of Egyptian soldiers as an escort. When she reached Veracruz, the Egyptian regiment gave her a 101-gun salute, while French marines and Austrian riflemen lined the street as the Belgian empress made her way to her lodgings in the port. This cosmopolitan reception did little to burnish her credentials as a Mexican monarch, and so Carlota ostentatiously refused to travel on the luxurious Austrian corvette that had been hired for the trip, preferring to board a dilapidated Mexican steamer. This patriotism did impress locals, who welcomed Carlota more enthusiastically than they had done eighteen months earlier when she first set foot on Mexican soil.

Maximilian seized on Carlota's positive description of her time in Veracruz, seeing in it proof that his empire was growing in popularity; however, he ignored Carlota's report about her entry into the nearby town of Orizaba. "Politically," she wrote, "things do not go well here". There were all kinds of rumours that the city was on the verge of falling to Juaristas and that Carlota had been sent ahead in preparation for Maximilian's abdication and flight to Europe. Her reception, she complained, had not been properly prepared, few admirers turned out to greet her, and it was, in short, a "disgrace". Not only that, but the few cries of "vivas!" were "Viva la emperatriz de México", not, as Carlota preferred "Nuestra emperatriz" ("Long live the empress of Mexico" as opposed to "Long live our empress").[36]

Carlota soon forgot this setback when she reached Yucatán. She was driven from the port to the state capital, Mérida, in a coach pulled by four white horses, stopping off in a small indigenous village where traditional festivities captured her imagination. The next day, down a newly repaired road, carefully lined with the arches and flowers so lacking at Orizaba, Carlota travelled triumphantly to the cathedral at the centre of town. Here, a large crowd had come out to see her, church bells rang, cannons thundered, and people cheered as the national anthem played.

In a simple white dress with blue trim, basking in the wall of sound and the tropical sun, Carlota was the popular empress she had dreamt she would be. As she walked up to the cathedral, a line of local dignitaries formed a guard of honour. Outside the doors, she knelt on a velvet cushion and kissed a crucifix. After a sombre Te Deum, she proceeded on foot to an elegant Spanish colonial mansion, where she was staying, followed by an excited crowd. Soon, by popular demand, she appeared on a balcony. As the noise died down, Carlota addressed the crowd. She apologised that Maximilian could not come in person, but continued, "I assure you from my heart that he deeply regrets that he cannot be here with me to tell you how great is his affection toward you."[37] The crowd broke out into cheers; crucially, the "vivas!" here were to the dynasty rather than the nation, a marked improvement.

The political message of the trip reinforced Maximilian and Carlota as the champions of the indigenous peoples of Mexico. Yucatán was home of the Mayans and, except for the port towns and churches, was largely untouched by Spanish and then Mexican governments. Carlota visited Mayan ruins as well as local hospitals, schools, and farms. One parish priest even introduced her to his congregation as an angel from across the seas who had come to bring them happiness. Mixing up her Mesoamerican civilisations, she felt that amongst the Mayans she could have been living at the time of Aztec emperor Moctezuma. The people of Yucatán were, she argued, natural monarchists, who respected authority and greeted her rapturously wherever she went.

Members of the Austrian Legion, who had passed Carlota on her way to Yucatán, told a different story about the region, one of hard fighting against Juaristas, burning villages, and summary executions. Not only that, but they had also lost almost half their company to yellow fever. Carlota was, of course, hidden from all this, but however buoyed she was by her trip, the unravelling reality of her kingdom was brought home to her on the voyage back to Mexico City. On December 15, 1865, Maximilian wrote to her, urging her to avoid the town of Jalapa. There were too many guerrillas and not enough imperialistas to guarantee her safety. Moreover, he advised arriving at Orizaba at night to avoid another embarrassingly cold welcome.

As so often when absent from his wife, Maximilian had fallen into a state of depression. When he heard news of Carlota's return on December 19, he wrote, "I felt so happy that I wanted to go out that same night to meet you in Veracruz", but the French warned that it was too dangerous, "so again I have to make another hard sacrifice." He was exhausted. "I am already very worn out by the endless, tiring issues and I am half spent; every day I have to preside over conferences. Meanwhile, I miss you with all my heart and with all my soul, my star, my life and my angel."[38]

With Carlota's return, he roused himself. Facing increasing criticisms from Paris, on December 27 Maximilian wrote a long letter to Napoleon III, justifying his rule. If his treasury was empty, he pointed out, it was a consequence of taking on onerous financial obligations that favoured the French, because "I believed, in all simplicity, that I was doing a real service to my best friend, the Emperor Napoleon". Maximilian asked his "best friend" for a service in return, that is, for the French government to cover, for a few months, the money Mexico owed under the Treaty of Miramar. Under mounting US pressure, Napoleon III now had to decide whether to waive the commitments Maximilian had promised to uphold or to abandon the emperor of Mexico to his fate.[39]

7

THE END OF THE AFFAIR

"Liberty", Napoleon III had declared after he proclaimed himself emperor of the French, "has never helped to found a lasting political edifice: it crowns the edifice when time has consolidated it."[1] By 1860 he felt the foundations of his empire strong enough to introduce liberal reforms. Rising from his seat at a seemingly routine cabinet meeting, he paced the room while reading aloud his proposals. Some of his ministers soon also rose, in amazement at the realisation that Napoleon III had granted the Corps législatif, the French national assembly, the right to debate, criticise, and vote on the annual address from the throne. Moreover, a later decree meant that any extraordinary expenditure beyond the agreed annual budget had to be discussed and voted on. Crucially, newspapers could also publish these parliamentary proceedings. In short, government policy was now open to attack. As the personal project of Napoleon III, immensely profligate in terms of men and money, the Mexican intervention was a gift to the opposition.

Not that there was much opposition, at least initially. To be a deputy in the Corps législatif required swearing an oath to the imperial constitution, which republicans refused. From 1857, however, five republicans were elected and took their seats in the assembly.

Most famous amongst these was a lawyer, Jules Favre, who made his name defending Felice Orsini, the Italian who tried to assassinate Napoleon III outside the opera in 1858. Master of the dramatic gesture, with thick, luxurious hair and a beard that framed a sombre face, Favre specialised in pointing out the hypocrisies in government policy. The Mexican intervention was, therefore, the perfect cause célèbre.

As early as March 1862, Favre's stentorian voice struggled against jeers in the assembly to argue that France was not, as the government claimed, simply setting out to redress wrongs committed against its subjects and ensure that Mexico paid its foreign debt. Rather, it was going to overthrow the legitimate president, Benito Juárez. Worse, his replacement, Maximilian, a foreigner to the customs of Mexico, would be a pawn in a civil war neither he nor France understood. "There is the combination for which the French government sends an expedition; there is the interest for which the treasure and blood of France will be wasted."[2]

Over the next three years, the government maintained the official line that the French army was welcomed as liberators, that monarchy was the free choice of the Mexican people expressed through universal male suffrage, and that the intervention would soon be over. Why, then, asked Favre in January 1864, were military operations still necessary? The lawyer answered his own question: it was because the French were supporting the Conservative Party, which was detested by the Mexican people. At enormous cost to the French treasury, the intervention had raised defeated murderers like Miguel Miramón and Leonardo Márquez to the rank of generals. "We were mistaken—Let us withdraw! Our brave soldiers, our officers," Favre insisted, "should have nothing to do with these tainted and bloody adventurers".[3]

One year later, in January 1865, Napoleon III confidently declared to the Corps législatif: "In Mexico, the new throne is consolidated, the country is pacified, its immense resources are being developed: the happy result of the valour of our soldiers, the good sense of the Mexican population and the intelligence and the energy of the sovereign!" He went so far as to say that the intervention was reaching its end. "We will be able to proudly put these words on a new triumphal arch: to the glory of French armies for the victories won in Europe, Asia, Africa and America."[4]

It was, therefore, somewhat embarrassing when only a few months later Napoleon III was forced to ask the Corps législatif for another 35 million francs to prop up Maximilian in Mexico. As Favre made clear to the assembly, between the words of the government and the truth, there was an enormous chasm. Reports of General Castagny's brutality in Sonora had reached Favre. Loud cheers resounded in the assembly as he read out the general's proclamation: "Mexicans! I have come in the name of the Emperor Maximilian in order to establish peace, protect property and to deliver you from criminals who oppress you in the name of liberty!" But the cheers soon died, as Favre asked how burning a village of four thousand people could be protecting them. The reality, he argued, was that the French army was not coming home; forty thousand troops would be needed in Mexico for at least ten more years and hundreds of millions more francs required to sustain them. "It is the work of Penelope that we have undertaken, but with this difference: Penelope was not killed by the shroud that she wove."[5] The Mexican policy of Napoleon III, Favre concluded as he had many times before, was madness.

Favre was not a lone voice: by January 1866, what little sympathy the French public and even Napoleon III's own ministers had for Maximilian was exhausted. An editorial in the influential *Revue des deux mondes* captured the mood when it simply asked: "For how many years are we to persevere in this gigantic thoughtless blunder, which has already lasted so long?"[6]

And Napoleon III now had much more than just domestic criticism to consider. In the United States, Ulysses S. Grant increased pressure on President Johnson to act, arguing that to allow Maximilian's rule in Mexico "is to permit an enemy to establish himself", and "Americans, instead of being the most favoured people of the world throughout the length and breadth of this continent, will be scoffed and laughed at." He did not consider the American Civil War finished while the French remained in Mexico, he informed the president. Grant began to take matters into his own hands, authorising the Civil War hero General John Schofield to recruit US volunteers and prepare to lead them in battle against Maximilian's empire. Lest events spiral beyond his control, on December 4, 1865, Johnson used his annual address to Congress to placate hawks like Grant and threaten France: "We should regard it as a great calamity to ourselves, to the cause of good government, and to the peace of the world, should any European power challenge the American people".[7]

On December 16, 1865, to ensure the point came across, Seward instructed the US representative to France, John Bigelow, to make known to the French government two points: First, the United States desired friendship. Second, this friendship was impossible unless France ended armed intervention in Mexico. Aware how bellicose anti-French sentiment had become in Washington, the French envoy to the United States sent a diplomat, Le comte René de Faverney, to inform Napoleon III in person that the choice was now between supporting Maximilian and war with the United States.

To add further steel to the US position, Seward summoned Schofield. The former commander of the Army of Ohio would not be organising the army Grant had envisaged. Instead, Seward dispatched him to Paris. "I want you to get your legs under Napoleon's mahogany, and tell him he must get out of Mexico", Seward told Schofield. Schofield's view was that "a long and bloody war, resulting, doubtless, in final success in America and probably in a revolution in France", was apt punishment for Napoleon III, but diplomacy should be tried first.

When Schofield arrived in Paris in December 1865, rumours circulated that this famous Civil War commander had come to present France with an ultimatum: leave Mexico, or fight the United States. Staying at the Grand Hotel, Schofield gave a toast at a banquet for US citizens. Six tables placed lengthways held some 250 people, including the press, who, after "Yankee Doodle" was played, punctuated Schofield's speech with cheers and applause. The general pointedly remarked that now the US government was "one of the strongest in the world, raising and maintaining armies and navies vaster than any ever before known".[8] The message did not go unnoticed.

Napoleon III, though, refused to grant the general an audience. Schofield instead met with Napoleon III's politically influential cousin, underscoring that the US government was ready to uphold the Monroe Doctrine, whatever the cost; public opinion in the United States demanded a more aggressive policy, and the government must follow suit. These conversations were reported to an increasingly anxious Napoleon III. Then on January 2, 1866, Napoleon III received the French diplomat who had come from Washington. Faverney explained that France must leave Mexico or go to war with the United States.

On January 15, 1866, faced with catastrophe or humiliation, Napoleon III wrote to Maximilian. "It is not without painful emotion", the letter began, "that I am writing to Your Majesty". Pleasantries out of the way, the French emperor cut to his decision. The impossibility of asking the Corps législatif for more money and Maximilian's own inability to provide the necessary funds, Napoleon III wrote, "force me to fix a definitive limit to the French occupation." Napoleon III tried to disguise this as a blessing: "The departure of our troops may be a temporary weakness, but it will have the advantage of removing all pretext for intervention on the part of the United States."[9] After spending four years fighting to create his kingdom, and almost as many persuading him to take the throne, in abandoning Maximilian, Napoleon III was, he claimed, doing his friend a favour.

It would take weeks for this letter to cross the Atlantic and reach Maximilian, but Napoleon III did not bother to wait. On January 22, 1866, the emperor had to open the annual session of the Corps législatif with a speech. It was a fine and mild January afternoon as the emperor made his way in a state carriage, with his young son, the prince imperial, at his side, on the short journey from the Tuileries to the Louvre. Senators, deputies, marshals, admirals, members of the Grand Cross of the *Légion d'honneur*, and foreign ambassadors, all in their elaborate uniforms replete with jewelled medals, watched on, and cries of "Vive l'empereur!" rang out as Napoleon III took his seat on the throne. Once silence had been restored, Napoleon III, used to public speaking by now, began in a clear, confident voice with a few banal remarks on foreign policy. What he said next shocked his audience: "In Mexico, the government founded by the will of the people is consolidated; the dissidents, vanquished and dispersed, no longer have a leader; the [French] troops have shown their valour, and the country has found guarantees of order and security . . . our expedition is coming to an end. I will come to an understanding with the Emperor Maximilian to fix the time of the recall of our troops".[10]

A delighted Schofield listened to the speech in person, and at a dinner held that same evening Napoleon III's cousin asked him whether the declaration would prove satisfactory for the United States. Unreservedly, the US general replied, it would.

WITH THE NEWS yet to reach Mexico, Maximilian remained ignorant that the man whom he considered his best friend had deserted him. Confident the letter he had sent on December 27, 1865, would buy him time, Maximilian's focus was now on interior design and landscape gardening. He was overseeing the finishing touches on luxurious retreats for himself and Carlota outside of the capital.

A lover of hot climates, Maximilian found even Mexico City's mild winters too cold. In these months he kept the stoves burning all day, at Chapultepec, or the National Palace, making the rooms as hot as a Russian bath, according to José Luis Blasio, Maximilian's private secretary, who added that his Mexican employees could not stand the heat. As soon as Maximilian left the room, Blasio would open the nearest window, hurriedly closing it when he heard the emperor's returning footsteps. When Maximilian caught him in the act, he chastised his secretary: "Don't you see that we're freezing?" The emperor continued, "These youngsters who have hot blood do not realize that an old man of thirty-two, like me, is as cold as ice. Close the window, and if you open it again I'll have a carpenter nail it shut."[11]

A longer-term solution for the heat-sensitive emperor presented itself at a picnic, an activity Maximilian enjoyed most Saturdays. With a train of mules carrying food, wine, tables, and chairs, and a militia of servants to deploy these accoutrements, Maximilian would forget his government duties. The fine foods were washed down with equally fine wines. During one of these well-lubricated lunches, a member of Maximilian's entourage held forth on the beauty and, crucially, the climate of the nearby town of Cuernavaca. So taken was Maximilian with the description that he decided to visit.

"Picture yourself", he wrote afterwards to a friend, "a broad level valley, blessed by heaven, stretching out before one like a golden bowl, surrounded by a variety of mountain ranges rising one beyond the other in the boldest outlines and bathed in the most glorious shades, ranging from the purest rose-red, purple and violet to the deepest azure". More important, he continued, "Imagine this golden bowl filled at all seasons—or rather all year round, for there are no seasons here—with a wealth of tropical vegetation . . . a climate as lovely as the Italian May, and handsome, friendly, loyal natives."[12]

Maximilian was so enraptured with Cuernavaca that he restored a mansion there and built another house, El Olindo, nearby. The first, the Garden of Borda, had been created in the eighteenth century for a wealthy mining magnate. This once magnificent palace and its gardens had fallen into disrepair, but, at great expense, Maximilian restored them to imperial grandeur. Vivid tropical plants lined the corridors, vines and orchids were arranged on the walls, and fish swam in crystal globes, while exotic birds in cages were hung from the ceiling.

At Cuernavaca, Maximilian and Carlota could relax in a more informal setting, their court reduced to a few trusted individuals, amongst them Blasio, Carlota's favourite ladies-in-waiting, and officers from the Austrian Legion. Here Maximilian could indulge in his taste for Austrian cuisine—schnitzel and goulash were staples, even at breakfast—although guests complained that the cooking was bland and the Hungarian wine atrocious. Maximilian preferred champagne and madeira, but the imperial cellars had run out of the latter. During one meal, desperate for a glass of port, the emperor lamented that there was none to be found in Mexico. At this point, an Austrian officer reluctantly admitted to having a case.

"You must be in the good graces of Bacchus," replied the emperor, "or else in secret relations with Mephisto". After the case was fetched, Maximilian declared it excellent and pressed the officer to explain how he came by it. When the Austrian refused, Maximilian laughed, "I see you have been smuggling like the French; but wait—after dinner I shall put you in a confessional". True to his word, later that evening, Maximilian took the officer by the arm and strolled with him in the gardens. "Now, confess; where did you get it? I promise not to betray your accomplices". Eventually, the officer admitted that he had bought a case from a shop near Chapultepec. "That is indeed hard", said Maximilian. "I know, of course, that I am constantly robbed, and I do not care as long as I have all we require and as long as they only take the *beaux restes*; but not to leave me a single bottle of my favourite wine, and to sell it, so to say under my very nose, is indeed more than I can stand. But you have my word and they shall not be punished".

Returning in good spirits to the dinner, Maximilian told Carlota, "I have confessed the culprit and given him absolution—the least I could do after he bribed me with madeira". Maximilian added that they should now put a sentry on the wine-cellar door or they would be drinking nothing but *pulque*, before asking, "I wonder how much they would charge me for my own stuff"? Carlota replied, "The Robbers!" before admonishing Maximilian for being too lenient. After dinner, cigarettes and cigars were smoked on the veranda, Carlota the centre of animated conversation, Maximilian pacing up and down while talking excitedly to guests.[13]

At Cuernavaca, Maximilian and Carlota were frequently joined by an eccentric Austrian botanist, Dominik Billimeck. Very tall and fat, with grey hair and beard, and thick, heavy spectacles, Billimeck rarely joined in conversation unless it had to do with natural history, insects, or reptiles—God's "little creatures" as he called them. He spent his time hunting for specimens, armed with an enormous yellow umbrella, a cork helmet, and a linen duster jacket with vast pockets. He could be seen in the distance, "bobbing about like a gigantic mushroom under his umbrella and helmet".[14] Returning for the evening, he placed the snakes he caught into alcohol-filled jars and unpinned the centipedes, scorpions, and flies attached to the lining of his hat. Maximilian loved spending time with Billimeck, but Blasio, whose bedroom was next to the naturalist, lay awake at night in fear that the poisonous creatures next door would escape their cages and invade his quarters.

Carlota found Cuernavaca just as idyllic as Maximilian. A keen rider, she often did the fifty-mile journey from Mexico City on horseback rather than carriage. Tents were pitched for lunch en route to avoid the midday heat and admire the picturesque countryside. At the Garden of Borda, she could relax, enjoying tranquil, lazy days, visiting beauty spots, picnicking in the beautiful grounds, and visiting local dignitaries. After one visit, her entourage was in a good mood, she wrote to Maximilian, sleeping in hammocks, eating with great appetite, and occasionally going to the theatre in town. She rekindled a youthful interest in butterflies, in hunting them at least, sending numerous specimens to Mexico City and enjoying the praise she received from Billimeck for her discoveries.

The gossip around Maximilian's second residence at Cuernavaca, El Olindo, however, was deeply hurtful to Carlota. Rather than climate, rumour had it that Maximilian's fondness for Cuernavaca was because an especially handsome and loyal "native", the seventeen-year-old daughter of his gardener, was installed here. El Olindo became known locally as La Casa de la India Bonita. Widely shared gossip had it that when his mistress became pregnant with Maximilian's child, she was hastily married off to prevent scandal.

Curious about such rumours, Blasio questioned Maximilian's valet, who said that the imperial couple had become estranged from each other after Maximilian returned from a trip to Vienna. This explained why they slept in different beds, but Carlota wanted to avoid public scandal—hence, they appeared united in public. Responding to Blasio's assertion that he had never seen anything suspicious, the valet answered, "You may have seen nothing, but I saw a good deal. The emperor's bedroom was visited many times by ladies of the court, who slipped in and out so mysteriously that only I saw them, and frequently without knowing who they were. How many of them, who no one would believe capable of it, yielded to [Maximilian's] desires!"

A sceptical Blasio conceded that at the National Palace in Mexico City this may have been possible, for there were many secret doors in the warren-like maze, but not at Chapultepec or Cuernavaca. Maybe not at Chapultepec, the valet conceded, but "at Cuernavaca the guards were so stationed that they might not have seen a woman going in or coming out. Did you never observe in the garden wall a narrow door, scarcely wide enough to let one person through[?] . . . [T]hat door could tell you many curious things about the persons who used it".[15]

Likely, there was little truth to these allegations, but, whatever the case, Maximilian and Carlota increasingly spent weeks apart. And time away from the capital sparked more gossip. For instance, Carlota was accused of going to Cuernavaca rather than Mexico City after her trip to Yucatán because her return would have coincided with a rapturous reception prepared for a famous Mexican soprano. Jealous, so the accusation went, of another woman receiving more attention than her, Carlota preferred to hide outside the city. More seriously, Maximilian's stays at Cuernavaca confirmed for the French their prejudices, namely, that he preferred luxury to government. To allay these suspicions, Maximilian and Carlota decided, as much as possible, that one of them should remain in Mexico City, while the other enjoyed time at Cuernavaca. This, of course, merely fuelled further speculation about their private lives.

The strain was beginning to tell on Carlota. She was often alone, and, even when in the same residence, Maximilian's routine meant he saw Carlota only twice a day, at mealtimes. Her worries about their precarious position in Mexico were multiplying, and the enormity of her role in the empire was a heavy burden. Her dinners, which Maximilian attended even more rarely now, had lost their shine. One attendee related how Carlota perfunctorily greeted guests, asking banal questions. Although the Christofle silverware was impressive, budget cuts meant that the meal was badly cooked, the wines mediocre. Silence reigned throughout the evening, the empress solemn and only occasionally exchanging a few words with her immediate neighbours. While remaining outwardly regal at public events, she was careful to make sure her face never betrayed her innermost anxieties.

But when, in January 1866, she found out that her beloved father had died, there was nothing she could do to hide her emotions. Carlota knew that Leopold had been ill, and when she heard Maximilian sobbing after receiving the mail she guessed what had happened. They then cried together, both extremely close to the Belgian king, an unswerving champion for their cause. Carlota sequestered herself away in her apartments for four days. Reading about her father's death in the newspapers, she wept uncontrollably. After the official mourning period ended, Carlota continued to wear black, except on exceptionally hot days, when she would wear white with black ribbons and a bracelet with a black cross that her mother-in-law, Sophie, sent from Europe.

Maximilian organised an official memorial for his father-in-law on January 15, the same day that Napoleon III sat down to write his letter announcing the evacuation of French troops. Comparing himself to Leopold I, whose Belgian kingdom had been founded with French support and governed as a liberal constitutional monarchy, Maximilian used the opportunity to make a rousing speech: "Confident in my faith I march towards my goal with indefatigable perseverance, my strength may fail me, my soul—never!"[16]

The effect, however, was somewhat undermined because he used the occasion to publicly humiliate Achille Bazaine, thereby confirming the fractures in the French alliance for all to see. Maximilian made his disdain for the marshal apparent by demoting his order of precedence at the ceremony, putting him behind his own ministers. Given Maximilian's well-known obsession with etiquette, this was almost as bad as insulting Bazaine to his face, which he did next. The infamous leader of the counterguerrillas, Charles du Pin, whom Maximilian had personally requested return to France because of numerous atrocities, had just come back to Mexico. After the ceremony, Maximilian greeted the members of the diplomatic core. When he reached the French diplomat Alphonse Dano, Maximilian raised his voice: "Why is du Pin here? I wrote that he was not to come. Be informed sir, that this is the first time since I am Emperor that anyone has disobeyed me. I am much displeased. Say so on my behalf to Marshal Bazaine."[17]

Dano smoothed things over, explaining that the recall of du Pin was nothing to do with Bazaine. Dano was right. After reading the charges of what today would amount to war crimes, the French minister of war had thought a man like du Pin would be useful in Mexico and reassigned him to active duty. Dano arranged a private dinner where Maximilian apologised in person; however, the gossip in political circles was of an open rupture with the French army. Worse, for Dano it confirmed what he had now long thought: Maximilian was disrespectful to his French allies. Compounding this view was Dano's belief that Maximilian surrounded himself with Austrian officers and neglected the government of his empire amidst the luxury of Cuernavaca. He was there when news reached him on

February 14 that a French envoy had arrived in Mexico City carrying an urgent letter from Napoleon III.

FEARING THE WORST, Maximilian pleaded sickness to delay the meeting. But the Frenchman made his way to Cuernavaca anyway and handed over the letter announcing the end of the French intervention to Maximilian in person. After reading it, Maximilian flew into a rage. First he threatened to immediately abdicate. Then he resolved that after the French withdrew, he would rather die fighting as a guerrilla against Juárez than return to Europe.

Once slightly more composed, he penned a short, petulant reply to Napoleon III: "Your Majesty believes that sudden pressure makes it impossible for you to observe the solemn treaties which you signed with me less than two years ago, and inform me of this with a frankness which cannot but do you honour." In a fit of pique, Maximilian then offered his own ultimatum: "I am too much your friend to wish to be a cause of the peril to Your Majesty or your dynasty, either directly or indirectly. I therefore propose to you with a cordiality equal to your own that you should immediately withdraw your troops from the American continent." Whatever happened, the emperor of Mexico resolved to conduct himself "worthy of a Habsburg" and "place my life and soul at the service of my new country's independence."[18] Despite his anger, Maximilian still refused to believe his friend Napoleon III had forsaken him and sent instructions to Félix Eloin, already in Europe on a diplomatic mission, to plead with the French emperor.

Another blow then crashed into Maximilian's Cuernavaca paradise a week later with the death of the French finance virtuoso Jacques Langlais, who had a heart attack on February 23. Maximilian had placed great hope in Langlais, expecting him to resolve the empire's considerable financial problems. Before he died, in an attempt to balance the budget, Langlais had finally proposed the reorganisation the Mexican treasury needed: cuts to government expenditure—not least Maximilian's own profligacy—and new taxes to increase revenues; however, the financier had not had time to implement these reforms. Indeed, French wits said it was the Sisyphean task of reshaping Mexico's treasury that had killed Langlais. Just as important to Maximilian as these reforms, Langlais was also willing to make plain to the French government that Maximilian's financial problems were not entirely of his own making, but rather the one-sided agreements favouring the French into which he had entered.

Despite losing an important ally, Maximilian did not attend the funeral. On February 27, 1866, a small crowd gathered in the central square of Mexico City as Langlais's body was brought from the cathedral and placed in a wagon that would transport it to Veracruz. Twenty Mexican soldiers escorted the hearse to the windows outside the National Palace, where it stopped, waiting for more troops to join. The bored soldiers thoughtlessly threw their bags into the wagon next to the dead body and then ate tortillas and tamales. Langlais's son and a few of his French coworkers looked on, horrified at this lack of respect that they felt epitomised Maximilian's attitude towards the French. As a report was sent back to Napoleon III detailing the careless funeral arrangements, this further damaged Maximilian's cause.

Weeks later, there was yet more bad news. Leopold II, now king of the Belgians, had sent a deputation to Mexico City to formally announce his accession to the throne. After completing their mission, a party was held for the diplomats the night before their departure. In white tie, military uniforms, or elegant ball gowns, the cream of Mexico City sipped iced champagne and waltzed, inevitably, to Strauss. The centre of attention was the Belgian aristocrat Baron d'Huart, a close friend of Carlota's younger brother and the man with whom all the women wanted to dance.

At five on the morning of March 4, the small group of Belgians left Mexico City on their way back to Europe. Only forty miles from the capital, where the road went through steep mountain passes thickly forested with trees, their carriage was ambushed. D'Huart reached for his pistol, but before he could grasp it a volley of fire rang out; his body was riddled with bullets, one smashing into his forehead. The other passengers, many of them wounded, managed to get some shots off, scrambled out, and laid down a defensive fire before charging the attackers with their swords. Fortunately, a second carriage was not far behind, and the assailants fled when they saw it approaching.

Upon hearing of the attack, Maximilian rushed to the scene and offered his personal physician to help the wounded. In a nearby chapel, lit with candles, he saw d'Huart's body laid out. After staring forlornly at the corpse, Maximilian, over a cup of coffee, interrogated the soldiers on the scene about what had happened. Carlota stayed in Mexico City, where she was due to host a dinner party that evening. Still without news, she was just about to greet her dinner guests when a member of the Austrian Legion informed her of the death of d'Huart. A solitary tear welled in her eye before she steeled herself and swept into the dining room, no emotion showing. The next day, though, Carlota wept wildly at the funeral.

Maximilian's enquiry into the incident suggested that it was not a robbery but a targeted attack to discredit the empire abroad. In this it succeeded. Maximilian went to the scene with only a couple of officers to demonstrate that he was not afraid of assassins. In Europe, however, the emperor's small guard was, obviously, not the story. As one Belgian newspaper reported with some understatement, "News from Mexico is not completely satisfactory." The attack on the Belgian mission, the article added, so close to the capital, did not "inspire great confidence in the current order of things".[19]

This was a significant setback because, dependent on European credit and volunteers, Maximilian had gone to great lengths to favourably influence opinion across the Atlantic. Above all, the *Times*, "cost what it may," he had written to his representative in Britain, "for, though it seems almost absurd to say so, it is nonetheless a political fact that whoever can rely on this paper can also rely on public opinion in England. Every true son of John Bull reads *The*

Times regularly at breakfast every morning, adopts the views of this paper, and imagines himself to be a great statesman for the rest of the day."[20] That April, however, every true son of John Bull read about the attack on the Belgian diplomats.

Even its most ardent backers could no longer pretend that Maximilian's kingdom was secure. José Manuel Hidalgo y Esnaurrízar, the man who had first brought the idea of a Mexican monarchy to Napoleon III's attention and now Maximilian's representative to the French government, had been recalled from Paris. Loath to leave his luxurious, well-paid, and, above all, safe post amongst Parisian high society, the Mexican monarchist did everything to avoid returning. When Maximilian insisted, Hidalgo pleaded for a strong military escort from Veracruz to the capital because, as one of the chief architects of the new regime, he had received death threats. Finally arriving in Mexico City, the usually debonair Hidalgo proved constantly nervous in the monarchy he had done so much to create. Accepting Maximilian's invitation for a ride through the city, Hidalgo came heavily armed. The emperor laughed this off. More serious was the fact that Hidalgo had failed to warn his sovereign of the attitude of the French government. Maximilian, therefore, sacked Hidalgo, but to soften the blow appointed him a counsellor of state. So terrified was Hidalgo of remaining in Mexico that he fled overnight from the capital to Veracruz. Without even informing the emperor, and under a false name, he arranged for passage to Europe.

Maximilian still maintained a regular—and lengthy—correspondence with another architect of his empire, José María Gutiérrez de Estrada. He had remained in Europe, incessantly chastising Maximilian for abandoning the Conservative Party and the Catholic Church. Gutiérrez de Estrada now recommended that Maximilian roll back his liberal reforms. In reply, Maximilian defended his conduct, blamed the empire's problems on the French, and invited Gutiérrez de Estrada to Mexico to discuss his concerns in person. Gutiérrez de Estrada declined, preferring to stay in the monarchies of the Old World rather than go to the one he had helped create in the New.

As his fury at Napoleon III's decision subsided, Maximilian threw himself into feverish activity to save his empire. The French emperor sent mixed messages: on the one hand, he had announced the withdrawal of his troops; on the other, as he wrote to Maximilian in April, "it is my most earnest desire, beside being to my interest, that the Mexican empire should be maintained. I shall therefore do all in my power to help Your Majesty". Crucially, Napoleon III promised that the French Foreign Legion would stay in Mexico, at his expense, and that he would waive all but the interest on 25 million francs immediately due to France.[21]

If Maximilian's empire were to survive, it would have to rely on its own resources. That made it all the more urgent that he overhaul its finances and create an independent army. This realisation finally spurred Maximilian into action. He spent days poring over military reforms. Combining Austrian and Belgian volunteers with Mexican imperialistas and the French Foreign Legion, he still had a formidable force, estimated at twenty-eight thousand men. After a conference with his generals, a buoyed Maximilian wrote to Carlota, "We will have a magnificent army".[22] So proud was he of the resulting proposals that he sent a copy to his older brother. Franz Joseph had advised his brother not to involve himself in military affairs because had had no interest in them, let alone experience. Yet in his note to the Austrian emperor, Maximilian pompously remarked that the European powers might learn from his Mexican example.

Despite his personal differences with Maximilian, Bazaine too felt that the empire could survive. He had a powerful incentive to make sure that it did. His wife's fortune, and his own—as a wedding gift Maximilian had given him a palace in Mexico City worth $100,000—were tied to the regime's fate. To give the empire every chance of success, he planned to draw out the French army's evacuation for as long as possible. The last contingent would not leave until the end of 1867. This gave Maximilian eighteen months of continued French military support. With the French still defending the most important parts of the empire, Maximilian's newly organised Mexican army would be free to take the offensive against Juárez.

Turning to foreign affairs, Maximilian then put his newfound energy into drafting a treaty with France to replace Miramar. Encouraged by Napoleon III's April letter, Maximilian could still not bring himself to believe that the French emperor had abandoned his dream of a monarchy in the New World. "It seems to me impossible," he wrote, "that the wisest monarch of the century and the most powerful nation in the world should give in to the Yankees in this somewhat undignified way."[23] Writing to Napoleon III, Maximilian attributed the misunderstandings to the distance between France and Mexico. A new entente cordiale between the two emperors, he suggested, would consolidate the Mexican empire.

Maximilian's entente cordiale, however, went far beyond informal goodwill. Instead, it envisaged French troops remaining in Mexico until the country was pacified, whenever that might be, although allowing for gradual reductions. Maximilian also demanded that Bazaine be sacked and replaced by a general who would obey orders from the Mexican emperor. To sell this plan in Paris, Maximilian turned to Juan Nepomuceno Almonte, who had earlier so beguiled Napoleon III with a vision of a Mexican kingdom. Almonte had been sidelined since May 1864 with a ceremonial position in Maximilian's court, but, as a trusted confidant of Napoleon III, Maximilian felt sure that he was the man to negotiate the entente cordiale.

Having resolved diplomatic and military affairs to his satisfaction, Maximilian now turned to finances. In April 1866, Maximilian, with much pride, announced the implementation of Langlais's reforms. As Maximilian's own ministers realised, however, the disjuncture between what was on paper and reality was astronomical. The imperial troops remained unpaid and without provisions. The Austrian and Belgian volunteers were owed $1.5 million in back pay. The salaries of government officials had been in arrears for months.

At an emergency cabinet meeting to discuss this financial disaster with Dano and Bazaine present, Maximilian interrupted his ministers and exclaimed, "Doing away with all detail, the question may be summed up in very few words—it is either the bankruptcy of the empire or the hope of saving it". The former, Maximilian implored, was surely against the wishes of Napoleon III.[24] Bazaine advanced the necessary sums from the treasury of the French army.

Yet the outraged letter Maximilian had sent in response to the news that the French were leaving Mexico had done nothing to change the wishes of Napoleon III. After reading it, the French emperor summoned Eloin. Visibly shaken, Napoleon III said it was obvious that "Maximilian is angry. I am not offended at this. I understand the impression that reading my letter must have made upon him. But what can be done?" He then criticised Maximilian: "All the reports which we receive concur in the opinion that the emperor Maximilian is lacking in energy; he confines himself to drawing up and promulgating decrees, without realising that they often cannot be carried into effect. It is alleged that, urged by his eagerness to achieve something, he loses himself in utopian schemes".[25]

Nonetheless, it was Almonte's mission to Paris in which Maximilian placed his greatest hope of persuading Napoleon III to change course. On May 20, Almonte formally presented himself as Maximilian's representative to the French government, handing over the treaty for the new entente cordiale that Maximilian had spent weeks drafting. Although the agreement accepted a slow withdrawal of French forces in the future, essentially it amounted to a request for more money and soldiers now. The French foreign minister made Almonte wait more than a week before giving a damning reply: "It is difficult to account for the persistency of illusion which must have guided the conception of this scheme."[26] Maximilian's plan went so far beyond what Napoleon III would allow that the Foreign Ministry told Almonte there was no point in even discussing it. To avoid any further misunderstanding, the minister of war ordered Bazaine to refuse any more payments to Maximilian's government from French funds.

These were not the only hopes dashed in Europe in the spring of 1866. The reorganisation of the army that Maximilian was so proud of depended on fresh volunteers from Belgium and Austria. But the Belgian king, Leopold II, cared little for his sister or her position in Mexico. Moreover, the US secretary of state, William Seward, indicated that Washington regarded the recruitment of European volunteers to fight in Mexico as an unfriendly act. Leopold II's indifference and US pressure ensured the Belgian government prohibited any further volunteers for Maximilian's armies.

Although her brother's refusal was a personal insult to Carlota, the Belgian forces in Mexico were few in number. In contrast, the Austrian Legion amounted to some six thousand troops, and Maximilian turned to his homeland in his hour of need, signing a convention for enrolment of another four thousand men in 1866 and then two thousand annually until 1870. In May 1866, around a thousand troops swore an oath of allegiance to Maximilian and gathered at Trieste, ready to sail to Mexico. When news reached Washington, Seward was outraged. He informed the Austrian government that if any volunteers left for Mexico, relations between the United States and Austria would be seriously damaged. Bowing to US demands, Franz Joseph ordered the men at Trieste to disband, many of whom had to be physically restrained such was their anger at breaking their oath.

Maximilian was incensed when he found out that his brother-in-law—and, worse, his brother—had abandoned him. It was "unpardonable weakness" on the part of the European powers towards the United States. "If all the governments of Europe," he resolved, "desert Mexico, I shall not leave my fatherland". What he saw as his brother's cowardice and betrayal came in for especial disdain: "If Austria had been loyal", he wrote to his diplomatic representative at Vienna, "she would at once have embarked the troops, but such a nerveless and faithless government could naturally not behave otherwise."[27]

Partly to maintain appearances to friends and family, but partly because he remained optimistic, Maximilian had always represented his situation in Mexico positively. In a letter to a friend, for instance, he grandiosely declared, "I would not for anything in the world give up my position and return to the old life." It was true, he reflected, that there were difficulties, "but fighting is my element, and the life of Mexico is worth a struggle." Moreover, he added, "On this continent one at least reaps a harvest from one's work which I never knew in Europe—gratitude. One finds something which I sought in vain in earlier life—recognition." To his former private secretary, he wrote that even if he had known in Europe what he knew now in Mexico, he would still accept the Mexican crown. The empire may collapse, he concluded, and he might perish with it, "but nobody can deprive me of the consciousness of having worked devotedly for a sublime idea, and this is better and more comforting than to moulder in inactivity in old Europe. There are those who consider the life led by my younger brothers a philosophic one; to me such an existence would be death in life, and worse still, I find it ridiculous. There is nothing more pitiable than an appendaged prince, leading what is called a care-free life."[28]

This optimism—some called it delusion—about his life in Mexico was destroyed on June 28, 1866, when news from Paris arrived. After reading that his entente cordiale had been dismissed out of hand, Maximilian at first grew angry and then, resigned, fell back into his armchair. Staring into the distance, he decided, there and then, he would abdicate.

When he told Carlota, she was furious. The granddaughter of Louis Philippe, the French king who abdicated in 1848, Carlota believed that her grandfather had "ruined" himself and his family when he gave up his throne. She had felt shame as an eight-year-old when she had heard what her grandfather had done, and she was not going to allow her husband to make the same mistake.

She put her thoughts in writing to ensure Maximilian understood them; even on paper, her rage was terrifying. Abdication, she insisted, "amounts to pronouncing sentence on oneself, and writing oneself down as incompetent, and this is only admissible in old men and idiots, and is not the thing for a prince…full of life and hope in the future." Renouncing the throne was only ever "a mistake" or "cowardice". "I say that emperors do not give themselves up. So long as there is an emperor here, there will be an empire, even if no more than six feet of earth belong to him." Money could be found and success won, she argued. "One does not abandon one's post before the enemy, why should one abandon a crown? Kings of the Middle Ages waited at least till someone came to take their states away from them before giving themselves up". Carlota added that abdication was not "worthy of a Habsburg", and if Maximilian did leave Mexico it would prove critics right—she named Jules Favre specifically—an admission that the empire had been "the greatest absurdity under the sun."

Counselling her husband to hold his nerve, Carlota took the decision out of Maximilian's hands. Where Almonte had failed, she resolved to succeed. She would go to Europe to argue with Napoleon III in person. "They may play with single individuals, but they must not play with nations, for God avenges this." "It is impossible," she insisted, "that Napoleon III abandons us, abandons himself and breaks his word. . . . I will go, I will speak to him, I will expose the truth that has been hidden from him. He has a generous heart and he will listen to me."[29]

Despite the personal and political tragedies that had landed one cruel blow after another, Carlota was not broken. The empire was still possible: "What will become of it, god alone knows, but it will not be our fault if it fails." Asked whether private life at Miramar would be preferable to being empress, she replied, "No, a hundred times no, and I prefer for my part a position which offers activity and duties, even difficulties if you want, to contemplating the sea until the age of seventy."[30]

Such was the enormity of her mission that Carlota even permitted her ladies-in-waiting an *abrazo* before she departed. After a tearful farewell with Maximilian, Carlota left Mexico City early on the morning of July 9 for Europe. Determined not to relinquish power, she had taken on the ultimate responsibility: the survival of the empire.

THAT SUMMER OF 1866, the tectonic plates of European power were shifting. Under the guidance of Otto von Bismarck, Prussia, the rising Germanic power, declared war on Austria, as did Prussia's ally the recently created nation-state Italy, which was determined to finally drive the Habsburgs out of the peninsula. It was not, therefore, only Maximilian who needed French help but also Franz Joseph. Napoleon III, however, remained neutral. At a secret meeting with Bismarck at Biarritz in October 1865, the French emperor had been promised territorial gains if he left Austria isolated. Hoping to profit while the two major powers of central Europe ground each other down, Napoleon III stood back.

Thus, two days before Carlota arrived in France, Maximilian wrote to her that "you will find Europe very changed", but "wise Napoleon in a better position than ever". It was, reasoned Maximilian, a propitious time for Carlota to negotiate for French troops to remain in Mexico, more financial support, and the replacement of Bazaine as commander in chief. To counter accusations that his government did not favour French interests, he had sacked much of his cabinet and appointed two French officers as ministers of war and finance. Having done this, he believed that Napoleon III could not refuse Carlota's requests. "We have done everything possible", Maximilian wrote. "Now the person who has to act is him." Putting pressure on his wife, he added, "It would be deplorable for the country and for yourself if you leave Europe with promises, but without achieving results."[31]

By the time Carlota reached the port of Saint-Nazaire in early August, Napoleon III appeared neither wise nor in a good position. After a lightning Prussian campaign, Franz Joseph's army had suffered a crushing defeat. Developed and trained under Maximilian's tenure as commanding officer, its navy was the only positive for Austria, for it had defeated an Italian fleet. Nonetheless, the war lasted only seven weeks, with Prussia emerging as the powerhouse of continental Europe. Napoleon III, his health painfully deteriorating, had committed a foreign policy miscalculation of catastrophic proportions. In August, Napoleon III tried to claim the territories that Bismarck had promised, but the Prussian chancellor responded with the diplomatic equivalent of laughing in the French emperor's face, pointing out that the Prussian army was already mobilised. Now it was war not only on the other side of the Atlantic that Napoleon III had to worry about now, but across the Rhine, where Bismarck martialled the forces of German nationalism behind a militaristic regime.

France was in a state of feverish crisis, and attacks on Napoleon III's policy towards Prussia were rife—even Napoleon III's wife, Eugenie, berated him for being outwitted by Bismarck. The last thing the French emperor wanted was an unpleasant reminder of another unpopular foreign policy disaster. He tried to delay meeting Carlota. Pleading illness, he urged her to visit her brother in Brussels first, but Carlota had already telegrammed the courts at Brussels and Vienna, informing them that she would not be visiting because of their refusal to send more volunteers. Ignoring the French emperor's excuses, she proceeded to Paris.

When she arrived, Napoleon III's aide-de-camp and officers were at the wrong railway station. Luckily, Almonte, with the irrepressible Gutiérrez de Estrada, was at the right one, gare Montparnasse. From here, Carlota drove to the Grand Hotel, a luxurious symbol of Georges-Eugène Haussmann's new Paris where Schofield had stayed. Finally reaching the hotel, Napoleon III's breathless aides made their apologies, enquired as to what time Carlota would like to receive Eugenie, and, pointedly, asked how long the empress of Mexico intended to stay in Paris. Carlota gave her answer: as long as it took.

The next day, at two, Eugenie travelled from the Saint-Cloud palace on the outskirts of Paris to Carlota's hotel. Entering the lobby, Eugenie saw Carlota at the top of the main staircase. Walking slowly down, Carlota embraced and kissed her French counterpart. The two empresses then retired to Carlota's rooms, where they spoke for an hour. Carlota pressed her case, arguing for more men, time, and money. Eugenie, sympathetic but evasive, spoke only in generalisations. Exasperated, Carlota asked when she might return the visit.

"The day after tomorrow", said Eugenie.

"And the emperor," asked Carlota, "shall I not be able to see him too?"

"Oh, the emperor is still unwell", replied Eugenie.

Carlota would not take no for an answer. She must see him, she insisted, or she would break into his apartments.[32]

As she wrote to Maximilian, this first meeting was not promising. "What struck me was that I know more about China than these people here know about Mexico". It was a revelation that might have been more useful two years earlier. She was less than chivalrous about Eugenie, writing, "I noticed that the Empress has lost much of her youth".[33]

She had at least been granted an audience, and on August 11 carriages arrived at the hotel to take Carlota to the emperor. She was nervous, but looked imperious, dressed in a long, black silk dress offset with a dazzling white hat. A crowd had gathered outside, which cheered her as she left the hotel and climbed into her carriage. Shaking with anxiety, Carlota held tightly onto the arm of Almonte's wife, who rode with her.

By time she arrived at Saint-Cloud, she had regained her composure. Greeted with the sound of drumrolls, with the soldiers of the Imperial Guard lining the driveway to the palace, Carlota bowed graciously as she passed the French flag before the carriage came to a stop outside a staircase that led up to the emperor's private apartments. The imperial household stood at the bottom of the steps to greet her, and when Napoleon III's son, ten years old, ran to open the carriage, she noticed the Mexican Order of the Eagle hanging around his neck. Eugenie then escorted Carlota into a study with the French emperor.

She had come to save a cause that was his own, announced Carlota, before handing Napoleon III a letter from Maximilian. She then produced a long memorandum that her husband had written, justifying his conduct in Mexico, along with numerous other documents. Appealing to Napoleon III's honour, vanity, and pride, she reminded him of the promises that he had made to Maximilian, described his desperate situation, and implored the French emperor not to abandon his faithful friend.

As she spoke, Carlota thought how much weaker the emperor seemed, both physically and mentally, than two years earlier. Napoleon III, who listened silently during this lecture, turned to his wife with a hopeless look in his eyes and began to cry. There was, he said, nothing he could do, whatever his personal feelings. It was no longer in his gift to help Maximilian. But, Carlota insisted, surely a country as rich and powerful as France could easily aid Mexico? Before Napoleon III could respond, the interview was interrupted by a servant entering the room with a decanter full of orangeade. Everyone was taken aback at this unexpected intrusion, Eugenie embarrassed, Carlota irritably refusing refreshment before finally being persuaded to take a glass.

Shaken by this interruption, the force of her argument seemed to diminish. Napoleon III's ministers, she now declared, had coerced him into abandoning Maximilian against his will. She resolved to speak to them, change their minds, and then meet again. Napoleon III, relieved at the prospect of getting Carlota out of the room, agreed to this, promising to make a final decision only after consulting his ministers. Wearied from the passionate discussion, her eyes tired and anxious, Carlota left the study. She walked to her carriage, declining the hand of an aide-de-camp as she climbed in, and then fell back into the cushions. This time when she passed the flag, she did not salute.

A series of conferences with the foreign minister, finance minister, and minister of war followed. All were courteous and sympathetic; all promised nothing. Undeterred, Carlota resolved to call on Napoleon and Eugenie again.

On August 13 she met with Napoleon III a second time. She wanted the emperor to authorise monthly payments of 500,000 francs to the Mexican empire. Without this, Maximilian could not pay government employees, let alone his army. To shame Napoleon III, she then laid two letters he had handwritten to Maximilian on the table. The first read, "I beg you always to count upon my friendship. . . . You may be sure that my support will not fail you in the fulfilment of your task." The other was yet more shaming: "What, indeed, would you think of me," Napoleon III had written when desperate for Maximilian to go to Mexico, "if, once Your Imperial Majesty had arrived in Mexico, I were to say that I can no longer fulfil the conditions to which I have set my signature." Napoleon III was visibly shaken, but he maintained that he could not comment until his ministerial council had met and returned its decision. The pain this meeting caused him was apparent to Eugenie. She ushered Carlota out of the room and into one with the ministers of war and finance.

When the ministerial council met the next day, it merely confirmed what had already been decided, namely, that no more French money or soldiers would be wasted in Mexico. Carlota's mission had made no difference. She remained, however, convinced that she could still rescue the situation. On August 15, Carlota wrote to her husband. "It is my conviction," she asserted against all evidence, "that we shall be able to accomplish something". She told Maximilian that Napoleon III and Eugenie were "childish", often weeping. She had, she admitted, failed to get the 500,000 monthly subsidy, but "I have not played all my cards with the Emperor Napoleon."[34]

Napoleon III had hoped that Carlota would leave Paris once informed of his decision. She refused. Her final card was to demand that the French emperor personally explain that French support was over, hoping that this would shame him into a last-minute repreive. So it was that on August 19, Napoleon III came to the Grand Hotel. Carlota once more pleaded with him to change his mind. If the Corps législatif would not vote the necessary funds, he should dissolve the assembly and put the matter directly to the French people. Finally, she appealed to the vision of an empire in Latin America loyal and profitable to France, which had lured Napoleon III to Mexico in the first place.

Napoleon III began to speak, but Carlota could not bear to hear him refuse. She interrupted. When she had finished, the emperor paused before coolly stating that Carlota could no longer be under any illusion. "Your Majesty," replied Carlota, "is immediately concerned in this affair, and ought not to indulge in any either."[35] Not deigning to respond, the emperor rose, bowed stiffly, and left the room.

This outcome deeply disturbed Carlota. She had done so much to encourage Maximilian to accept the Mexican crown, sustain him in it, and persuade him that he must stay even when he wanted to abdicate. Already exhausted and under enormous stress—she felt the future of Maximilian's empire depended on successfully bringing Napoleon III around—her mental state began to deteriorate. She suffered excruciating headaches, which, compounded by anxiety, meant she slept little. When she did, she had feverish nightmares, the apocalyptic book of Revelations combining with ghoulish scenes from Albrecht Dürer's engravings, which she had seen as a girl growing up in Belgium, haunting brief moments of sleep.

From Paris, she wrote a letter to Maximilian on August 22 that showed her mind unravelling. "I have the satisfaction of having upset all their arguments, brought all their false pretexts to naught, and thereby given you a moral triumph, but He [referring to Napoleon III] curtly refuses, and no power can aid us, for he has hell on his side and I have not." The true reason for Napoleon III's betrayal was not, as he claimed, the unwillingness of the Corps législatif or the threats from Washington. Rather, she wrote, "He means to commit a long premeditated and evil deed . . . because he is the evil principle upon earth and wants to get rid of the good, only humanity does not see that his deeds are evil and they adore him". For Carlota, Napoleon III was "the devil in person", and when she saw him last he had an expression that would make one's hair stand on end. "He was hideous, and this was the expression of his soul. . . . And so he has never loved you from beginning to end, for he neither loves nor is capable of loving; he fascinated you like the serpent, his tears were as false as his words, all his deeds are treachery." She claimed her meeting with Napoleon III reminded her of the apocalypse, and Paris of Babylon, and added that "it is enough to make any unbeliever believe in God to see this Devil so near."

Carlota now saw Napoleon III's betrayal in biblical terms, but she still urged Maximilian not to abdicate. "I think you ought to maintain yourself as long as possible, for if hell is thrown out [that is, Napoleon III's regime], it would be in the interest of France and the whole of Europe to make a great empire in Mexico, and we can do this. Things in the Old World are sickening and depressing. *He* is so near, and one smells him in all the bloodshed." Maximilian should not come to Europe, she argued. "You cannot exist in the same hemisphere as He, he would burn you to ashes, he can hardly bring himself to mention your name."[36]

Despite her mental state—and increasing paranoia, which led her to allege that the orangeade at the first meeting in Saint-Cloud had been poisoned—Carlota resolved to continue her mission to Rome. If the pope could be persuaded to sign a concordat with Maximilian, then it would heal the religious divide that tore Mexico apart, undermine Juárez, and rally Catholic Mexico behind the emperor.

Before Rome, she rested at Miramar. On her way there, she travelled through the Italian countryside, which reminded her of happier times with Maximilian as governor of Lombardy-Venetia. The journey calmed her, and she became less restless. Furthermore, she was well received wherever she went, met as she was with crowds of well-wishers flying the Italian tricolour alongside that of the Mexican flag. Arriving at Miramar in September, she was moved to tears on seeing home again. She cried even more when she received a letter from Maximilian in which he had enclosed a photograph of himself.

She responded to Maximilian's letter with a wildly optimistic, or deluded, review of the situation. The loss of French support, she now maintained, was a positive. Without Napoleon III, the United States would recognise Maximilian's empire and end its support for Juárez. The republicans would then renounce their struggle. With the rebellion over, only a few troops would be needed and credit would flow to Mexico, solving the financial situation. Maximilian would have "the finest empire in the world, for Mexico must and will inherit the power of France". The letter ended with an incoherent reverie on Napoleon III, who, Carlota wrote, would "cease to exist", leaving Maximilian as the "heir to his greatness in both hemispheres."[37]

Blasio, whom Maximilian had sent to Europe with important documents, arrived at Trieste on September 14. He quickly sensed all was not well with Carlota. She was annoyed that it had taken him so long to reach her; however, she was most concerned about whether anyone could have tampered with the letters from Maximilian on Blasio's journey. "I am always fearful of Napoleon, who is our mortal enemy", she told him.[38] The letters were securely sealed with wax, but this did not allay the empress's suspicions. After speaking with the treasurer of the imperial household, who had travelled with Carlota from Mexico, Blasio discovered that she now took all her meals in her room. She usually ate alone, although occasionally with Manuela Gutiérrez Estrada del Barrio, her lady-in-waiting and daughter of Gutiérrez de Estrada.

For those who had not been with her for the previous few weeks Carlota still appeared a commanding empress. On September 16, the anniversary of Mexican independence, she held a party at Miramar to celebrate. Blasio observed how that night she hosted dinner, elegantly dressed and smiling with unusually brilliant shining eyes beneath a shimmering crown of diamonds.

Two days later, she set out for Rome. Travelling slowly, she did not arrive until a week later. Dressed in black, she stepped off the train late at night in the pouring rain. The pope had sent a scattering of cardinals to meet her at the station alongside various other dignitaries before she was driven by torchlight to Rome's own Grand Hotel, where she had reserved the entire first floor.

The next day came Cardinal Giacomo Antonelli, the pope's most trusted adviser. Arriving in a luxurious carriage, and attended by servants in their Vatican uniforms of knee breeches, three-cornered hat, and powdered wig, the cardinal entered the hotel dressed in the distinctive purple cassock. A crowd had gathered, falling as one to its knees in reverential silence as Antonelli passed. Blasio thought he looked majestic; Carlota described him as sick and decrepit. For an hour, she discussed Mexico and the concordat with the cardinal. Carlota remained calm, composed, and determined throughout the interview, as she did with many other visitors that day.

Her audience with the pope was arranged for September 27. She was confident. Everyone she had met in Rome, she reported, had told her that the concordat would be approved. Napoleon III, though, continued to haunt her, even in her more lucid moments. He "will soon pay for his evil", she warned, claiming again that his regime would collapse. Within her dreams and delusions, there was one truth: Napoleon III had deceived Maximilian. "If it were not so," she wrote to him, "we would never have gone" to Mexico.[39]

At eleven on September 27, the pope received Carlota at the Vatican. She made her way through the palace, the Swiss Guard in their navy-blue and bright-orange uniforms lining the stairway that led up to the papal throne room. At the far end, decorated with frescoes celebrating the lives of the pontiffs, was the throne itself. Seated upon it, dressed in white, was Pope Pius IX.

When Carlota approached, bending to kiss the pope's foot, Pius rose to stop her. Seventy-four years old, tall, well built, and with lively eyes, the pope extended his right hand so that she might kiss the papal ring. After the pope invited her to sit at his right, the rest of Carlota's entourage then approached one by one, knelt, and kissed his sandal. Finally, he blessed everyone in the room before dismissing them so he could speak alone with the empress.

Although she handed the pope Maximilian's concordat, Carlota did not discuss ecclesiastical affairs in the hour and a half they spoke together. Instead, she confided that all those who made up her entourage were trying to poison her on Napoleon III's orders. Afterwards, Carlota returned to her hotel, refusing to speak to servants or friends, where she then shut herself up in her apartments. Two days later, the pope returned the visit. Carlota spoke with him for a long time alone in her room. After he left, she gave a dinner, but refused to eat anything except oranges and nuts, first making sure that neither had been tampered with before putting them in her mouth.

Early the next morning, she summoned Manuela Gutiérrez Estrada del Barrio and went for a drive. With Carlota still dressed in black mourning clothes, wearing a small bonnet with black silk ribbons tied under her chin, Blasio saw her before she left the hotel, her face haggard, eyes sunken, cheeks shining. When her carriage reached the Trevi Fountain, Carlota got out and filled a pitcher with water. She refused to drink anything at the hotel.

Then, suddenly, she demanded to be driven to the Vatican. At the entrance to the palace, she dismissed the driver, walked up the stairs, and insisted on an audience with the pope. As it was still early in the morning and the visit was unannounced, there was some debate over what to do, but eventually she was taken into the pope's room. Immediately, she flung herself at Pius's feet. With tears streaming down her face and sobbing uncontrollably, she begged for help. Her life was in danger, she screamed. Everyone who had travelled with her from Miramar was trying to murder her. She pleaded for sanctuary in the Vatican, the only place where her life was safe. Astonished, the pope tried, unsuccessfully, to calm her. Shrieking now, she said that no one could force her to leave; she would be safe only if she stayed the night, and if there was nowhere for her to sleep she would do so in the corridor.

Exhausted, Carlota finally grew calmer. Pius offered her breakfast, but she refused a cup of hot chocolate, declaring that she would rather die of hunger than fall into a trap set by her persecutors.

A second cup was brought, but then, as if nothing had happened, she drank from the first and began to talk of Mexican affairs quite sanely. Hoping to get her to leave, Pius indicated that he had urgent business. Carlota, however, refused to exit the palace, again claiming that assassins waited for her outside. In the end, the pope persuaded her to move into the library and, while she was talking to a colonel in the Vatican police, slipped away. Carlota asked the colonel to take her to the gardens, where she drank from a fountain. Next, she wrote down the names of three of her travelling companions and asked the colonel to have them arrested.

Still Carlota refused to leave, although she agreed to have some lunch on the condition that she ate from the same plate as Manuela Gutiérrez Estrada del Barrio, whom she allowed to stay with her. As the day drew to a close, Carlota even now would not return to her hotel. This presented the Vatican officials with something of a problem: women were not allowed (in theory) to stay overnight in the palace. Nonetheless, Pius IX ordered two beds to be set up in a library. There Manuela Gutiérrez Estrada del Barrio watched over Carlota, who fell asleep almost immediately.

The next day, convinced she would die, Carlota made her will, leaving everything to Maximilian. She then wrote to him: "Dearly beloved treasure, I bid you farewell. God is calling me to him. I thank you for the happiness which you have always given me. May god bless you and help you win eternal bliss."[40]

Again refusing to return to her hotel, she was persuaded to visit a nearby convent. Initially, the visit went without incident, and it was hoped her health was improving. When she went to the kitchen, the nuns offered her some food. "The knife and fork have been poisoned!" she cried out.[41] Then, in front of the astonished sisters, she knelt down and gave thanks to God for saving her from death. Rising to her feet, desperately hungry, she plunged her hand into a boiling pot of stew. Badly burned, she passed out from the pain as her hand was bandaged. She was carried unconscious back to her carriage, which took her to the hotel. She then locked herself in her room. Here she insisted her servant obtain a small stove, a basket of eggs, and two live chickens, which had to be killed, prepared, and cooked in front of Carlota. When even these measures struck her as insufficient, she somehow procured a cat, which she pressed into service as her personal taster before she would eat anything.

After a few days, Carlota summoned Blasio. In the empress's room, amongst hens tied to table legs, he was asked to write out decrees that charged Carlota's closest entourage with trying to murder her. In order not to excite the empress, Blasio agreed, wondering how the decrees could be carried out given that she wanted them to be signed by the head of the imperial household—who was also to be dismissed for treason. Eventually, he took his leave, and with tears in his eyes he kissed her hand and looked at her face, "haggard, the cheeks sunken and flushed; her eyes had a wild expression and, when her attention was not fixed, roamed vaguely and uncertainly as though in search of absent figures or far-away scenes."[42]

On October 8, 1866, Carlota's younger brother, Philippe, Count of Flanders, arrived from Belgium and escorted her from Rome to Miramar, where she was to convalesce. A message was sent to one of Maximilian's confidants in Mexico, informing him of the empress's sickness. Those who had witnessed Carlota's breakdown were convinced that as soon as her husband heard the news, he would abdicate and return to Europe.

8

ABDICATION CRISIS

Abandoned by Napoleon III and isolated internationally, Maximilian's fragile kingdom soon faced further setbacks in 1866. As French troops retreated towards Mexico City, the imperial flag still flew, precariously, over the empire's distant outposts. In Matamoros, Tomás Mejía clung on despite guerrillas controlling much of the countryside surrounding the town. Across the Rio Grande in Brownsville, Juaristas met to plot Maximilian's downfall.

Here, two US citizens took commissions in the liberal army, opened a recruiting office, and offered fifty dollars plus expenses to anyone who would sign up to invade Mexico. As one report concluded, this offer attracted the usual outlaws, adventurers, and border riffraff. In January, this ragtag force attacked Bagdad, a port downriver from Matamoros, which was Mejía's only point of resupply by sea. Taken by surprise, the few imperialistas guarding the docks were soon overwhelmed. A French gunboat anchored nearby opened fire, but the invaders turned a captured artillery piece on the boat, forcing it to retreat. The adventurers then looted the docks and warehouses, ferrying their plunder across to the US side of the border. For days, wagons loaded with goods made their way along the north bank of the Rio Grande into Brownsville as imperialistas watched on helplessly from the other side. The raid was not coordinated with other Juaristas, and, without reinforcements, the mercenaries who occupied Bagdad melted away, allowing Mejía's forces to retake the port some weeks later. Nonetheless, the earlier unexpected victory showed liberal general Mariano Escobedo how weak imperial control in the region was and convinced him to renew the struggle for Matamoros.

Escobedo looked more like an intellectual than a general. His steel-rimmed spectacles, a sprawling beard that was not entirely under the command of the face it sat on, and a kindly expression belied a determined soldier. He had fought the Americans, the conservatives, and now the empire. Towards the end of 1865, Benito Juárez had sent him to the frontier to command the Army of the North, where his first task had been to unite disparate republicans behind the constitutional government and against the empire.

With men and money pouring over the border to boost Escobedo, Mejía continued to hold out with his ever-dwindling garrison. Ernst Pitner, an officer in the Austrian Legion tasked with defending Matamoros, was not enamoured with his posting. The town was a "hole", wrote Pitner to his mother. Besieged by mosquitoes, with cats howling outside his lodgings, Pitner described how the unpaved streets formed standing canals when it rained, with horses sinking to their chests in the mud and some mules even drowning. At night the heat was stifling. Pitner recalled walking out of one terrible play because he could no longer stand the temperature in the packed theatre, made all the worse as the performance re-created a cool Alpine scene, replete with giant cotton wool balls for snow.

Pitner would not have to endure the town much longer. With the empire in danger, the three hundred Austrians who complemented Mejía's garrison were needed closer to the capital. It was decided that they should join an escort of fourteen hundred men protecting a convoy, which would take them part of the way to Mexico City before the Austrians made the rest of the journey on their own.

Convoys were necessary because guerrillas made it unsafe for merchants to travel alone.

The one Ernst Pitner and his men were charged with guarding was huge, made up of two hundred wagons, pulled by more than two thousand mules, and filled with commercial goods worth some 11 million francs. Stretching six miles front to back, the caravan had to lumber its way west to Monterrey, the state capital of Nuevo León, more than 180 miles away. The plan was to rendezvous with two thousand imperialistas coming from the opposite direction, who would then guard the convoy. Not only was the route through the rough, coarse, and arid bushland of northeast Mexico, but the undulating landscape was also infested with Juaristas. "In a word," wrote Pitner, "it was one of the most awful marches".

On June 7, 1866, the convoy began its journey, crawling through the searing heat under a punishing sun. Five Austrians died of sunstroke on the first day, three more the next. In the heat and the dust and the dirt, without sufficient water, the soldiers resorted to eating the fruit of prickly pear cacti that lined the route, but many suffered from terrible diarrhoea as a result. They raided one of the wagons for wine, which may have temporarily lifted their mood, if not their thirst. The state of the roads meant the wagons frequently had to pause while engineers repaired the route.

On the thirteenth the shooting started. The imperial soldiers could not see the Juaristas, but sporadic shots rang out from distant bushes, tearing into wagons, mules, and men alike. Occasionally, the Austrian artillery fired grapeshot back into the chaparral, with little effect. In desperate need of water, the convoy pressed on towards a nearby river. Guerrillas had intercepted communications between Matamoros and Monterrey, and Escobedo knew exactly where the convoy was headed. Sending a small force to harass and delay the imperialista troops trying to rendezvous with the convoy, Escobedo now had the time, and the men, some three thousand, to set the trap. Two days later, at around five o'clock, the convoy's advance guard came under heavier fire. Unable to advance, the convoy camped for the night. Extremely hungry and, worse, still desperately thirsty, Pitner recorded that he went to bed that night with "fairly gloomy thoughts".[1]

As there was no choice but to press on for water, the convoy began to move the next day. With the wagons grouped into fours in the middle and the soldiers surrounding them, the imperialistas advanced cautiously. Soon bullets smashed into the convoy, but the enemy was nowhere to be seen, except for occasional horsemen appearing on the crests of nearby hills. Pitner's company crawled upwards towards them. When they reached the top, Escobedo launched his ambush. The enemy infantry, concealed in a thicket, threw itself into the attack, while the cavalry charged its imperial counterparts with equal ferocity. Pitner's Austrians, outnumbered, were raked by crushing fire from the infantry in front of them. As they tried to launch a bayonet charge, another mass of republican soldiers outflanked them. In the cross fire, half the company fell to the ground, dead or wounded.

The only hope for the exposed legion was to run to the wagons and form a defensive perimeter. Before he could reach them, however, Pitner found himself surrounded by cavalry. Sabre in one hand and revolver in the other, he shot one officer attacking on horseback. When another aimed a blow at Pitner's head, the Austrian parried with his left arm before shooting his attacker in the stomach with his right. Still rushing towards the wagons, he felt an acute pain in his neck, fell to the ground, and then rolled under the mules, blood dripping everywhere. He had been shot through the throat. Somehow, he managed to climb into the temporary safety of a wagon.

Outside the sounds of battle thundered. Escobedo's men gave no quarter and greatly outnumbered the Austrians, whose corpses were soon strewn across the ground. The groans of the dying mingled with the cries of the wounded, desperately calling for water. Eventually, the slaughter ended, and the surviving imperialistas were taken prisoner.

In fact, few had fought. Unlike the Austrians, most of the Mexicans, many of whom had not been paid for months, took the view that Maximilian's empire was not a cause worth dying for and had surrendered before fighting. Escobedo took the enormously valuable convoy and the remainder of the legion, including Pitner, into captivity. Equally precious to Escobedo were the muskets, artillery, and military equipment, which included the cornets, clarinets, and drums of the imperial band. Of the 300 Austrians who had set off with the convoy just over a week earlier, around 120 died in this battle.

For Escobedo, and Juárez, it was a stunning victory. Not only did the value of the seized goods provide a much-needed injection of cash for their war chest, but the victory demonstrated that the empire could no longer guarantee security or commerce for its subjects in the north. Equally as important from a propaganda point of view, it showed that foreign soldiers could be vanquished. Escobedo proclaimed as much to his army: "You have brought the usurper's Austrian mercenaries to your feet to implore you for clemency". The contrast with a year ago was marked: "We were fighting almost without hope, with nothing but our patriotism to sustain us. . . . [N]ow that the northern army is everywhere victorious, who will dare oppose us?" Escobedo urged his troops on to Matamoros.[2]

He need not have bothered. A week later, Mejía surrendered. With only a few hundred troops remaining, he could not hold it. A Juarista general, Antonio Carvajal, came over from Brownsville to negotiate the terms, and Mejía proposed to abandon Matamoros as long as his troops were allowed to leave with their weapons. This was agreed on June 22, and the next day, flags flying and drums beating, Mejía's forces marched to the port of Bagdad, where they boarded a French ship. The last town on the Rio Grande loyal to Maximilian had fallen.

This loss hit Maximilian hard. It deprived his empire of much-needed customs revenue, and it meant that Juárez's forces could now be easily resupplied by sea or overland from the United States. With the French everywhere in retreat, Monterrey was evacuated on

July 26. Next, without a shot fired, Juárez reoccupied Chihuahua. Within weeks, after a brief siege, the last port in imperial hands in the northeastern state of Tamaulipas fell. On the Pacific Coast, French troops similarly deserted hard-won ports. The income lost from these towns was bad enough, but the message it sent was even worse: the empire was everywhere in flight. Porfirio Díaz, now escaped a second time from captivity, rallied the Juaristas in the south. Juárez's forces began to constrict an ever-tighter circle around Maximilian's empire. The French maintained only a precarious corridor to Veracruz, their escape route.

While the liberals were in the ascendant, their own affairs were far from straightforward. As of November 1865, Juárez's term of office had expired, and, under the 1857 constitution he had sworn to uphold, the presidency technically should have passed to the head of the supreme court, Jesús González Ortega, who had surrendered Puebla to the French in 1863. To keep power, Juárez decreed that, as it was impossible to hold elections, he would remain president. Unfortunately for him, Ortega viewed this as unconstitutional and counterdecreed himself president. Now Mexico had one so-called emperor and two so-called presidents.

To make matters worse, only weeks after ousting Mejía, Matamoros had descended into chaos. Furious at Carvajal, who had cut the deal allowing Mejía to escape, Escobedo complained to Juárez, who declared the surrender unlawful. Carvajal was to be court-martialled. To speed up justice, another officer, Servando Canales, then launched a coup d'état in the city and proclaimed himself governor. Warned beforehand, Carvajal shot the officer sent to arrest him and quickly fled to Brownsville. Upon hearing the news, Juárez in turn declared Canales's actions illegal and summoned him to Chihuahua to answer for his crimes. Canales ignored the invitation and on September 23 declared for Ortega. After the dust settled, Juaristas had lost whatever nominal control they had briefly enjoyed over Matamoros. Just as the tide seemed to be turning, the anti-imperial coalition looked like it was falling apart.

MAXIMILIAN DREW SOME comfort from the infighting amongst his enemies, but, as reports of his shrinking empire flooded in, he isolated himself at Chapultepec. To compound matters, he now suffered from frequent enervating fevers, which his doctor diagnosed as malaria. Without Carlota, all semblance of court life had ceased; the emperor shunned society even more than usual, only appearing when required at rare state occasions.

Many of his closest confidants had left with Carlota, so Maximilian had few trusted advisers with him. One friend, a former comrade from the Austrian Navy, Stefan Herzfeld, had recently arrived from Europe. A loyal courtier, he knew little of the situation in Mexico. Maximilian's recently appointed physician, Dr Samuel Basch, was also constantly at his side. Born in Prague, he studied medicine in Vienna. Thoughtful, intelligent, and with Maximilian's welfare his main concern, Basch was frequently consulted, but he had just turned twenty-nine and had been in Mexico only since February 1866, and consequently his opinions carried little weight. Dominik Billimeck was still part of Maximilian's entourage. While the professor's understanding of botany was second to none, his knowledge of Mexican politics, and Spanish, was limited.

In fact, Maximilian's most trusted counsellor at this stage was a forty-one-year-old Jesuit priest named Augustin Fischer. Born in Germany, he had emigrated to Texas in the 1840s, where he had scratched out a living as a farmer before panhandling during the California gold rush. In the end, he found it more profitable to convert from Protestantism to Catholicism, train as a Jesuit, and then make his way to Mexico, where he worked as a secretary to a bishop. His religious dedication was called into question after he seduced and ran off with a married servant of his employer, but as a German-speaking priest he somehow managed to charm Maximilian, who sent him to Rome to help negotiate a concordat. In this, he failed, although he convinced Maximilian that it was no fault of his own. He did not come from the ascetic school of Catholicism. A corpulent figure with a ruddy complexion, he loved to eat, drink, and talk.

Recently arrived back from Rome, his garrulous positivity appealed to Maximilian, who appointed him court librarian and brought him to live at Chapultepec. He was, wrote Maximilian, "a great support to me because of his pleasant spirit."[3] They dined together most evenings and then played billiards, with Fischer bringing figurative and literal spirit to table.

Fischer, however, did not provide impartial advice. He was entirely in league with the Conservative Party. His detractors—and he had many—claimed that his great intelligence was matched only by his immorality. Sara Yorke Stevenson described him as "an obscure adventurer of low degree, and of more than shady reputation, whose shrewdness and talent for intrigue had impressed themselves upon the weakened mind of the Emperor."[4]

While Maximilian secluded himself with this inner circle of a whiskey priest, a doctor, a courtier, and a botanist, the cream of society were laughing at him in Mexico City. A penniless French aristocrat and court wit, sometime playwright and occasional soldier, Philippe de Massa had come to Mexico seeking rapid promotion and better pay as an aide-de-camp to Achille Bazaine. In Paris, he had been at the heart of court life, where he penned plays and songs to amuse French high society, including Eugenie and Napoleon III. His lighthearted—and lightweight—art gently lampooned the French elite, much to the amusement of the court where his work was performed.

In 1866 he arrived in Mexico and soon produced a vaudevillian farce that took aim at the empire. Targets for satire were legion and ranged from Maximilian's financial reforms to his attempts to organise a national Mexican army. It was the rousing final chorus that was cruellest. After ridiculing hopes of bringing order to the empire, the final ironic refrain rang out: "Have courage, quickly to work! France is here to help us". Written by a member of Bazaine's staff, the main parts were played by French officers, including Bazaine's nephew (in drag as a passable soubrette). In September, the play was performed in Mexico City to a packed audience, including the marshal and his wife. Maximilian took care to avoid the production; however, he was hurt by reports of what seemed to him like a callous French-backed satire lampooning his empire.

Yet Maximilian held on to the conviction that Carlota would succeed in her mission, bringing meaningful French help to his ailing regime. He still had not received definitive word from Europe and refused to believe, as he wrote to a friend, that illness and the rise of Prussia "have so far crushed the poor Emperor Napoleon that he is tottering helpless and perplexed towards the abyss. He will recover his accustomed fortitude; and the cool judgement of the Empress, who stands before him like a living conscience, will succeed in reviving in his sick soul the memory of the sacred duty of abiding by his plighted word."[5]

Even with French support, Maximilian recognised that as Juárez's fortunes were reviving the empire could no longer depend on the loyalty of its more liberal ministers. In a reversal of policy, the emperor turned back to the Conservative Party. This process had begun in April 1866, when he sacked his most prominent liberal ministers, including the gluttonous José Fernando Ramírez, but was completed in September when he appointed a new cabinet. At the head of this cabinet was the sixty-year-old Teodosio Lares. A conservative of the purest water, his appointment sent a clear message: the liberal empire was finished.

Maximilian's volte-face was entirely counter to his political principles as well as his personal tastes, but he felt it was his only hope. Maximilian wrote to Carlota that his new cabinet crushed his soul. "They are very worthy men", he added, "and for love of the country I make the sacrifice to govern with them, but they are dull and bore me to death."[6] In return for power, conservatives—and, crucially, the Catholic Church—would back Maximilian throughout Mexico with or without the French army.

With the conservatives on board, the clergy following, and faith in Carlota, Maximilian was more optimistic than he had been in June. Then he contemplated abdication; now he was ready to celebrate

211

Mexican independence again on September 16. He had not appeared before his subjects for some time, but that morning the national anthem rang out as he attended a military parade in the Zócalo and then a Te Deum in the cathedral, which, Maximilian noted, lasted only twenty minutes—"thank God".[7] These were merely preliminaries to the official celebrations later that day at the National Palace, which was packed with the highest dignitaries of the empire.

As the emperor walked onto a balcony, an expectant silence fell on the crowd below. Lares gave a short speech, and then Maximilian responded in a strong, deliberate voice: "Mexicans!" he declared. "I still stand firmly in the place to which the will of the nation called me: unmindful of all the difficulties, without faltering in my duties, for a true Habsburg never leaves his post in the moment of danger."[8] The audience erupted into cries of "Viva el Emperador! Viva la Emperatriz!"; the enthusiasm, he predictably added, "was enormous" and "thundered through the beautiful, vast hall." By now, superlatives seemingly having lost all meaning, these celebrations were, Maximilian claimed, "better and more brilliant than ever". The day ended with a spectacular banquet and toasts to the empire and its sovereign; everything, concluded Maximilian, went perfectly.[9] Maximilian thus publicly put an end to the rumours that he would follow his wife to Europe and abandon Mexico. He had resolved to stay and govern in whatever way would keep him in power. Then the post arrived.

CARLOTA'S TIME IN Paris had upset Napoleon III. He did not like to be reminded of his failure, even less so of his promises, but her presence showed that his message was not getting through to his protégé in Mexico. On August 29, he wrote a letter to Maximilian in plain language: "It is henceforward impossible for me to give Mexico another *écu* [a small denomination of French currency] or another man." This being settled, continued the French emperor, the only question remained of whether Maximilian could maintain himself with his own strength, or would he be forced to abdicate? In the first case, French troops would stay, as promised, until the following year. If the latter, then "other measures" would be necessary. In that scenario, Napoleon III suggested that Maximilian publish a manifesto explaining that "insurmountable obstacles" had thwarted his attempts in Mexico. After that, the French army would organise a national congress that would elect an interim government. "Your Majesty will understand how painful it is for me to enter into such details," concluded the emperor before adding, without irony, but "we can no longer lull ourselves with illusions".[10]

Weeks after writing this, however, the latest complaints from the US government reached Paris, suggesting Maximilian remained as deluded as ever. When Secretary of State William Seward had heard that the French army was now officially at the heart of Maximilian's civil government, with two of its officers as ministers, he had lodged a diplomatic protest. Upon receiving this in September, Napoleon III was furious. He immediately ordered the officers to resign their posts, wrote a letter berating Bazaine for allowing the appointments, and published a disavowal of the whole affair in the official French government newspaper.

To make sure the message that there would be no more support from France finally got through, Napoleon III now decided to send an aide-de-camp, General François Castelnau, to Mexico. Before he left, the emperor explained that the general must persuade Maximilian to abdicate. The best way, reasoned Napoleon III, to avoid further embarrassment was for Maximilian to voluntarily give up his kingdom. If he left of his own accord, under the protection of the French army, then the French emperor could hardly be accused of betraying his ally. Napoleon III would stay in close communication with his aide. That summer, a transatlantic cable became operational, and now messages could be sent to Mexico via the United States in days rather than weeks. Ever the optimist, Maximilian celebrated what he called the greatest scientific triumph of the age by sending Napoleon III a telegram. He did not get one back.

Castelnau had another role in Mexico. Maximilian and Carlota's constant briefings against Bazaine had planted doubt in Napoleon III's mind. Castelnau was, therefore, to observe the marshal, evaluate his performance, and privately report back. Napoleon III went so far as to break with centuries of military tradition, giving Castelnau, a mere brigadier general, the right to remove Bazaine as commander in chief. Castelnau was to keep this fact hidden and make it known to Bazaine only if the actions of the marshal were contrary to Napoleon III's preferred outcome: Maximilian's abdication. Castelnau left France on September 17 to pressure Maximilian into surrendering his throne, the day after Carlota had celebrated Mexican independence at Miramar and Maximilian in Mexico City.

THE LATEST MAIL from Europe arrived in Mexico at the beginning of October. Two letters dated late August came from Carlota, which confirmed she had been unable to change Napoleon III's mind. Maximilian also received news from her stating her intention to go to Rome before departing for Mexico, arriving at Veracruz in the second week of November. But it was Napoleon III's August 29 letter that stunned Maximilian. Categorically crushing any hopes Maximilian still held with regard to his former ally, the French emperor also openly discussed abdication. In disbelief, Maximilian read the letter over and over again. Finally grasping the reality of his situation, he asked Herzfeld and Fischer for advice. The former plainly stated that Maximilian should abdicate; remaining in Mexico now was simply too dangerous. Fischer, on the other hand, urged Maximilian to redouble his efforts and push on with his new conservative ministry. Free from French interference, but with the Foreign Legion, the Austrian and Belgian volunteers, and the nation rallied behind the church, he argued, Maximilian was well placed to weather any storm.

Maximilian, as ever, was indecisive, choosing a middle path. He declared that he would call a national congress to deliberate on whether the empire should continue. He would await the outcome at

Orizaba, close to Veracruz. Here he could receive news more quickly from Europe and meet Carlota at the port when she arrived in November. Explaining the plan in a letter to his wife, he wrote that, if the vote were favourable, "we shall return to the capital with legitimate and untrammelled power". If the vote went against them, "we shall retire with dignity, with the pure and elevating consciousness of having done our duty honourably." Concluding, he wrote, "In a few weeks' time, joy of my life, I hope to press you to my suffering heart! Your ever faithful Max."[11]

Then, on October 18, two cables arrived from Europe. Herzfeld began to decipher them, but, when he realised they announced Carlota's illness, he pretended that he was unable to make them out. He merely said that someone at Miramar was sick, but it was not clear whom. Maximilian knew he was lying. "I know that it must be something frightful. Please inform me; I expect the worst", he said to Herzfeld. Basch diplomatically left the room, but after a few minutes Maximilian called him back. With tears in his eyes, Maximilian asked the young physician whether he knew a Dr Riedel from Vienna, as he was looking after Carlota at Miramar. "He is the director of the insane asylum," Basch forced himself to reply.

The news broke Maximilian. All but disowned by his older brother and abandoned by the man who he thought was his friend, Napoleon III, Maximilian had always relied on the love and support of his wife. She had convinced him to stay in Mexico. Now, ill, depressed, and alone, without family and friends, Maximilian's universe shattered. Later that day, he asked Basch whether he should leave Mexico.

"I do not think," his doctor replied, "Your Majesty will be able to remain in the country."

"Will anybody really believe that I am going to Europe because of the Empress' illness?" answered Maximilian.[12]

Basch reassured him that people would understand, but an anxious Maximilian wanted to know what Basch thought Herzfeld and Fischer would recommend. Basch said that Herzfeld would back abdication but that Fischer would put Conservative Party interests above Maximilian's security and warned the emperor not to listen to his advice.

Desperate to get Maximilian out of Mexico City before he changed his mind, Herzfeld made the arrangements. The commander of an Austrian corvette anchored at Veracruz was informed of the emperor's imminent departure, Maximilian's possessions were packed up and sent to the port, and Maximilian settled his most important affairs. With dreams of founding an imperial dynasty vanquished, Maximilian now wrote to Alice Iturbide that he was returning her son, Agustín, to her care. He had, at least, been well looked after, embedded at the heart of the Mexican court and under the tutelage of an aunt happy to go along with an arrangement that gave her luxury and status.

On October 20 Maximilian informed Bazaine that he was leaving for Orizaba. As soon as word of this leaked out to his conservative ministers, they saw it for what it was: a prelude to abdication. They pressured him to stay. Basch had to stand guard in front of the emperor's room, insisting, often in heated arguments in the corridor, that Maximilian was too sick to see anyone. Despite this, Lares presented himself at Chapultepec on the same day Maximilian had written to Bazaine, insisting on an audience. Basch explained it was impossible. The politician then handed him a letter announcing that the entire ministry resigned in protest against Maximilian's departure.

That afternoon frantic messages were exchanged between Maximilian at Chapultepec and Bazaine in Mexico City. Herzfeld informed the marshal, "Lares has just tendered the resignation of all the ministry, and has stated that, as soon as the emperor leaves the capital, there will no longer be any government. As his majesty is in a state of extreme weakness, and insists upon leaving, it is necessary that some measures should be taken. I beg that your excellency will be pleased to consult with the emperor again this evening."[13]

Pacing up and down his room, Maximilian impatiently awaited the reply. At seven o'clock it was handed to him. Bazaine, who had received Napoleon III's letter indicating that abdication was now the preferred option, was all too happy to step in. He would pressure the ministers not to resign, but, if they did, the French army would take over the government. Relieved, Maximilian was free to depart.

Before daybreak on the morning of October 21, escorted by 304 Austrian hussars, three carriages transported the emperor towards Orizaba. Always with an eye for a teachable moment, the first stop was at a small village next to, so the emperor claimed, a mountain where the Aztecs had sacrificed humans. According to Maximilian, every fifty years the Aztecs prepared themselves for the end of the world. Priests would pray on the hill, offering victims to appease the gods. When the moment had passed, without the world ending, they would construct enormous bonfires that would be the signal for others to be lit across the mountains surrounding the valley of Mexico, celebrating another fifty years of existence.

At the next stop, Maximilian came face-to-face with more pressing events. In the town of Ayutla, still only a few miles from Mexico City, General Castelnau had arrived, travelling the opposite direction from Veracruz.

CASTELNAU HAD REACHED Veracruz on October 12 and the next day began the journey to Mexico City. Egyptian soldiers now guarded the train with swivel guns mounted on the carriage roofs. Once he reached the end of the railway, he made the rest of the journey, under strong escort, on horseback to better see the country. When he learned that Maximilian was at Ayutla on his way to Orizaba, Castelnau requested an audience. The emperor, still angry at Napoleon III, had no desire to meet with his aide. Basch informed Castelnau that Maximilian was bedridden, receiving no visitors.

The next day Castelnau arrived in Mexico City, where it appeared that his mission had already been accomplished. Bazaine received a letter from Maximilian dated October 21 in which he asked for three points to be arranged before he abdicated: no more courts-martial; the revocation of the Black Decree, allowing for the summary execution of Juaristas; and an end to the war in general. Once these were agreed, wrote Maximilian, he would send documents confirming his abdication. Thus reassured, a tall and attractive man of great charm, Castelnau settled in for what seemed like an easy job. He spent his time in style, securing his own box at the opera house and holding evening soirées. When not at leisure, he penned reports for Napoleon III on the situation in Mexico.

They were damning. The French army, he wrote to Napoleon III, was exhausted, demoralised, and all too aware that, despite heavy losses, they had not accomplished their task. "Most of the officers," explained Castelnau, "are even more discouraged than the soldiers." Castelnau reported that the Foreign Legion was worse than the regular army; men had enrolled for free passage to Mexico and then deserted at the first opportunity. Nonetheless, Castelnau wrote, the French army was at least an effective fighting force. He was less sanguine about Maximilian's own resources. The remaining Austrian and Belgian volunteers were, in his opinion, "without cohesion, without discipline, badly administered, poorly commanded, having all the vices belonging to foreign mercenaries." Even so, these foreign soldiers were an elite force compared to the "so-called" Mexican army, which was in "such a state of disorder and dissolution . . . that it is impossible to have any confidence in it." Desertion was rife, recruitment was forced, and surrender was the preferred method of engaging the enemy. That was just the men, for their officers were worse. Castelnau, whose preferred writing style was heavy with asyndeton, stated that these commanders were "without training, without experience, without morality, without honour, they are, in every sense, worthy of their soldiers."

Politically, Castelnau claimed, everyone agreed: Maximilian's cause was lost, and the responsibility lay squarely on the young emperor's shoulders. France was blameless. Still not having met Maximilian, Castelnau nonetheless condemned "his indecision, his blunders, his contradictions, his wasteful expenditure, above all his inertia". In case Napoleon III was confused as to Castelnau's views on Maximilian, the aide added "limited intelligence" and "procrastination" to his criticisms. Maximilian's abdication was, Castelnau concluded, the most urgent necessity, "no less for the interests of France than for those of Mexico." Not only that, but, Castelnau added, far from supporting monarchy in the Americas, France must now enter into negotiations with the liberals and the United States for an interim republican government to replace Maximilian.[14]

After two weeks in Mexico, Castelnau pronounced that the empire was dying. His report was designed to please, and exonerate, Napoleon III. Although the empire was in a grave crisis, Castelnau exaggerated every fault and invented others. Still, whatever his failings, at least Maximilian had promised to send confirmation of his abdication the day after the general arrived in Mexico City.

The letter never came. Castelnau, Bazaine, and Alphonse Dano waited anxiously in the capital for word from Orizaba. Finally, on October 31 a note from Maximilian arrived, but it merely reiterated that the fate of the Austrian and Belgian volunteers must be arranged before Maximilian left the country. Two more weeks of silence followed, until a letter dated November 12 reached the capital. Addressed to Bazaine, it requested a collective response. "Before I decidedly resolve what I must do," began the letter, "I must ensure the settlement of certain points".[15] Maximilian then outlined five areas that needed resolution before he abdicated, including the repatriation of the foreign volunteers, payments to the Iturbide family, and Maximilian's outstanding debts settled. Delighted, the three Frenchmen put their signatures to a letter agreeing to Maximilian's requests. They had achieved what Napoleon III had asked: the abdication of Mexico's emperor. All they needed now was the confirmation from Maximilian.

TWO WEEKS EARLIER, as the sun began to set on October 27, Maximilian approached the town of Orizaba. A crowd lined the road, some on horse, others on foot. Soon thousands had gathered, throwing flowers in front of the imperial carriage and filling the air with cheers. Encouraged, Maximilian ordered his escort to hang back so he could enter the town with only a small entourage. As he passed through the streets, the imperial army saluted him, while a cacophony of artillery salvoes, church bells, and fireworks drowned out the cheers. Maximilian was deeply moved. It seemed that his subjects had not deserted him after all.

Nonetheless, Maximilian had resolved to abdicate. Farewell letters were written to ministers and foreign diplomats, belongings were loaded onto the Austrian ship, and Maximilian drew up his travel arrangements, expecting to be in Europe by December. Unsure of the reception he would receive within Habsburg lands, he had decided to sail to Corfu, where Carlota would join him if she could. He drafted a press statement explaining his actions to influence public opinion, laying the blame on the French and stressing his wife's illness. He sent Herzfeld to arrange things in Europe.

But this was not the only reason Herzfeld left. While Maximilian's Austrian friend had been urging Maximilian to leave immediately, Fischer tried to dissuade him from a hasty flight. The priest convinced Maximilian that Herzfeld's insistence on a rapid departure was unhelpful when they needed to deliberate on how best to leave some order behind in Mexico. Fischer then ensured that Herzfeld did not receive his orders to depart from the emperor personally, preventing him from seeing Maximilian before leaving for Veracruz. From Havana, a desperate Herzfeld wrote to Fischer to put in writing what he was not allowed to say in person to Maximilian: "Every hour's delay involves the gravest danger. . . . Urge the Emperor to leave at all costs. . . . [T]he completion of the work is now allotted to you by providence. . . . Be firm—do not let yourself be influenced from Mexico [City]. . . . [S]ave the Emperor."[16]

No doubt, Fischer read this letter with a wry smile before putting it aside. By broadly agreeing with the abdication plan, Fischer had been playing for time. In Mexico City, Lares had withdrawn his ministry's resignation not because of pressure from Bazaine, but because of Fischer's counsel. To his conservative friends he argued that at this crucial time, it was critical that they remain in power to influence events. Even before Maximilian reached Orizaba, they did exactly that, orchestrating the welcome into the town that so moved Maximilian. Leading members of the party made all kind of promises: the empire was still popular; the church could miraculously raise money. Feverish and determined to leave, Maximilian refused to change his mind, but conservatives had not yet made all their moves.

On November 7, Miguel Miramón and his wife, Concepción Lombardo, arrived at Veracruz. They had no authority to do so, for Miramón had not been recalled from his mission to Berlin. In fact, he had not been there for nearly a year. Detesting the cold—and, worse, the German food—he had absconded to Paris and then to Austria. After hearing the desperate news from Mexico, he had resolved, against Concepción's wishes, to return to his homeland, to serve Maximilian—or, more accurately, the conservative cause. As he did not have papers to enter the country, at Veracruz he telegrammed Maximilian, who replied that he was delighted Miramón was back and asked him to come to Orizaba immediately.

Ahead of that meeting, Fischer briefed Miramón, urging him to do everything in his power to keep the emperor in Mexico. Miramón found Maximilian visibly anxious and upset, fearing even greater bloodshed if he remained, lamenting his lack of men and money. Miramón calmed him. The cause was not lost, he insisted, before explaining that when he was president, he had had fewer resources than Maximilian but almost pacified the country during the civil war with Juárez. It was not only Miramón who pledged his sword. Leonardo Márquez, now back from the Ottoman Empire, also swore his allegiance to the emperor, promising that he could raise thousands of soldiers. The new arrivals insisted that their combined military expertise, plus that of Mejía's, would find no match in republican forces splintering between Ortega and Juárez.

Only one other person was allowed to see the emperor, the British diplomat Peter Campbell Scarlett. After Scarlett's long career, the tumultuous events in Mexico proved enough for the Englishman, and he had decided to retire. Returning home, family in tow, he reached Orizaba on November 1. Maximilian, desperate for advice, welcomed Scarlett as a friend, and he ended up staying for weeks. On long walks together, Maximilian confided his innermost thoughts. "If the Empress dies," he admitted, "I shall not have the courage or desire to remain in Mexico. I came here more on her account than on my own, and I have no ambition to continue alone after her death, and especially, . . . as I have no children or successor."[17]

Fischer now spied an opportunity, taking great pains to befriend Scarlett. The diplomat did not see a dissolute whiskey priest but rather "a person of good reputation and capacity." Having won his confidence, Fischer explained to Scarlett that "evil counsellors" had taken advantage of Maximilian's weak state of mind after hearing news of the empress's illness. These evil counsellors—Herzfeld, Basch, and Billimeck—had urged Maximilian to abdicate. Moreover, had Fischer not managed to persuade him otherwise, the emperor would have signed a document renouncing the throne the day after he left Mexico City.

The priest then played on the anti-French sentiment latent in any self-respecting nineteenth-century English diplomat. The plan to force Maximilian's abdication had been devised in Paris to carve up Mexico with the United States. In return for the French delivering the northern states to Washington, the US government would take on the debt owed to France. There was enough truth in the allegation—France indeed hoped to enter into an agreement with the United States over Mexico's future—and enough prejudice in the Englishman to believe the allegation. Fischer "begged" Scarlett to "use all the influence he could to induce the emperor to return to the capital".[18] To defend the interests of Britain as he saw them, the diplomat agreed to do so.

Scarlett put his advice in writing: "Your Majesty was so obliging at Chapultepec as to show me an autograph [sic] letter written by the Emperor Napoleon", referring to the August 29 letter in which the French emperor had said that if Maximilian abdicated, then a convention should be called to decide on Mexico's next government. Scarlett, however, put a spin on this letter to which Maximilian was sympathetic, suggesting a congress be called to deliberate on whether Maximilian should abdicate in the first place. "It is clear", Scarlett wrote, that "the French Emperor never contemplated Your Majesty's sudden retreat without first making this appeal". In this misreading, wilful or otherwise, it was the wish of Napoleon III that Maximilian return to the capital. For good measure, Scarlett called abdication "ignominious flight". Returning to Mexico City, argued Scarlett, was the "only honourable and practical course."[19]

Maximilian was unmoved. He told Scarlett that the idea of governing Mexico with reactionary conservatives was anathema to his political beliefs. It would be "repugnant" to govern the country "in any other way than by liberal principles".[20] Furthermore, so tired was he of dealing with the French that Maximilian dreaded going back to Mexico City to face Bazaine, Dano, and Castelnau.

In a private letter to Fischer, therefore, Scarlett sharpened his tone. "I am really very much amazed," opined the diplomat, "that the Emperor has resolved upon a premature abdication. History will show that His Majesty has been the victim of an intrigue which he lacked the resolution to escape or crush." In a quite extraordinary claim, Scarlett said that even Juaristas would find Maximilian's departure "precipitate". Besides, there was every chance, Scarlett felt, that a national vote would be in favour of Maximilian if it meant the end of the French intervention, "to which everybody in the country is opposed. It is quite certain that after the departure of the French a strong party would prefer to rally round the imperial flag".[21]

Fischer, of course, immediately showed the letter to Maximilian. The emperor no longer trusted the French, and he knew the conservatives were looking to protect their party. But what possible interest could Scarlett have? Maximilian convinced himself that the diplomat would never have made such a strong statement unless under instructions from the British government in London. Ever the anglophile, Maximilian began to waver in his plans for immediate departure.

Maximilian hesitated even more because if he returned to Europe, he must do so as a private citizen. Speculation in the European press reached him at Orizaba suggesting that unless he reconfirm his renunciation to the Austrian throne, he would not be allowed into Habsburg territory, not even to Miramar. With his honour impugned, the conservatives pressuring him daily, and the British seemingly against abdication, life in Mexico began to seem preferable to that of an exiled, failed, and humiliated emperor living as a dilettante in Europe. Maximilian's determination to leave the country drained away.

Ironically, it was the French reply to his conditions to be met prior to abdication that convinced Maximilian to stay. Receiving this letter on November 16, Maximilian was horrified to see at the bottom of the document that in case Maximilian's debts could not be paid, they would be settled by the new government of Mexico. For Maximilian, this confirmed the French were negotiating with Washington and the liberals to constitute a government replacing his empire. The letter brought out all of his hatred for the French and Napoleon III. His response was to ban all Frenchmen from his entourage. Whenever possible, he even refused to speak French, insisting on Spanish. If he had to give up the throne, Maximilian decided, he would relinquish it not to the French, but only on his own terms.

On November 18, he put this decision, or lack of one, in writing to Bazaine: "I must thank you, as well as General Castelnau and M. Dano, for having arranged those points which concern me so closely. But one important point still remains to be settled: a firm government to protect the interests which are compromised."[22] Maximilian then explained that his fever meant that he could not return to Mexico City and so requested Bazaine come to Orizaba to discuss the situation in person. This was not the only invitation Maximilian extended; he also notified the marshal that he had summoned his ministers and advisers. In a cabinet meeting, they would vote on the future of the empire.

WHEN LARES, PRESIDENT of Maximilian's council of ministers, arrived at Orizaba on November 24 he was far more sprightly than he had been upon offering up his resignation just a few weeks earlier. This time, the sixty-year-old bounded up to the emperor, leaving him no time to avoid the *abrazo*. In private conversations, the conservatives now played on Maximilian's sense of honour. The whole country, they told him, expected him to remember his September 16 speech: "A true Habsburg never leaves his post in the moment of danger." Even José María Gutiérrez de Estrada weighed in with a timely letter, writing that Maximilian had made binding promises that he would remain. Despite Carlota's illness, "what general", Gutiérrez de Estrada wrote from the comfort of Europe, "would leave his position of command in the hour of battle for any private reason"?[23]

The day after Lares's arrival, twenty-three minsters and counsellors sat down to deliberate on whether Maximilian should abdicate. Notable by his absence was Bazaine. Castelnau and Dano feared that his presence would lend official French backing to whatever was decided and persuaded the marshal not to attend. At the start of the meeting, Lares read a handwritten statement from the emperor: he would accept any solution that ended the civil war, including the rumoured French-US settlement, but called on those present to resolve the matter.

Rather than listen to their deliberations, Maximilian went butterfly hunting. The lush countryside surrounding Orizaba proved too much of a temptation for Billimeck, who was not going to let a political crisis get in the way of useful scientific work. Maximilian, armed with enormous flycatchers and butterfly nets, proved a willing assistant. The local population looked on with incredulity as their emperor scrambled around putrefying tree stumps, searching for rare larvae.

Back in Orizaba, the two most liberal members left in Maximilian's government voted for immediate abdication. Lares and his conservatives, ten in total, voted against. This left eleven moderates with the deciding vote. They voted for abdication, but urged the emperor to postpone it until an interim government could be set up. Thus, the majority of Maximilian's own ministers and advisers had voted for the end of the empire. Read another way, however, twenty-one out of twenty-three had voted for Maximilian to remain as emperor for the time being.

The latter was Maximilian's interpretation. Replying to Lares, he announced that he was "deeply moved by the loyalty and sympathy" the council had shown. "To abdicate power into the hands of foreigners," Maximilian believed, "would be treason", and "no Habsburg would do that".[24] He then outlined (yet more) conditions that needed to fulfilled before he abdicated. The first and most important was to organise a national congress to decide on the future government of Mexico. In fact, as conservatives well knew, this was a victory for those who wanted the empire to continue indefinitely. Imperialistas did not control enough of Mexico to hold an election, and, even if they had, Juaristas were determined to settle the issue on the battlefield rather than through the ballot box.

Regardless, on December 1 Maximilian issued a manifesto. He would convene a national congress, candidates from all parties standing for election before voting on whether the empire should continue. It was a project that he had been contemplating for some time, even drafting a letter to President Andrew Johnson, asking him to recognise the empire. In return, Maximilian would leave Mexico if the vote went against him. In his proclamation, Maximilian assured the people that his ministers were making the necessary arrangements.

Not that you would know it from the conservative press. "The emperor does not abdicate; the emperor does not go", announced one newspaper. "We have faith in the future of the monarchy." Another editorial declared that "the doubts and uncertainty of the last 40 days are over" and that the emperor "by resolving to continue with us and at the head of the government makes a sacrifice greater than when he accepted the crown." But, the paper warned, if the emperor had sacrificed everything for Mexico, the nation must now sacrifice everything for the emperor. Rather than a congress, the first duty of the government was to raise an army, march into the interior, and "scatter the gangs of political criminals" that made up the enemies of the empire. The message was clear: it was to be a war to the death.[25]

Maximilian ignored his supporters' bellicose rhetoric. In a letter intended for the European press, he gave his reasons for staying. The French were in league with the United States, which threatened Mexico's independence. "People are disturbed by fear of the North American colossus" and therefore declare for the empire, ran the press release. "In the midst of this restless agitation, Maximilian lives modestly in Orizaba like a man in private life. Only dealing with a few trusted members of his entourage, he is without an imperial household." The message stated that Márquez and Miramón "have offered their swords", while other imperialistas remained loyal.[26] This, reasoned Maximilian, was support enough to maintain his throne until such a time as it could be put to a national vote.

AT THREE IN the afternoon on December 1, fireworks were let off and church bells rang out across Mexico City as an official paper was distributed throughout the capital announcing Maximilian's decision. Similar scenes played out in the few remaining towns loyal to the empire, notably Querétaro, Puebla, and Orizaba. Castelnau, Dano, and Bazaine, though, were not celebrating, especially once they read Maximilian's declaration. They were outraged at its anti-French tone, publishing a denial that they were negotiating an interim government with the United States, pointing out that the council at Orizaba was able to meet only because of the protection French bayonets afforded it.

On December 3 Lares informed Castelnau, Dano, and Bazaine that Maximilian would continue his government without the support of the French. The French triumvirate responded with a signed declaration on December 8 that it was, in their view, impossible for the empire to survive on its own resources; the emperor must abdicate. Castelnau then telegrammed Napoleon III of Maximilian's decision to remain in Mexico. When the French emperor heard the news, he was furious. He telegrammed back: "The evacuation must be completed by March [1867]. Repatriate the Foreign Legion and all the French, soldiers or otherwise, who desire to return as well as the Austrian and Belgian Legions, if they ask for it."[27]

Napoleon III had just broken more promises. In October he had already reneged on the agreement to keep the French army in Mexico until the end of 1867, insisting on March as the latest date. Now the Foreign Legion, which he had told Maximilian would stay in Mexico, would also leave. Not only that, but, as the French emperor knew, the Austrian and Belgian volunteers were unlikely to stay if given free passage to Europe. Finally, all French officials, from financial advisers to administrators, were ordered, if they were in the French army, or strongly encouraged, if they were not, to resign their posts. In short, as of December 1866, all meaningful cooperation with the French ceased. But the French insisted that the financial conditions they had agreed with Maximilian be met, taking half of the ever-dwindling customs revenues from Veracruz. If Napoleon III's decision was churlish, it was also tactical: with Maximilian further deprived of men and money, the French emperor expected him to reconsider and abdicate.

Maximilian left Orizaba on December 12 to return, slowly, to Mexico City. The night before there had been a party. Champagne had flowed freely, much to the delight of the bibulous Fischer, who sacrificed his health celebrating the empire. With an early start the next morning, the hungover priest struggled. Complaining to Basch that he was suffering from violent headaches, Fischer made it to only the first stop before announcing he could travel no farther. After a consultation with Basch, who reassured him that this kind of sickness usually passed, Maximilian pressed on without Fischer.

On December 14 Maximilian reached Puebla, staying just outside the city. Unhappily for Billimeck, the butterfly-hunting expeditions proved less fruitful here, and after a few disappointing outings these excursions ceased. Maximilian had also started shooting practice after dinner, and, more accustomed to the swishing of the net than the crack of a pistol, the botanist often retired because of his nerves. As far as government went, Maximilian met with his ministers and the now-recovered Fischer, who promised that the deficit would disappear and the army would be organised.

This was not the opinion of Castelnau, who after two months had finally been granted an audience. He arrived at Puebla on December 20, meeting with the emperor the next day. Maximilian received him coldly, positioning himself in the shadows so that when Castelnau entered the room, bright sun blinded him. Relishing this small victory, Maximilian then explained that he still wanted to relinquish the crown, but honourably—called by the people of Mexico, he would depart at their wish. Thus, he had decided on a national congress. Castelnau replied that this was a generous, great, and workable plan, a year earlier. Now, it was impossible. The only way to save Mexico, and Maximilian's life, was to abdicate immediately. Unmoved, Maximilian ended the discussion after about an hour.

Castelnau, this time with Dano, tried again the next day. As the French were taking half of what little revenue was left to the empire, a furious Maximilian heatedly complained about broken French promises. "Is it just", he asked, "that I must fulfil my engagements when you fail to fulfil yours?" Dano sidestepped this uncomfortable accusation, and then Castelnau again implored Maximilian to abdicate. The emperor had thrown himself into the arms of the "weak and impotent" conservatives, the strength of the liberal party was increasing daily, French soldiers were withdrawing, and the US Army was manoeuvring to help Juárez. After the French left, civil war would intensify in all its fury, leading, with terrible carnage, to the collapse of the empire. Maximilian had the power to stop all this.

He must abdicate, concluded Castelnau, in the name of humanity, and in the interests of Mexico.

No one, Maximilian replied, wanted power less than him. He was ready to give up everything if it could be done honourably, but he considered himself a soldier on sentry, and so he could not be relieved from his duty except by the people who had put him there. Returning to his idea of congress, and claiming that this was in fact Napoleon III's own view, Maximilian said that he knew very well that it would result in the election of Juárez. The emperor would be the first to congratulate the newly elected president, wish him a happier fate than he himself had enjoyed, and then take the road to Veracruz as a simple citizen of the Mexican republic before departing for Europe.

Dano and Castelnau stressed that the congress was an impossibility before handing Maximilian a note they had signed with Bazaine recommending abdication. Maximilian read it without emotion. Then, taking a note of his own from his desk, Maximilian handed it to Castelnau. It was a message from Bazaine that claimed nothing was possible in Mexico apart from the empire, which the marshal would do everything in his power to support. After Castelnau's astonishment wore off, Maximilian explained that he knew Bazaine well and had often been the victim of his dissimulation, but ultimately could count on his support. Seeing that further discussion was futile, Castelnau and Dano took their leave.[28]

Castelnau believed that Bazaine's own fortune was tied to the survival of the empire and had long suspected the marshal of secretly encouraging Maximilian to remain as emperor. "I know beyond doubt that Marshal Bazaine has betrayed the interests of Your Majesty to further his own", thundered Castelnau to Napoleon III, accusing Bazaine of treason.[29] To add a layer of farce to these intrigues, Bazaine came across a draft of Castelnau's letter accusing him of betraying France. A soldier, previously attached to the marshal's headquarters, stumbled across a crumpled copy on the floor while sweeping Castelnau's apartment, or, if Bazaine's aide-de-camp is to be believed, while on the toilet and in urgent need of paper. The serendipity of such a discovery suggests that Bazaine had Castelnau under surveillance, but whatever the case it gave the marshal the chance to refute the accusations and make some of his own.

Bazaine wrote to the minister of war to defend himself, insisting he had not covertly influenced Maximilian's decision. What he had said was that if the emperor showed energy, relied on the conservatives, and resolved to stay in power, then the Foreign Legion and the French who were helping organise the Mexican army would remain in Mexico. As Bazaine pointed out, this had been agreed to by Napoleon III, and it was not until his December telegram that government policy had changed. Castelnau and Dano, Bazaine argued, had prevented him going to Orizaba, which the marshal maintained was the crucial moment to sway Maximilian. Then they had gone without him to Puebla. Here, Bazaine claimed, they might have succeeded in bringing about Maximilian's abdication if they had been less arrogantly hostile.

Castelnau's accusations were indeed groundless. The only secret manoeuvres were his own likely attempts to bribe Maximilian's counsellors to recommend abdication—Fischer was allegedly offered $150,000. Even Napoleon III realised his aide had overplayed his hand and had telegrammed him a warning: "Do not force the emperor to abdicate".[30] All Napoleon III wanted now was the swift evacuation of French troops and to extract as much money from Maximilian's empire as possible.

At the beginning of January 1867, Maximilian finally returned to his capital. Will the "stay in Mexico City harm my health?" the emperor asked his doctor. Not his health, replied Basch, "but I fear that it could endanger Your Majesty's life."[31]

9

UNDER SIEGE

Maximilian's health was in serious question. He was not well. Sick with fever, distraught with anxiety about Carlota, the strains of the past months were written into his body as he quietly arrived on January 5 without fanfare to a dilapidated, ramshackle dairy farm on the outskirts of Mexico City. Here he would stay. The furniture at Chapultepec had been shipped to Veracruz, and he refused to sleep in the empty castle.

Maximilian drew some comfort from letters he received from home. His mother at least supported his decision to stay in Mexico. She wrote to him that when surrounded by the imperial family at a Christmas gathering in Vienna, she had been reminded of Maximilian and became tearful. Guessing the cause, Franz Joseph had turned away awkwardly. Even though she desperately missed her son, Sophie added, "I am bound to want you to stay in Mexico now as long as this is possible, and can be done with honour. Farewell, dear Max, we all embrace you from our hearts and send you best wishes for your happiness in the new year." Maximilian's younger brother, Karl Ludwig, had written the same day, "You have been quite right to let yourself be persuaded to stay in the country . . . so long as you are able to stay, do hold onto your present position."[1]

This was not the opinion of Achille Bazaine. Declining to see any French officials, Maximilian made an exception for the marshal. Although he had constantly briefed against him for more than a year, Maximilian now realised that compared to the contempt of François Castelnau, Bazaine was the most amiable of the high-ranking Frenchmen. Walking arm in arm, the two talked for hours. Bazaine's message, however, was simple: without the Foreign Legion, the Belgian and Austrian volunteers, and the French who had joined the Mexican army, Maximilian's forces would be defeated. The emperor must abdicate and leave now.

Maximilian again rejected this advice, repeating what he had told Castelnau and Dano. Above all, the emperor stressed, it was a question of honour: he had made promises he felt he could not break. Nonetheless, Maximilian recognised the weakness of his position in Mexico and asked Bazaine to repeat his prognosis to his conservative supporters at another cabinet meeting arranged for January 14. Once again, the fate of the empire hung in the balance.

On that day, Bazaine read aloud a prepared statement. The majority of the country, he said, was now under the control of Juárez. "What would be the point of launching a military campaign and spending enormous sums to reconquer lost territory?" He answered this question himself: "Nothing". The empire was, Bazaine argued, financially, militarily, and politically bankrupt. "It seems to me impossible", concluded the marshal, that Maximilian could "continue to govern the country". If the emperor stayed in power, it would merely be as the head of a faction fighting a civil war that would likely be lost.[2]

But conservatives were determined to fight this civil war, come what may. In reply to Bazaine, Leonardo Márquez promised that towns now in the hands of Juaristas would declare for the empire as soon as a military campaign was launched. As for resources, ministers pledged twenty-six thousand soldiers and $11 million a year to finance them. Archbishop Pelagio Antonio de Labastida y Dávalos declared the support of the Catholic Church. Monarchy was popular, the conservatives, and Fischer, who was also present at the meeting, maintained. If states had gone over to Juárez, it was because they hated the French invaders, not Maximilian's reign. The council resolved, twenty-eight votes against five, for the empire to continue.

If Maximilian hoped Bazaine's pessimism might temper the bellicosity of conservative ministers, or get them to take the idea of a congress seriously, he was disappointed. Instead, they prepared for the coming struggle, appealing to the Mexican nation, or the few parts of it that they still governed. All, rich or poor, must sacrifice themselves on behalf of the empire. In practice, this meant money, while those who had none should give their lives. These would not be voluntary sacrifices: forced loans raised the money; men were press-ganged into the army. This was in keeping with the practice of numerous previous Mexican governments, but it was far removed from Maximilian's earlier determination to reign above party, but not above the law. Instead, his ministers now declared that the emperor was a military leader, who held in his hands the national flag and was willing "to die with you, if it is necessary, for the independence and liberty of the nation."[3]

For many of his former liberal supporters, Maximilian was now exactly what Bazaine had said he was: no more than the head of the Conservative Party. Those who had not done so already abandoned him. The gourmand José Fernando Ramírez, who had served Maximilian faithfully as a minister for two years, wept when he came to say good-bye for the final time; Maximilian also had tears in his eyes. Fearing reprisals from Juaristas, Ramírez went into exile rather than stay behind to watch the civil war. Many other liberal imperialistas followed him; Mexico City no longer seemed safe.

After an epic march from the state of Sinaloa on the Pacific Coast, the final remnants of French forces under General Castagny reached the capital on January 15. Fever, sunstroke, and combat had killed many of these troops, and those who survived resembled walking corpses by the time they reached their destination. These were the last French troops north of Mexico City to make their retreat. With them came hundreds of imperialista refugees, many of whom had walked for weeks through the mountains and deserts.

February 1 was set as the last date that the French army could guarantee safe passage to Veracruz. Those who had the means made preparations to leave the capital, desperate to get out. Amongst high society, all the talk was of escape at joyless parties organised to say good-bye to family and friends. For Sara Yorke Stevenson, whose family was one of the first to leave, these festivities were more like wakes. "It was as though we were launching out in the night, and, like children in the dark, we sang aloud to keep up our courage."[4]

Despite the personal rapprochement with Bazaine, the French now seemed to be doing everything they could to obstruct the conservative war effort. Castelnau had resolved to undermine the emperor. Whether through spite, or because he thought that weakening the empire could still persuade Maximilian to abdicate, Castelnau ensured as little as possible of the customs receipts from Veracruz— by this point the empire's sole source of meaningful revenue—as well as military equipment the French could not transport to France, were available to imperialistas. Artillery was destroyed, gunpowder spoiled, and fortifications torn down wherever the French retreated. Towards the end of January, Teodosio Lares complained to Bazaine, questioning the honour of an army that behaved in such a fashion. This enraged even the normally patient Bazaine, who informed the minister on January 28 that he would no longer communicate with his government.

Bazaine did write personally to Maximilian to explain his actions. He assured him that whenever possible, he was helping the imperialistas as much as his instructions allowed. But, again, he cautioned Maximilian that his conservative ministers had little support, and if he remained with them it would be an era of "sanguinary reprisals, of grievous catastrophes, of complete ruin and anarchy".[5] This in turn was too much for Maximilian. Furious, he left it to the ever-present Fischer to write to the marshal: the emperor could not accept such insulting language towards his government. Maximilian now refused to have any dealing with Bazaine whatsoever.

At dawn, on February 5, 1867, the French flag was lowered from its headquarters in Mexico City where it had flown for nearly four years. Crowds lined the streets, staring silently as the French troops massed in a nearby public park before Bazaine and his officers led them out of the capital, a military band defiantly playing. Behind the troops came refugees, determined to follow in the safety of the French army's wake. The windows and doors of the National Palace remained pointedly shut. On the roof, the emperor, wrapped in a grey cloak against the morning chill, peered out from behind a parapet. Once the last French soldier was out of sight, he reportedly turned and said, "At last we are free!"[6]

Others in Mexico City were more uneasy. Márquez was placed in charge of the capital, and that evening a notice was pinned up in the squares. The text read more like a threat than the dawn of a prosperous new era: "As you know me," declared the general, "I believe it unnecessary to say more". He did, however, say more: "I would rather die than permit the least disorder". Should anyone have the "insane intention of disturbing the peace", then he would use the full force of his powers against them. Another communication followed immediately. "Although there is currently no cause for alarm," the decree began, somewhat disingenuously given what came next, the city must be prepared for any eventuality. The notice then outlined what the people were to do if the city was attacked.[7]

Whatever Márquez's protestations to the contrary, Juarista armies were fast closing in on the capital. Porfirio Díaz, commander of the Army of the East, was approaching from the south. In October 1866, he advanced on Oaxaca. Before the final assault, Díaz had received word that 1,500 imperial troops, many from the Austrian Legion, were marching to relieve the siege. Rather than meet them outside the city, Díaz moved to ambush them in the surrounding hills. Surprising the relief column, the Juaristas emerged triumphant after savage fighting. Díaz reported significant losses, but 396 Poles, Hungarians, and Austrians were taken prisoner. Mexican officers were shot under Juárez's January 1862 law. The captured guns and artillery were then turned on Oaxaca, which capitulated two weeks later.

Yet in the north things were not going well for Juárez. Here liberals were at war with each other. In the name of Juárez, Mariano Escobedo was besieging Matamoros, under control of the liberal Servando Canales, who served the rival claimant to the presidency, Jesús González Ortega. To further complicate matters, on November 23, 1866, the US Army crossed the Rio Grande (ostensibly to maintain law and order), occupied the main square of Matamoros, and raised the Stars and Stripes. The US colonel in charge hoped to bring Escobedo and Canales to an agreement; however, he managed only to broker a meeting where the two Mexicans swore at each for hours, refusing to compromise.

Having failed with insults, Escobedo then tried with bullets, attacking the town the next day, but vicious fighting resulted only in a tense cease-fire. Several hundred of the troops that had crushed Ernst Pitner's Austrian Legion months earlier fell. Although Canales still occupied the town, he realised he could not hold out indefinitely and came to an uncomfortable understanding with Escobedo. In return for submitting to Benito Juárez's authority, Canales let Escobedo briefly and symbolically occupy Matamoros before the latter headed south to fight the imperialistas.

In the end, it was the United States that helped put an end to these divisions within the liberal ranks. Ortega, then in New Orleans, published a manifesto announcing his imminent departure for Mexico to assume the presidency. Before he could do so, the US authorities intervened to protect Juárez, arresting Ortega. They held him for more than a month, during which time support for his cause withered. When he did eventually make it to Mexico, Juaristas imprisoned him again in January 1867.

Matamoros pacified, Escobedo rapidly advanced south. As Díaz approached Mexico City from the other direction, Juaristas were now encircling Maximilian's empire like a lasso tightening around the capital. The empire's territory had been reduced to little more than Mexico City, a few towns to the immediate northwest—Querétaro and Morelia were especially well garrisoned—and a ribbon of strongholds that ran eastwards to Veracruz. Then, at the end of January 1867, Juaristas took Cuernavaca. The loss of Maximilian's retreat was a personal blow and left liberal forces only a day's march from the capital.

It was left to the imperial army and the foreign volunteers to defend what was left of the empire. The latter, though, were demoralised, rarely paid, and increasingly mutinous. To avoid a complete collapse, Maximilian released the foreign volunteers from their oaths, hoping they would reenlist in the Mexican army. Out of some 8,000 volunteers who had gone to fight in Mexico, only 173 officers and 650 men chose to stay. Other than these forces, Maximilian was dependent on the military skills of Márquez, Tomás Mejía, and Miguel Miramón.

Determined to demonstrate his prowess, Miramón had left Mexico City on December 28, 1866, with only 400 men, planning to unite various imperialista forces under his command and then take the fight to the enemy. With speed that would have impressed the Prussians he had been attached to in Berlin, he went northwest from the capital to Querétaro. From here he toured nearby towns, recruiting as he went. Finally, on January 20, with a force of some 1,500 men, cavalry, and artillery, Miramón headed farther north.

Coming from the other direction was Juárez, who had followed close behind Escobedo's army marching south. On January 22, the president entered Zacatecas, where republicans proved as adept as monarchists in organising balls and fireworks to celebrate. These festivities, however, were cut short when news reached the town that Miramón was approaching. Taken completely by surprise, the president resolved to stay and organise the defences. Juárez could not countenance fleeing in the face of the enemy, especially not Miramón, whom he had defeated in 1861.

On the evening of January 26, Miramón's forces occupied key points around the town. The next morning they attacked. Juárez's generals warned that the town could not be held; the president must escape before it fell. As Juárez left the town hall, Miramón's troops appeared in the streets, firing on the president's escort, but he managed to reach his carriage. Imperialista cavalry, under the command of Miramón's brother, Joaquín, pursued Juárez for miles, but were unable to catch him.

Miramón watched Juárez flee from a nearby hill, then entered the town before telegramming the capital to report he had taken Zacatecas. "Artillery, weapons, carriages and prisoners have been left in my possession. Juárez has been saved by the speed of his carriage."[8] In Mexico City, Maximilian was elated. Miramón's boldness proved he could rely on his Mexican generals now freed from French command. The emperor even paid a visit to the house of the heavily pregnant Concepción Lombardo to congratulate her on her husband's success. It would have been a brilliant coup de main had he captured the president, but with too few troops to hold the town Miramón had to abandon Zacatecas after a few days and retreat, lest his small army be cut off in hostile territory.

He left too late. Through rapid, punishing marches, Escobedo caught up with Miramón some forty miles southeast of Zacatecas and forced him to fight at a remote hacienda. Outnumbering the imperialistas, many of the republicans were armed with the latest US-made repeating rifles, and their victory was almost total. Miramón managed to escape with some cavalry, but Escobedo seized weapons and money, leaving some two hundred imperialistas dead on the battlefield.

Miramón's brother, Joaquín, was captured, along with perhaps five hundred others. A few days later, Joaquín was executed. He was given barely enough time to write to his wife before, badly wounded in the leg, he limped to the firing squad. It was too painful to stand, and he had to ask permission to lean against the wall before he was gunned down. Reports reached Miramón that the body was later used for target practice. Amongst the other prisoners were about a hundred French who had volunteered to stay behind and fight for Maximilian. After several days in captivity, they were informed, while washing their clothes, that they too would be executed. So as to prevent any attempt to escape, they were marched in small groups to the execution site, hugging their comrades before they left. Reports emerged that one Frenchman, unharmed after the first volley, was added to another party. This time he was only lightly wounded before he was finally tied up and dispatched from point-blank range with a recently arrived third group. It took more than an hour to kill them all.

When Bazaine heard news of Miramón's catastrophic defeat, he sent word to the capital that he could still help Maximilian leave Mexico, but "in a few days it will be too late."[9] But Maximilian never saw this message; the French army left without him. It had been more than five years since the first French troops landed in Mexico. Now Bazaine was one of the last to leave, sailing from Veracruz on March 12, 1867.

Maximilian was not in Mexico City when Bazaine's message arrived, because Márquez had persuaded the emperor to take personal command of what remained of the imperial army and march to Querétaro. The plan was to rescue Miramón's beleaguered forces, awaiting Escobedo's imminent attack. If the emperor won a glorious victory over Juárez's best general, reasoned Márquez, confidence in the empire would be restored.

So it was that on the morning of February 13, Maximilian rode out from Mexico City at the head of fifteen hundred men and with only 50,000 pesos—earlier promises from Maximilian's minister of more men and money having proved wildly exaggerated. Wearing a general's uniform, black trousers with silver buttons down the sides, and boots that came up to his knees, Maximilian, who had never fought in an army before, let alone commanded one, did at least look like a soldier—and a Mexican one at that, his wide sombrero completing his battle dress. He was armed with a sabre and two revolvers at-tached to his saddle, while he always carried on his person an old naval telescope, which he used as a field glass. Much to the despair of the few Austrian officers who had chosen to fight with Maximil-ian after their legion was disbanded, Márquez had convinced the emperor that only Mexican officers should lead the relief force. The foreign volunteers remained behind to garrison the capital.

Thus, if Maximilian looked the part, his army was a far cry from the European parade drills that had bored him as a child in Vienna. Resembling a heavily armed crowd rather than a disciplined bat-talion, his soldiers did not march in step, the artillery lumbered far behind, and, as was the custom, women and children followed at a greater distance still. Pressed into service less than six weeks before, many of the troops still wore the ragged clothes in which they had been seized. What uniforms there were defied the meaning of the word, varying greatly according to availability and personal choice. Making their way through the rugged, hilly terrain between Mexico City and Querétaro, this slow-moving convoy presented a tempting target for the guerrillas who controlled the countryside.

Deprived of his Austrian officers, it was Márquez and Colonel Miguel López who would be at Maximilian's side for the 130-mile journey northwest. López, who had led the escort that brought Max-imilian and Carlota to Mexico City in 1864, was a personal favou-rite; Maximilian was godfather to his child. With thinning blond hair and blue eyes, López was an excellent rider who cut a dashing figure in his rich red dragoon jacket. He had impeccable manners, a quality always appealing to Maximilian. More usefully, he had so distinguished himself militarily that he was one of the few Mexicans to be awarded the French Légion d'honneur. He commanded the Empress' Regiment, an elite body of cavalry.

As his capital receded into the distance, Maximilian recalled Hernán Cortés's flight from Mexico City some 450 years earlier af-ter Aztec forces surrounded the few hundred conquistadores. Max-imilian reflected, "The man of iron wept with bitter tears". Taking comfort in this, Maximilian continued, this "teaches us . . . that men of the strongest and most domineering natures . . . have rare moments when they believe themselves abandoned". Cortés too had been forced to flee, but then "rose from his affliction stronger than before and retook Mexico City".[10] Maximilian drew solace from the parallel, although Cortés probably spent less time on his journey making notes about the local trees and fauna than the emperor did on his.

Only twenty miles from the capital, while dining with a local priest for lunch, shots were heard. After a brief skirmish, the guerrillas were repelled, but the next attack was more serious. Several hundred horsemen sprang an ambush. Maximilian galloped to the front of his troops. When he reached them, not three yards away, a bullet smashed into a sergeant, who fell to the ground. Samuel Basch, one of the few foreigners with the emperor, performed his first field operation, while Maximilian's army successfully fought off the attackers.

At the next stop, the village of Cuautitlán, Santiago Vidaurri, one of Maximilian's most trusted lieutenants, and one of the few more liberal supporters who had remained loyal, joined the imperialistas. Having been delayed in Mexico City, he had caught up after hard riding. With him was the improbably named Prince Felix Salm-Salm, a Prussian aristocrat turned soldier of fortune who had fought with great distinction for the Union. After the American Civil War ended, Salm-Salm had offered his services to the empire and enlisted in the imperial army. Thirty-eight years old, with a moustache reminiscent of Napoleon III's, Salm-Salm was brave to the point of recklessness and had convinced Vidaurri to put him on his staff to ensure he could join Maximilian regardless of Márquez's insistence that foreign officers remain in the capital.

Salm-Salm had been accompanied to Mexico by his American wife, Agnes. An unlikely princess, she had grown up in the circus before becoming an actor, but once married they were inseparable. She travelled on campaigns with Salm-Salm, sometimes even fighting herself; however, her husband had forbidden her to accompany him to Querétaro. After a heated argument lasting almost an entire day, she had resigned herself to staying in Mexico City, with her dog, Jimmy.

Once the army was on the move again, Maximilian came across an imperial soldier hanging dead upside down from a tree in a churchyard, his body mutilated and his skull crushed. He had been captured and executed; Juaristas had left his corpse as a warning. The column fought its way through to Querétaro, frequently under enemy fire. When the emperor's aides urged him to take cover, he replied, "What do you want me to do, run away the first chance I get?"[11] He showed enormous calm. As bullets whistled all around, he later told Dominik Billimeck, "I saw the most beautiful butterflies fluttering about", adding, "To go down sword in hand is fate, but not disgrace."

As well as sangfroid, Maximilian demonstrated the rallying spirit of a military leader. On February 17, four days after leaving Mexico City, he halted the march and issued a proclamation to his soldiers. He had wanted to be their supreme commander for a long time, he told them. Finally, free from foreign interference, he could now lead them. Trusting in God to protect Mexico, "let us fight with indomitable spirit under this sacred cry: Long live independence!"[12]

The staunchly conservative, religious, and proimperial town of Querétaro had been anxiously awaiting relief. Scenes of jubilation therefore greeted Maximilian's entry. Imperial troops lined the streets from the southern gate to the house where Maximilian was staying, while balconies and rooftops were full of people cheering the emperor. The requisite artillery salvoes, fireworks, and bells added to the noise, which, predictably, Maximilian described as more enthusiastic than ever. When the procession reached the centre, Maximilian got off his horse and warmly greeted Miramón and Mejía, who had reached the town beforehand. The requisite Te Deum and banquet followed.

Spirits were raised even higher the next day with the arrival of General Ramón Méndez, the imperialista commander whose three thousand or so battle-hardened veterans had been fighting in the state of Michoacán. Undefeated, they had abandoned the state capital when news reached them of the emperor's journey and made for Querétaro. Maximilian was deeply impressed with these well-equipped, well-trained, and well-disciplined soldiers who greeted him with shouts of "Viva el Emperador!" as he reviewed them.

Over the next few days, the most devoted imperialistas gathered one way or another in Querétaro. Austrian Ernst Pitner, whom Escobedo had released on his own parole after eight months' imprisonment, even broke his word and joined Maximilian rather than leave for Europe. The emperor now had the most famous names of the Conservative Party at his side, Mejía, Márquez, and Miramón, as well as the liberal Vidaurri, who remained popular in the north of Mexico. Although the troops were of varying quality, some press-ganged into the army weeks before, others with decades of experience, and still plenty of foreign volunteers in the rank and file, Maximilian now had roughly nine thousand men at his command.

The question was how to employ them, for three separate republican armies were converging on Querétaro. General Ramón Corona approached from the west with eight thousand men, Escobedo from the north with twelve thousand, and General Vicente Riva Palacio was some way behind the other two with another seven thousand. Once combined, the Juaristas would outnumber the imperialistas three to one. Although nominally in overall command, Maximilian brought his usual indecision to the role and delegated to his generals. Miramón urged an immediate attack on Escobedo's troops to scatter them before Corona arrived with reinforcements. Miramón, however, had fallen from Maximilian's favour after his recent defeat, and Márquez's advice was now preferred. His plan was to send for reinforcements and money from Mexico City and await their arrival before taking any action against the enemy.

While he awaited further support capital, Maximilian mingled freely amongst the people of Querétaro. When not in military uniform, he dressed in a plain blue tunic with a walking stick rather than a sabre. Fond of cigars, he would often ask unsuspecting people in the street for a light and talk informally with them while smoking. His accommodation was a far cry from the luxury of Chapultepec. He had two simple rooms, one a bedroom, the other a study. Even on campaign, he maintained a strict routine: dinner with a few friends followed by billiards and then bed at nine before waking at five.

Until more resources arrived from the capital, it was left to Vidaurri to organise what financing he could in Querétaro. The $50,000 soon ran out. Squeezing enforced loans out of the forty thousand inhabitants, he somehow managed to provision an army of nine thousand, but these emergency measures were only a short-term solution. Despite these hardships, life in the town continued much as before: the theatre remained open, a French coffeehouse became the preferred meeting place for officers, and there was even a bullfight to enjoy. The people of Querétaro warmed to Maximilian, who himself was in good spirits.

Then, on March 4, news reached the imperialistas that the enemy was approaching. Feverish military activity replaced coffeehouse discussion the next day when the enemy appeared massing on the plain to the west of the town. Any hope of defeating the republican armies separately was now ended; a siege had begun.

LAID OUT IN typical Spanish colonial style, Querétaro lies in a valley surrounded by hills on three sides and an open lowland to the west. A river ran through the north of the town, while a magnificent eighteenth-century stone aqueduct supplied the city with freshwater from the east. As Salm-Salm noted, though, it was the worst place in the world to defend because if the besieged did not hold the high ground, then the enemy would have every building within gunshot range—and Maximilian did not have enough troops to occupy the hills.

Instead, the imperialistas resolved to defend strongpoints in the town. The river provided a natural defence to the north; to the south, a stone farmhouse known as the Casa Blanca and the Alameda, a public park, were fortified. To the east, the thick-walled Convent of Santa Cruz was turned into a citadel. Finally, to the west, a small, isolated rocky hill covered with cacti, the Cerro de las Campanas (Hill of the Bells), which rises gently out from the town before dropping off more steeply over the plain, was garrisoned. Nine thousand soldiers and perhaps thirty thousand people were crammed into a space that, west to east, could be walked across at a brisk pace in a half hour, north to south in twenty minutes. The imperialistas did not even hold the whole town, for across the river the suburb of San Sebastian was quickly occupied by Escobedo's men.

With a commanding view over the city and the plains, the Cerro de las Campanas was where Maximilian made his headquarters in anticipation of an immediate attack. Here, he slept out in the open. During the day, much to his delight, he found a hollow in the rocks, a small cave, shaded from the sun and surrounded with high cacti. It was a place of respite from reviewing troops and military preparations. When Basch arrived on the hill, Maximilian excitedly showed him the spot. "Do not tell anyone about this treasure. I should like to be alone here," he told his doctor.[13] No doubt part of the attraction was that the cave was a perfect spot to watch hummingbirds that darted around the hill. To the soundtrack of intermittent gunfire, Maximilian breakfasted at ten here daily. The town was well provisioned, and Maximilian enjoyed roast turkey, cold meats, eggs, cheese, bread, and wine.

Maximilian's generals predicted the liberals would attack immediately, but when the expected onslaught failed to materialise, it was decided to move headquarters to the thick-walled convent, known to the defenders as La Cruz, which provided more comfort and security. On March 13, therefore, Maximilian moved into a former nun's cell divided into two rooms. In one he had a table and two chairs as an office, and the other served as his bedroom. An iron camp bed, washstand, clothes rack, and some chairs were all that furnished the chamber. Maximilian's general staff took rooms

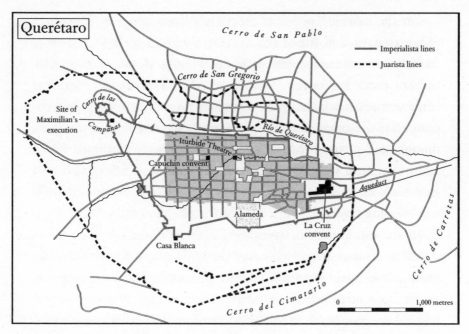

Siege of Querétaro

nearby. While nonmilitary members of Maximilian's inner circle like Fischer and Billimeck had chosen to stay in the relative safety of Mexico City, Maximilian's private secretary, José Luis Blasio, recently returned from Europe, had insisted on accompanying the emperor to Querétaro. Here he took a cell with a connecting corridor to Maximilian's and managed to procure provisions, including, crucially, wine.

Escobedo was in no hurry to attack. He spent the time reconnoitring Maximilian's positions, occupying the surrounding high ground and placing his artillery. Once the encirclement was complete, republican troops cut the aqueduct that brought freshwater into the city. Well supplied with US arms—and volunteers in the American Legion of Honour—Escobedo had assembled some thirty thousand troops ready to attack Querétaro. Juárez, 120 miles or so north at San Luis Potosí, was impatient that Escobedo should begin, insisting that his general accept only unconditional surrender from Maximilian and his supporters.

On the morning of March 14, Maximilian reviewed his troops in the courtyard of the convent. While he was delivering a speech, artillery from the nearby republican guns crashed into the walls. The Juarista attack had begun. With explosives falling around them, the emperor and his adjutants ran through the gardens to a less exposed square on the other side of the convent. They were still in range, though, as an explosive landed a few paces away from Maximilian and his general staff. While everyone dropped to the ground, the emperor remained standing serenely, and the bomb detonated without harming anyone.

In the convent's bell tower, an officer with a telescope shouted down the enemy movements to Maximilian and the commanders below, desperately coordinating the defence. The town was under attack from three sides. Cavalry was advancing from the south, infantry bore down on the convent from the east, and liberals had brought an artillery piece up to secure a bridge and pour over the river from the north.

To the south, Mejía launched his cavalry into an immediate counterattack. Leading the charge himself with lance and sabre, such was its furious impetuosity that the imperial cavalry drove the Juaristas back to their own camp, killing many and taking more prisoners. The liberals regrouped for a second attack, but this one proved even more disastrous than the first.

Meanwhile, the fighting was fiercer at the bridge to the north. There, too, an attack had been beaten off, but the Juaristas had occupied the houses on the other side of the river, and their sharpshooters kept the imperial troops pinned down. Under this cover, the republicans then brought up an artillery piece, which began firing on the imperial battery defending the bridge. Salm-Salm was ordered to rush the gun and drive the liberals from the streets and houses on the north side of the river. After speaking to his men in broken Spanish, a cry of "Viva el Emperador!" rang out from his troops as they ran across the bridge towards the gun. The liberals manning it held their ground but fell under heavy fire, and the few survivors were bayoneted or clubbed to death. The liberal infantrymen in the street then barricaded themselves in nearby houses. Salm-Salm's men broke down the doors and massacred those inside. The Prussian recalled how one man had already killed four people in a room when he came across another on his knees praying for mercy. "All the mercy I will grant you", said the imperialista, is that "I will give you the honour of a bullet" before shooting him.[14]

As the areas to the north and south were secured, Escobedo's men were attacking the convent. Across the gardens to the east was a chapel, which Márquez, not expecting an attack from this direction, had left poorly defended. Liberal troops soon occupied it and some surrounding houses, only a few hundred yards from the convent itself. To retake the building, imperial soldiers made a hole in the east-facing wall, but in their haste they made the opening too narrow. As they squeezed through, bullets tore into them. Some made it into the gardens, but their officers and many more soldiers were killed. As the retreat was sounded, the soldiers tried to push back through the opening, scrambling over the bodies of their dead comrades. When the republicans closed in, Márquez personally commanded the counterattack. Rising from behind a barricade when his troops faltered, the general directed their advance as shells and bullets whistled past. The imperialistas concentrated their artillery and eventually retook the chapel and nearby houses.

Miramón then arrived at the grounds of the convent, having co-ordinated the defence along the rest of the lines. Announcing that the liberals had been repulsed, Maximilian embraced him. In the early evening, the emperor went to inspect his troops. As he rode past his soldiers holding the line, they saluted him with wild cheers, potshots from sharpshooters kicking up the dirt near his horse. By six the bells of Querétaro were ringing, trumpets sounded victory, and his troops sang the national anthem. Maximilian was a hero. As one artillery officer recorded, "Everyone was swept up in the emotion. The empire had been saved. . . . These moments were sublime. I will never forget them. It was the beautiful side of war".[15]

Hundreds of prisoners were taken that day, some of them Americans, one of whom was paraded before Maximilian. In an act of defiance, the captive refused to remove his hat in the emperor's presence. Such an egregious breach of etiquette naturally pained Maximilian, and an awkward silence ensued before Méndez tactfully removed the American's headwear.

"Why do you fight against us?" asked Maximilian.

"Because I am a republican."

"If you are really a republican", Maximilian replied, then he should have fought with the constitutional president Ortega.[16]

For all the euphoria of victory, the town remained besieged. These prisoners added more mouths to feed. The need for reinforcements and money from Mexico City grew more urgent still when the third Juarista army under Riva Palacio reached Querétaro. Now Escobedo had roughly forty thousand men. The theatre's lead roof was turned into musket balls, while church bells were melted down to make artillery shells. So desperate were Maximilian's gunners for ammunition that rewards were offered for unexploded projectiles; women and children salvaged them.

This was not enough to sustain a long siege, though, and a council of war held a week after the Juaristas had been repulsed decided that Márquez and Vidaurri would break out with a small force and make their way to Mexico City. Maximilian, who realised his conservative ministers had badly let him down in the capital, providing him with only a fraction of what they had promised, granted Márquez extensive powers. The emperor appointed him lieutenant-general of the empire, essentially regent. This would give him sufficient authority to raise money, gather reinforcements, and then return to Querétaro within two weeks. For himself, Maximilian requested some good books, copies of his speeches and legislation, as well as a map of the surrounding country amongst other personal effects.

On March 22, Miramón led a diversionary attack on the western plain. The general took the liberals by surprise, capturing wagons laden with food, sixty oxen, and nearly two hundred sheep and goats.

With the republicans in disarray, Márquez and Vidaurri slipped out unnoticed that night with eleven hundred cavalry. The defeat of the republicans, the provisions Miramón seized, and the ease with which Márquez broke through the lines boosted the imperialistas' confidence to endure another fortnight of siege warfare.

While he waited, Maximilian, ever a creature of habit, went for a daily walk between six and seven thirty. Soon the liberals became aware of the routine and concentrated their artillery on the convent to coincide with this stroll. Often insisting Blasio accompany him so he could dictate notes, as the shells and bullets flew around them, Maximilian outlined to his secretary the details for emergency court etiquette to be observed under siege conditions. Eventually, Miramón persuaded the emperor not to expose himself so carelessly, arguing that to die on the battlefield was glorious, but to die unnecessarily was foolish.

Márquez had promised to return within two weeks, but on April 10, the third anniversary of Maximilian's acceptance of the throne, there was no sign of him. Undeterred, the highest civilian authorities that could be scraped together in Querétaro presented themselves before the emperor to congratulate him on his reign. The minister of justice read a speech, which began, presumably without irony, "On this day Your Majesty deigned to accept the crown of Mexico, by this memorable deed forever opening the gates of hope for this unhappy land". Despite some evidence to the contrary, the minister insisted that the empire was the "will of the nation", the republic but the "will of the few".

Extraordinarily, given the circumstances, Maximilian's speech in reply maintained that he still wanted a national congress. Until that was possible, he would defend his empire. He reminded his audience of his previous September 16 speeches. In 1865 he had declared that every drop of his blood was Mexican and that he would fight for the nation's independence. The following year, he had said that no Habsburg would leave their post. "Those that surround me in the difficult days of Querétaro see that I have kept my word."[17]

With the empire reduced to a few streets in Querétaro, there was something tragic about these declarations. Excepting hyperbole, however, there was nothing dishonest about the celebration of Maximilian's bravery. On the same day, Miramón, Mejía, and Méndez, amongst other generals crammed into the town, presented Maximilian with a written commendation to go with a medal for valour they had awarded to him earlier. More speeches followed, these praising Maximilian's courage living amongst his subjects in the midst of danger. To the loyal imperialistas who defended the town, these speeches were not meaningless, but still with no word from Márquez morale began to drop. Without money to pay the troops, Maximilian's generals were forced to extract funds however they could. Taxes were levied on windows, balconies, and then simply whatever was left. With food now running out, horses and mules were slaughtered.

Desperate for news of Márquez's movements, spies were sent out from Querétaro to discover his whereabouts. Those caught were killed and then strung up on poles with placards declaring them "the emperor's courier".[18] With the situation deteriorating each day, it was decided that a force must break out and discover what had become of Márquez.

After a conference on April 15, it was agreed that Mejía would punch a hole through the liberal lines, find Márquez, or push onto Mexico City. Mejía, however, was sick, and Salm-Salm was appointed in his place. Maximilian gave the Prussian secret instructions broken down into twenty points that he was to execute once he reached Mexico City. So pressing did the emperor feel was the position that he gave Salm-Salm orders for the capital to be abandoned if there were not enough soldiers to garrison it and relieve the siege. But, indecisive as ever, Maximilian wanted to keep his options open. Salm-Salm was authorised to start negotiations with the Juaristas. He was also to find out if the Austrian corvette that was to have taken Maximilian to Europe months earlier if he had abdicated was still in Mexican waters. Maximilian again asked for some good books, preferably about history, to relieve the tedium of siege warfare.

At two, under a bright moon, the small contingent of the imperialistas began to move. The plan was to cross the river and then ride hard east towards the Sierra Gorda range, where any pursuers could be easily lost. A Mexican officer who knew the terrain would lead the march. The river was deep and its banks steep, which meant that it had to be forded slowly. Salm-Salm brought up the rear as the soldiers crossed. As soon as he reached the other side, enemy fire opened up all around, while rockets went up into the sky to alert the liberals and illuminate the imperialistas' movements.

Undaunted, Salm-Salm pressed along the riverbank for ten minutes before gunfire hit the troops head-on as well as from the flanks, a bullet grazing the Prussian, while another hit his horse. The march came to standstill. Salm-Salm rushed to find his fellow commanding officer, who was crouching behind a ditch. Dense columns of infantry had blocked off their route; it was impossible to cut through. There was no option but to go back. "Never in all my life was I so furious and mortified as on this retreat," Salm-Salm recorded, blaming the timidity of his fellow officer. If he had acted with more speed, Salm-Salm reasoned, they would have broken through. Once news of the failure spread through Querétaro, the already low morale began to collapse. Fifteen officers signed a letter urging Maximilian to surrender—three of them were imprisoned because of fears they would sap the defenders' confidence further. A few days afterwards, another imperialista spy appeared hanging from a tree on the other side of the river, a placard around his neck. But Maximilian still had faith. "Márquez will come yet", he told Salm-Salm.[19]

Finally, the imperialistas managed to get a spy into the liberal camp and, more important, back across their lines. Márquez was not coming. Disobeying orders, he had been catastrophically defeated trying to relieve Puebla, which was itself under siege from Porfirio Díaz's troops. The republican general took the town and had then routed Márquez's forces. The lieutenant-general of the empire had managed to retreat to Mexico City, but was now himself encircled in the capital with the few thousand troops who remained to the empire outside Querétaro. No help was coming.

The imperial army knew none of this. "Without a doubt General Márquez will stand before this city within a few days, and . . . Querétaro will soon see the day when its suffering will end", ran a bulletin in the official newspaper. Now that breaking out from the siege was the only option, Maximilian kept news of Márquez's defeat to only a few generals, and they resolved that the whole army would fight its way out on April 27. The night before, Maximilian even lied to Basch, "Márquez will attack tomorrow and we will do likewise at the same time".[20]

This time Miramón orchestrated a do-or-die attack to the south of the city. Before dawn, the imperial troops, outnumbered three to one, stared into the murky hills where the liberals were entrenched. As the reveille sounded in the enemy camp, the signal for the assault was given; artillery exploded into action on both sides. Emerging from the clouds of smoke, two imperial columns, one cavalry, the other infantry led by Ernst Pitner, rushed the enemy lines.

Taken by surprise and outflanked, the republicans broke and fled. General Corona, second in command of the liberal forces, saw his camp overrun, his soldiers completely dispersed. The imperialistas seized twenty guns, hundreds of prisoners, and, most important, ammunition and provisions. The starved townspeople of Querétaro dashed to the deserted enemy lines and looted what food was left.

Maximilian, who had been waiting for news at the convent, soon arrived on the scene. Congratulating Miramón, who rode alongside him, he inspected what had been the enemy lines. The victorious Miramón turned to his troops and shouted, "Soldiers! Long live his majesty the emperor!" The massed ranks of imperialistas roared the cry back. Miramón had defeated the republican troops, the southern hills of the city were clear, and, as it would take hours for Escobedo to redeploy soldiers, the road to Mexico City was open.

Miramón, however, wanted to secure the flanks prior to escape. While he reorganised his troops, Escobedo frantically dispatched soldiers to seal the hole in republican lines. He sent thousands of men, including a crack division known as the Supremos Poderes, Juárez's personal guard, round the city to reoccupy the lost position. It took Miramón hours before he was prepared to occupy the heights beyond the liberal trenches. When he was finally ready, Maximilian decided to lead the march himself, with Miramón on his right and Salm-Salm to his left, advancing slowly up the steep incline.

Only two-thirds of the way up the hill, thousands of Escobedo's men appeared at the crest and formed a defensive position. With enemy cavalry flanking them, a tremendous volley of fire hit the imperialistas, halting their march. Maximilian stepped out in front of his troops and urged them forwards, bullets flying past. Salm-Salm grabbed his left arm and insisted on retreat, which Maximilian reluctantly did. As Salm-Salm noted, "The hill offered a spectacle which cut me to the heart. It was covered with our troops flying in disorder". Worse, the enemy cavalry now turned the retreat into an even bloodier rout, with Salm-Salm estimating that some 250 men were lost during the panic. The imperialistas made it to their previous positions, and the republicans contented themselves with reoccupying their own lines, cutting off escape from the south. Salm-Salm believed a small force could still break out to the east, where liberal lines were weaker after Escobedo had moved his troops. Maximilian refused, asking, "What will become of this unfortunate city, which has been so faithful to us and of our poor wounded who we cannot take with us?"[21]

Conditions in Querétaro worsened. Even with the captured supplies, the staple diet of tortillas and frijoles ran out, and soldiers began to starve. Desertion became a serious problem, with ten to twenty soldiers crossing the lines daily into the well-fed liberal camp. The official bulletins maintained that Márquez was on his way with help, but no one in the town believed them anymore. Constant fighting, disease, and desertion had reduced the imperialista ranks so much that it was no longer possible to man the trenches. Cavalry, whose horses had died of starvation, were brought forward to make up the numbers.

Maximilian's once fine dining now consisted of roast mule marinated in vinegar. On one occasion, according to Blasio, a delicious pie was brought into dinner. As Maximilian's guests were halfway through eating it, Miramón appeared, asking how they were enjoying the food. When the response came back that it was delightful, the general replied, "When you want another one, there are still plenty of cats at my place".[22] Maximilian, warned in advance, had eaten only the pastry and enjoyed the joke. Probably it was funnier because there was still wine, for a local store had been relieved of its supply, and some champagne had been found.

In stark contrast to those starving in Querétaro, on May 5 wild celebrations could be heard from the liberal camp, where soldiers were raucously drinking to celebrate the anniversary of the French defeat outside Puebla in 1862. That evening, in place of a firework display, republican artillery coordinated and intensified its shelling. The flashes of more than a hundred guns lit up the dark hills surrounding the town as the projectiles briefly burned fiery arches into the night sky before exploding into the streets below.

Although particularly intense that night, the town was under near-constant artillery fire. Women and children were frequently killed or maimed, adding yet more agony to the besieged. Moreover, any citizens who still had money were forced to make contributions to the imperial coffers, dropping whatever they had off at headquarters at six every afternoon. Provisions were nearly exhausted; horses and mules received no rations whatsoever, although López had somehow managed to find fodder for the emperor's horses. The situation was clear: the imperial army was weakening every day and would soon disintegrate unless it could fight its way out.

This was what was decided at another council of war. The army would repeat Miramón's success of April 27, but to the east and, this time, with no delay, evacuating once the enemy lines were breached.

To disguise the concentration of forces, a call went out for the people of Querétaro to join a volunteer legion. This unit would man the lines, while the main army broke out into the hills of the rough Sierra Gorda, mountainous territory where Mejía had lured and then destroyed previous liberal armies. Here Maximilian could get information from the rest of the country, recruit more soldiers, and rally his forces. If it all proved hopeless, he could make his way to the coast in the hope of finding the Austrian ship and escaping to Europe.

The attack was set for May 13. After Mejía had trouble recruiting the civilian force, however, it was agreed that the mission be pushed back to midnight the following day. As everything was readied, Maximilian, in case he was captured, divided his money and possessions amongst his closest entourage, Salm-Salm, Blasio, Basch, and López. The latter would personally guard Maximilian with his Empress' Regiment. At ten another council of war was convened to agree on the plan of attack, but still Mejía did not feel his volunteers were ready and requested yet another twenty-four-hour delay. Although the generals agreed, Maximilian insisted that this should be the final postponement. Salm-Salm complained that Mejía had enough men to cover their escape. "Well," Maximilian replied, "one day, more or less, will be no matter."[23] Before retiring to bed, Maximilian asked to see López. Giving him a medal for bravery, the emperor ordered that if he fell wounded and could not escape López was to end his life with a bullet.

Maximilian, suffering from dysentery, did not go to bed until one in the morning, but could not sleep because of stomach cramps. He called Basch to his bedside at two thirty, and the doctor stayed with him for nearly an hour before retiring. Meanwhile, Salm-Salm, still annoyed about the delay, drained a bottle of champagne before going to sleep.

AT FIVE IN the morning López burst into Salm-Salm's room. "Quick!" he shouted. "Save the life of the emperor, the enemy is already in the [convent]". Salm-Salm, who slept in his uniform, grabbed his sword and revolver as Maximilian's servant came into his room, asking him to go to the emperor.

At that moment, Basch ran in, asking the Prussian what was happening. "We have been taken by surprise", replied Salm-Salm. "Tell the hussars to mount and be ready" outside.

After relaying the order, Basch went to Maximilian, who said calmly, "Nothing will happen. The enemy has broken into the kitchen gardens. Take your pistol and follow me out into the square." Basch hurried out of the room to fetch his gun.

"Salm," Maximilian, still composed, said to the Prussian when he arrived, "we will go to the [Cerro de las Campanas], and see how we can arrange the matter. I shall follow you directly."

Running outside to ready the horses, Salm-Salm was astonished to find the square in front of the convent deserted. Eventually, he ran into the commanding officer of the hussars and ordered them to muster in the square. As he turned to go back inside, in the dim morning light, Salm-Salm made out the grey uniforms of the Supremos Poderes, Juárez's elite soldiers, approaching the convent. Salm-Salm then bounded back to the emperor, who himself was coming down the stairs, with a greatcoat over his military uniform, sword at his side, and a revolver in each hand. Taking Maximilian's arm, Salm-Salm pointed to the door at the bottom of the staircase and shouted at the emperor, "The enemy is there!"

It was too late. As they left the convent into the main square, liberal soldiers, who had occupied the plaza, stopped them. Salm-Salm raised one of his revolvers, but Maximilian gestured with his hand to lower it. Then a Juarista officer stepped forward and looked over the emperor and his companions. "Let them pass", he told his men. "They are civilians".[24]

Querétaro had descended into chaos, as liberal troops attacked imperialista lines and shells rained down. In the confusion, Maximilian, having left the grounds of the convent, was determined to march across the city to the Cerro de las Campanas, where he hoped to rally his troops. He sent messengers to Mejía and Miramón to join him there.

As they reached the town's main square, López appeared on horseback.

"What is it?" Maximilian asked.

"Everything is lost. Your Majesty can see the enemy troops closing in around us."[25] López urged Maximilian to hide in a nearby house to save his life.

"Never! We will keep on to the Cerro de las Campanas."[26]

As they reached the foot of the hill, more and more imperialistas joined them. The Cerro de las Campanas was held by a few officers and a hundred or so infantry with four artillery guns. Maximilian scrambled up the hill. As he did so, a Mexican officer collapsed, exhausted. Salm-Salm took one arm and Maximilian the other, dragging him up the steep incline, as shells burst all around them.

At the top, Mejía, Ernst Pitner, Salm-Salm, and a few other officers were with the emperor. One of them informed Maximilian that Miramón had been shot in the face trying to fight his way through the streets and was lying wounded in a house below. By now it was a wonderfully bright, clear morning, the whole town visible to Maximilian. Looking down, he saw thousands of liberals swarming towards the hill with cavalry behind them; three separate artillery batteries opened fire.

As the shells crashed around him, the emperor turned to Salm-Salm and said, "Now for a lucky bullet."[27]

Then, speaking to Mejía, Maximilian said, "Let us get on our horses and try to get through", before adding, "If we cannot get out we can at least die in the attempt." Mejía gestured that this was hopeless. While they were speaking, a shell landed a few paces away, throwing dirt over Maximilian. When Maximilian asked again if they could escape, the general replied, "I care but little whether I am killed; but I will not take on the responsibility of leading your majesty to certain death."[28]

Maximilian could see that the town of Querétaro had fallen, his army surrendering. After burning some papers, he ordered an officer to raise the white flag. Unbuttoning his greatcoat to reveal his military uniform, and leaning on his sword, Maximilian awaited the republicans.

A few moments later, a deputation arrived to take him to Escobedo. Maximilian was escorted down the hill and out of the town to the western plain. Finally, he reached Escobedo's headquarters. "I am your prisoner," said Maximilian. Then the archduke Ferdinand Maximilian, born at the Habsburg palace of Schönbrunn, offered his sword to Escobedo, a former farm labourer from the harsh sierras of Nuevo León. If blood must be spilt, Maximilian said, then let it be only his, before pleading for his closest officers and friends to be spared. Juárez's government, replied Escobedo, would decide everyone's fate.

Maximilian was then taken back to the convent. His former room became his prison cell. He was kept company by Salm-Salm, Blasio, and two other officers. Basch, who had been captured before he could escape the convent, was reunited with Maximilian. When he saw his doctor, he embraced him, tears rolling down his cheeks. Regaining his composure, Maximilian pressed Basch's hand and then turned away with a deep sigh.

Breaking the long silence, Maximilian said, "I am happy that everything has happened without more bloodshed. I have done what I intended to do. I have cared for you all." He told the small group how impressed he was with Escobedo's conduct, remarking that his own clemency seemed to have had a good effect on the liberals.

With that Maximilian doubled up in pain, still suffering from dysentery. Basch put him to bed, surprised to find that the emperor had on his person a box of opium pills grabbed from his bedside table that same morning. "You see," he remarked, "you must never lose your head. This, morning when I already knew that we were betrayed, I did not forget to bring that with me."[29]

MAXIMILIAN WAS RIGHT: he had been betrayed. The previous night, Colonel Miguel López, commander of the Empress' Regiment, had crossed the lines into the republican camp. Claiming to be an intermediary for Maximilian, López said he would deliver the convent if Maximilian was allowed to go free. Escobedo told him that he could accept nothing short of unconditional surrender. The counteroffer was that López's own life would be guaranteed, and enriched by $30,000, if he guided liberal troops into the emperor's headquarters.

So it was that at three on the morning of May 15, López met the commander of a detachment of liberal forces, José Rincon y Gallardo, and had led him into the grounds of the convent. There the imperialista colonel had ordered the emperor's guards to stand down. When liberal troops had silently occupied the grounds, López calmly entered the convent before sprinting to Salm-Salm's room, shouting that the enemy was upon them. This was why when Basch ran into the courtyard to find his horse, he was greeted by republican bayonets and placed under arrest. But Rincon y Gallardo had thought it shameful to take Maximilian prisoner after such deception. It was Rincon y Gallardo that Maximilian and Salm-Salm had encountered that morning—he was the officer who had allowed them to escape from the convent, where they now waited to see whether Juárez's government would be as lenient.

10

THE TRIAL

When Maximilian's health worsened, it was decided to move him to more salubrious imprisonment, another convent nearby. Too weak to walk, Maximilian went by carriage, his generals on foot. As the other prisoners caught up with him, respectfully removing their hats, Maximilian laughed and said, "No monarch can boast of a larger court."[1] This court, made up of José Luis Blasio, Samuel Basch, and Felix Salm-Salm along with several other high-ranking imperialistas, was now crammed into a room adjacent to Maximilian's.

Some of the emperor's commanders refused to surrender themselves and hid in the town. Mariano Escobedo decreed that those who did not present themselves within twenty-four hours would be shot, but General Ramón Méndez refused to give himself up. It was not long before he was discovered. The next morning he was marched past the prisoners watching from the convent's windows. Smiling and smoking a cigar, he offered his former comrades a cheerful wave. Later that day, he was escorted into the street, pushed to his knees against a wall, and then his guards readied to shoot him in the back as a traitor. As the order to fire was given, he turned round to face the guns on one knee and shouted "Viva Mexico!" before collapsing under the bullets.

This little reassured Maximilian and his fellow prisoners, but they at least received news of the outside world on May 20 when Felix Salm-Salm was reunited with his wife, Agnes, who had made her way to Querétaro from Mexico City. Seeing her husband for the first time in months, she recalled, "He was not shaved, wore a collar several days old, and looked altogether as if he had emerged from a dustbin".[2] She wept as they embraced, nearly fainting. Felix then introduced her to the sick and pale emperor. It was from her that Maximilian learned of Márquez's betrayal.

Maximilian already knew that instead of returning with men and money to Querétaro, his lieutenant-general had disobeyed orders and marched to Puebla, where his forces were routed. What Maximilian did not know was that Márquez still held Mexico City. Although Porfirio Díaz's army surrounded the capital, Márquez not only had refused to surrender but, in a reversal of roles, now lied to the population, claiming Maximilian would soon relieve Mexico City. Hearing this, Maximilian offered to abdicate, surrender Mexico City to Juárez, and leave for Europe, swearing never to return. In informal conversations, Escobedo was amenable if noncommittal. Soon, however, the general received the order from Benito Juárez's government that Maximilian was to be prosecuted under the law of January 25, 1862.

Put simply, this law condemned to death anyone who supported the French intervention. As the principal agent of that intervention, Maximilian was, of course, guilty. In case Escobedo was under any doubt, the order from Juárez's government stated that the "notorious facts of Maximilian's conduct include the greatest number of liabilities specified in this law."[3] Moreover, under this law, a court-martial, not a civil trial, passed judgement. Military officers appointed from the republican army would decide the case. Maximilian was moved to a more secure prison, another former convent, this time a Capuchin one. As his room had not been readied, Maximilian spent the first night in the crypt. Deep in the convent, the names of dead nuns carved on the walls, he spent the night amongst their tombs. It was to remind him, so a republican officer remarked, of what was to come.

The next day he was moved to a six-by-four-foot cell on the upper floor, with an uncovered window looking onto a large patio below where orange trees grew. With no more than a bed, a washstand, and a table, Maximilian made himself at home as best he could, hanging a serape over the window to give himself some privacy. A trunk with a few personal possessions had been found, and Maximilian arranged these neatly on the table alongside a silver candlestick holder. Whenever a visitor dislodged his possessions on the table, Maximilian became upset, hurriedly rearranging them. Mejía and Miramón, who were to be tried with Maximilian, were given adjoining cells.

On May 24, the prosecutor visited the emperor and read aloud the charges before, somewhat farcically, asking Maximilian to confirm his identity, place of birth, and parents. The humiliation did not faze Maximilian. The indictment, he told Basch, was "laughable, clumsy and spitefully made". Determined to defend himself, Maximilian told his doctor, "I am something of a lawyer myself. They will have a hard fight with me. I do not give up easily."[4]

As local lawyers prepared Maximilian's defence, a telegram was sent to Mexico City to engage two prominent attorneys and request that foreign diplomats hurry to Querétaro to give international weight to the appeal. The capital, however, was still held by Márquez and under siege. Even if anyone could get out, the court-martial was due to start before they would arrive. Agnes Salm-Salm therefore went to San Luis Potosí to plead before Juárez for more time.

Although well aware of his wife's powers of persuasion, Felix Salm-Salm was convinced that the court-martial would merely deliver a prejudged verdict of death. Escape, he explained to Maximilian, was the only way to save their lives. At first, the emperor was horrified, arguing that to run was dishonourable, but Salm-Salm convinced him that his honour had been satisfied through the heroic defence of Querétaro. The trial was a farce. He must save himself.

Salm-Salm's bonhomie made him a favourite with the guards. He arranged to meet a liberal officer, plied him with wine, and then brought him into the plan. Opening the conversation, Salm-Salm said that he knew the officer had not been paid for months, but if he helped Maximilian escape he would give him $3,000. Salm-Salm then showed him the money before adding that once they reached Havana, he would receive another thousand ounces in gold. Thus having bought off the guard, Salm-Salm began to put the plan into effect. As they were under constant surveillance, Maximilian's servant, who brought the prisoners breakfast every morning, hid coded notes in the bread. Salm-Salm's task was made all the more difficult because Maximilian now insisted he would not flee without Mejía and Miramón. Undeterred, Salm-Salm managed to secure horses and revolvers for all of them.

On the morning of May 30, Salm-Salm discovered a note with his breakfast. Maximilian requested spectacles as a disguise for the escape. "On the horse must be fixed two serapes, two revolvers, and a sabre. Not to forget bread or biscuit, red wine and chocolate."[5] The emperor refused to shave his distinctive beard, but agreed to tie it behind his neck and put on the glasses. The plan was to ride into the Sierra Gorda and then make for the coast and get to Veracruz, which was still under imperial control. There an Austrian ship would take Maximilian to Europe. The bribed officer, though, insisted that escape was not possible unless the commanding officer of the cavalry guard was also won over. Salm-Salm offered this man $5,000, and Maximilian signed a bill of credit for the sum. Everything in place, the guards bribed, early in the afternoon on June 2, Salm-Salm confirmed with Maximilian that they would slip away that same night.

One week earlier, outside Mexico City, the republican general Porfirio Díaz received a telegram addressed to the two lawyers Maximilian had nominated as well as one to Baron Anton von Magnus, a Prussian diplomat, requesting they come to Querétaro. For four days, Díaz held onto the telegram, unsure as to how to deliver it while the city was under siege. Eventually, a way was found, but Márquez would not let the diplomats or lawyers leave. Although privately he knew the emperor was imprisoned, Márquez publicly denied it. Augustin Fischer interceded, pleading with the general to let the lawyers defend Maximilian, but Márquez refused. After they threatened to reveal to the people of Mexico City that Márquez was lying, he reluctantly allowed the diplomats—Maximilian requested the Belgian and Austrian representatives as well—and lawyers to pass through Díaz's lines. Alphonse Dano offered to go, but was told a French presence would only harm Maximilian's defence. He therefore sent a former consul, Antoine Forest, as an unofficial envoy, charging him to do everything in his power to help.

On June 1, the representatives of the most powerful monarchies in Europe, and Belgium, made their way to the outskirts of the defence perimeter on their mission to save a Habsburg. When hundreds of desperate and starving citizens tried to evacuate the city with them, the republican artillery opened fire, mistaking the crowd for an infantry assault. Shells exploded around the lawyers and diplomats, and then a secretary in the Prussian legation seized a horse, improvised a white flag, and galloped to the soldiers. Finally, the party was allowed through.

Meanwhile, in San Luis Potosí, Agnes Salm-Salm had secured an audience with Juárez. She asked the president for more time, at least until the lawyers made it to Querétaro from the capital. It is unlikely she had much sway over him—she spoke no Spanish, and one of Juárez's ministers had to translate—but other appeals had reached the president. When he had learned that Maximilian was under siege in Querétaro, Franz Joseph, anxious for his brother's safety, had asked Secretary of State William Seward to use US suasion to urge Juárez to be lenient. After speaking with President Andrew Johnson the same day, Seward warned the liberals through diplomatic channels that executing Maximilian would damage Mexico's reputation and the republican cause throughout the world. Juárez recognised that the trial of Maximilian must not appear rushed. He approved the delay. The trial was now scheduled for June 13.

Determined to give the news to Maximilian in person, Agnes Salm-Salm travelled overnight to Querétaro. The weather made the roads so bad that she often had to get out and walk, the stones cutting her feet through her thin boots. Arriving at the town on May 31, her boots torn to pieces, hair dishevelled, and, in her own words, looking like a "scarecrow", rather than change she hurried to Maximilian. When she told the emperor that the delay had been granted, he took her hand, kissed it, and said, "May god bless you, madame!"[6] After exchanging a few more words, Maximilian abruptly turned away and walked to the window. Staring out of it, his back to Agnes, he broke down in tears.

In the days that followed, Felix and Agnes disagreed over what to do next. The former remained convinced that flight was the only way to save Maximilian's life; however, Agnes argued, heatedly and in front of the emperor, that the time was not right and the plan badly flawed. Maximilian, as ever, wavered, but told Felix to not yet cancel the arrangements made for June 2.

In the early afternoon of June 2, Salm-Salm confirmed that the plan was set. They could slip away quietly that same night. But later that day Maximilian received a telegram announcing that the diplomats and his lawyers were on their way. Hours before the escape, he summoned Salm-Salm to his room at five o'clock. "What would the ministers, whom I invited here, say if they arrived and did not find me!" Salm-Salm replied that they would be happy he escaped, but Maximilian answered, "A few days more or less will be of no account".[7] But, the next day, the bribed guards were replaced, the number of soldiers on duty trebled, and surveillance intensified with random inspections of the prison cells. With escape now impossible, Maximilian's life depended on the court-martial.

After Maximilian's lawyers discussed the case with him, they concluded that the military tribunal at Querétaro was only a show trial. It was in Juárez's cabinet where things would be decided, and so they went to San Luis Potosí to sway the outcome there. Maximilian had chosen his legal representatives carefully. Mariano Riva Palacio, the father of Vicente, the general who had taken part in the siege of Querétaro, and Rafael Martínez de la Torre were well-known liberals connected with the upper echelons of the party. While there was no chance they could persuade Juárez that Maximilian was innocent, they were confident that their influence combined with the weight of international opinion would prevent the death penalty. After all, heads of state were not executed in the nineteenth century. Napoleon I, who had the entire continent of Europe united against him, was twice exiled rather than killed. More appositely, Jefferson Davis, president of the Confederacy, was currently imprisoned in Virginia for treason, but would ultimately be released and granted amnesty. And this was exactly what the man who had done so much to put Davis in prison recommended. If he were Mexican, Juárez's most passionate US supporter, Ulysses S. Grant, reasoned, he would try Maximilian and then pardon him.

Awaiting the trial in prison, feverish and suffering from stomach cramps, Maximilian often stayed in bed until midday and then returned to it at about five. In the hours between, sunlight turned the small cells into furnaces, driving the prisoners into a gallery outside their rooms. There Mejía, Miramón, Salm-Salm, and Basch played dominoes with Maximilian to pass the time. When available, wine and cognac provided further relief. Although suffering mentally and physically, Maximilian still had hope for the future. Walking amongst the orange trees in the courtyard of the convent with Blasio, he told his secretary that they would go to London together. "We'll stay there a year, have my papers brought from Miramar and write the history of my reign. Then we shall go to Naples, and rent a house in one of the beautiful suburbs". Taking out Maximilian's yacht, Billimeck and Basch would join them sailing to Greece. He told Salm-Salm that he would go to Europe with Miramón and Mejía and settle them in Spain before going to meet his mother and Carlota.[8]

Yet for all the talk of the future, Maximilian's past still haunted him. He told Dano's representative, Forest, that he wanted it to be known in Europe that his "improvised army" was loyal to the end and, somewhat contradictorily, that it had been defeated only by treachery. "The wretched [López] sold us for 11 *reales* a head. However, his betrayal is less despicable to me than that of General Márquez", Maximilian said with passion. "If I could punish one I would chose Márquez! He is responsible for everything, even López's crime!" It was not only Márquez that upset Maximilian. Referring to his final meeting with Dano, where the Frenchman had insisted he abdicate, Maximilian said, "Once, at Puebla, we had a heated exchange. I was angry, but not with him, with his instructions, which badly hurt me". "Deep in my heart", the emperor insisted, "there is no bile or bitterness".[9]

This was less evident in conversation with the other diplomats. Now that he was a soldier, Maximilian told the Prussian representative, Baron Anton von Magnus, he would enrol in the Prussian army when he returned to Europe and fight against France, such was his hatred for the country. Maximilian maintained that he had been deceived and then abandoned by Napoleon III in Paris, while Bazaine had betrayed him in Mexico. From memory, he quoted the letter the French emperor had written: "What, indeed, would you think of me if, once Your Imperial Majesty had arrived in Mexico, I were to say that I can no longer fulfil the conditions to which I have set my signature?" The perfidy of France would be a key part of Maximilian's public defence.

Not that Maximilian wanted to hear this defence in person. On June 12, the eve of the trial, he exclaimed, "I do not want to appear before the court. Never, never will I sit in the dock!" When Forest, Dano's representative, tried to calm him with the (hardly reassuring) examples of Louis XVI and Marie Antoinette, Maximilian, interrupting, shouted, "I will not go to the court!" Stressing how weak and sick he was, the emperor cried, "Oh, it is impossible for me to go to the court!"[10] After Basch exaggerated his illness to the doctor appointed by the liberals, Maximilian was granted a certificate exempting him from appearing.

AT EIGHT ON June 13, the court-martial began. Held in a theatre, named after Agustín de Iturbide, the first emperor of Mexico, executed in 1824, the symbolism was hardly subtle. The panel of judges comprised six captains, none older than twenty-four, with a lieutenant-colonel, in his midthirties, presiding. The trial took place on the stage, lit as for a performance, with the accused on stools. Mejía, who was seriously ill, and Miramón, despite the bullet wound to his face, were forced to attend. They appeared at nine, before an audience of a few hundred, mostly made up of military officers.

The prosecution accused Maximilian of thirteen counts under the January 25, 1862, law. The most important charges held that he had taken up arms as a traitor against the republic and that he had signed the Black Decree on October 3, 1865, which resulted in the unlawful deaths of thousands of Mexicans. The emperor's defence denied the competency of the court, before refuting the charges against him and ending with an appeal to compassion.

Antoine Forest watched from the audience. At about four, as Miramón's lawyer was reading his defence, Baron Eduard von Lago, the Austrian envoy to Mexico, found Forest and asked him to leave the theatre. As guards followed them, the Frenchman engaged the Austrian diplomat in banal conversation until they found a safe place to talk. When they entered a large public square, the Austrian made Forest swear not to reveal what he was about to say to anyone. After the Frenchman agreed, Lago explained that Maximilian's escape had been arranged for that evening.

He then outlined the plan. At ten Maximilian would visit a chapel within the former convent. The two colonels in charge of his guard, Villanueva and Palacios, had been bought off with $100,000 each. Lago had the bill of credit on him, which he and Maximilian had signed. All that was needed now were two things. First was $8,000 in gold to bribe the rest of the guard. Forest assured Lago that he had that sum available to him. The second was the signature of another diplomat to the bills of credit to prove to Villanueva and Palacios that they would be honoured in Europe.

Maximilian had managed to get hold of a list of the judges prior to the trial. When he saw that he was to be tried by captains, he now believed that they had been appointed to sentence him to death, a pardon unlikely; escape was his only option. The whole plan had been orchestrated by Agnes Salm-Salm, who had befriended Colonel Villanueva. He spoke good English and had agreed that in return for $100,000 and money to bribe soldiers, he would slip away with the emperor, even providing him with an escort. Basch, Agnes and Felix Salm-Salm, Mejía, and Miramón would flee with Maximilian, who had asked that the Frenchman Forest accompany them as well.

Maximilian, however, had lied to the diplomats so that they would give him the money. Palacios had not yet been won over, and Villanueva refused to do anything unless his fellow officer joined the conspiracy. It fell to Agnes Salm-Salm to bribe Palacios the evening of the escape. After visiting Maximilian, who gave her his signet ring to prove that she spoke on his behalf, Agnes asked Palacios to escort her home from the prison. When they reached her house, she invited the young officer inside.

After twenty minutes of nervous small talk, trembling, Agnes came to the point. She made him swear on his word as an officer and a gentleman, and on the life of his wife and child, that he would not reveal anything to anyone. Then she explained that if the emperor did not escape that night, he would be shot. In return for $100,000, he could save Maximilian's life. Taking the cheque in his hand, Palacios stared at it for some time. Returning it, he said that he could not make a decision that night, but would need to reflect before giving his answer first thing tomorrow morning.

"Isn't the sum enough?" Agnes is reported to have replied. "Well, then colonel, here am I", she said, undressing.[11]

Palacios was unmoved, insisting again he would give his answer the next day. Shortly afterwards, Villanueva arrived to see what the decision was. Then, after ten, Basch came to the princess's house to get news. When Agnes Salm-Salm saw him, she ushered him into another room, returned the signet ring, and said that escape was not possible that night, but to be ready for the next day. Basch then went to Maximilian, returning the ring.

At seven the next morning, Basch, on his way to Maximilian, walked through the streets of Querétaro. A liberal officer stopped him and escorted him to Escobedo. When Basch entered the room, Escobedo smiled at him. "We know what you have been doing. I make you responsible for everything that happens with Maximilian; you are the first I will have hanged."

"Señor," replied Basch, "whatever pleases you."[12]

That same morning, June 14, the European diplomats were on their way to the theatre to watch the second day of the trial. As they approached it, they too were accosted and frog-marched before a general. They had two hours to leave Querétaro, they were told. If they returned within three days, they would be shot.

After meeting with Agnes Salm-Salm, Palacios had gone to Escobedo and told him everything. Thankfully for them, the diplomats had refused to sign the cheque, with the others convincing Baron Lago, who had already signed, to cut his name off the bottom of the document. When Maximilian found out about the conduct of the representative of the Habsburgs in Mexico, he thought it cowardly. "What would it matter if he were hanged?" he remarked.[13] It was, however, a serious blow for Maximilian to have the diplomats sent away in disgrace, their ability to influence Juárez's government now discredited. Fortunately, some days earlier, the Prussian envoy Magnus had gone to San Luis Potosí and could not be tied to the conspiracy.

It took only a day and a half for the court-martial to hear the prosecution and defence. They reached their verdict just before midnight on June 14, but would not release it publicly until Escobedo confirmed it. Maximilian's legal representatives in Querétaro held out no hope and telegrammed Riva Palacio and Martínez de la Torre in San Luis Potosí to act as though the sentence were death. They immediately petitioned Juárez's government to pardon Maximilian, receiving the reply that he could not be pardoned until the sentence was officially released.

At eleven on the morning of June 16, the prosecutor entered Maximilian's cell and read the sentence. With a pale but calm face, Maximilian listened as he was told that he was condemned to death by firing squad. The officer as he left the room turned to Basch, tapped his watch, and said that the execution would be at three. "You still have more than three hours and can settle everything with ease."[14]

Forty-five minutes later, in San Luis Potosí, Maximilian's lawyers received a telegram: "Six o'clock in the afternoon is named for the execution."[15] With Magnus, the two lawyers raced to the palace to make one last appeal to save Maximilian's life. En route they were informed that the telegram had been mistaken; the execution was at three, not six.

Back in Querétaro, a priest arrived at midday to hear Maximilian's confession. Mass was then performed in Miramón's cell before the three condemned men received holy communion. In their final few hours, Miramón, Mejía, and Maximilian spoke with each other, trying to keep each other's spirits up. Maximilian had Basch write letters of farewell, including one to Carlota. "Death is to me a happy release," it ran. "I shall fall proudly as a soldier, like a king defeated but not dishonoured. If your sufferings are too severe, and God calls you to come and join me soon, I shall bless the hand of God which has been heavy upon us." Fifteen minutes before the execution, Maximilian said his final good-bye to Basch. Handing the doctor his wedding ring, he said, "Go to Vienna. Speak to my parents and relatives and report to them about the siege and the last days of my life. Especially you will tell my mother that I fulfilled my duties as a soldier and that I died a good Christian."[16]

As the clock struck three, no one arrived to take the men to the execution. Minutes passed, then an hour. Finally, Colonel Palacios appeared, telegram in hand. It was from Juárez's government in San Luis Potosí. Palacios read it aloud. Maximilian's execution had been postponed for three days. Upon hearing the news, Felix Salm-Salm, in prison awaiting his own trial, procured a bottle of wine to celebrate. Smoking a cigar and humming a tune, he paced up and down his cell excitedly. The postponement of the execution, he reasoned, could only be prelude to a pardon.

Everyone rallied to ensure this happened. Miramón persuaded the tearful Concepción Lombardo, baby and young children in tow, to go to Querétaro to plead for Maximilian's and her husband's lives. The irrepressible Agnes Salm-Salm accompanied her. Meanwhile, Maximilian's lawyers protested that the three condemned men had confessed, received the sacrament, and thus already died morally. "It would be horrible to put them to death a second time".[17] Magnus also reminded Juárez's government that Prussia, all of Europe, and the United States wished Maximilian's life spared. Finally, for his part, Maximilian telegrammed the president to ask for a pardon for Mejía and Miramón. If a victim was necessary, as he had said many times before, it should be only him.

The day before the execution, Agnes saw Juárez. When the president refused the pardon, she fell trembling and crying to her knees, desperately pleading for mercy.

When she stopped, Juárez replied, "I am grieved, madame, to see you thus on your knees before me; but if all the kings and queens of Europe were in your place I could not spare that life. It is not I who take it, it is the people and the law, and if I should not do its will the people would take it and mine also."[18]

Concepción Lombardo, Maximilian's last hope, was not even granted an audience. "Excuse me, gentlemen, from that painful interview", Juárez told Maximilian's lawyers who requested it. As they left the room, Martínez de la Torre suddenly turned and said, "Señor President, no more blood!"

"At this moment," replied Juárez, "you cannot comprehend the necessity for [the execution], nor the justice by which it is supported. That appreciation is reserved for time."[19]

The last-minute intervention on June 16 had been no prelude to pardon. Juárez had merely felt that the execution gave the condemned men insufficient time to put their affairs in order and postponed it for three days. After all, Maximilian represented monarchy and foreign intervention, Miramón the aristocratic creole elite, Mejía indigenous popular and religious conservatism. Juárez had fought against all these forces for more than ten years. Their deaths, he believed, would mark the final triumph of republican liberalism after nearly fifty years of political chaos.

"I am at peace with the world," Maximilian told Magnus the day before his execution. Maximilian's only regret was that he had not been shot two days earlier. "We were completely prepared for death", he remarked, and the delay was very hard to take. It had been a beautiful day, the sky clear and bright. "I have always wanted to die on a very clear day with good weather."

Still sick and weak, false rumours reached Maximilian that Carlota had died. "The only concern I had left in the world", he told Magnus, "was having to leave her alone in the fatal state of mind she was in, but she has already preceded me. Tomorrow I will be reunited with her, so I will die peacefully." In a letter to Magnus, Maximilian wrote that the news of her death had broken his heart, but was also a consolation: he had no other desire left on earth other than to be buried alongside Carlota's body. "I no longer belong to this world," he told Magnus. "I am only an intruder here."[20]

That evening Maximilian read Thomas à Kempis's *Imitation of Christ* before blowing out the candles at about ten and somehow falling asleep. An hour later, he was woken by Escobedo's arrival. But this was no last-minute reprieve. The Mexican general had come only to pay his final respects. Irritated, Maximilian remarked to Basch that he had just gone to sleep. It was another hour before he dropped off again.

He woke at three thirty, and his confessor arrived shortly afterwards. At five, he heard mass with Mejía and Miramón and then breakfasted on coffee, chicken, bread, and a half glass of red wine. Shortly afterwards, the carriages arrived to take the three men to the Cerro de las Campanas, where they would be shot. Remaining serenely calm, Maximilian took off his wedding ring and handed it to Basch for the second time. The doctor broke down, unable to follow him out of the room. Seeing Miramón and Mejía waiting in the corridor, Maximilian asked, "Are you ready, gentlemen?" After they replied that they were, he hugged both men, and they made their way down to the street.

Dressed in black, with a buttoned frock coat and carrying a crucifix, the former emperor of Mexico climbed into the first of three black closed carriages. Under infantry and cavalry escort, this sombre procession made its way slowly towards the execution site, stopping at the foot of the hill. Getting out of his carriage, Maximilian saw a former servant in the waiting crowd. "Now do you believe that they are going to shoot me?" he asked.[21]

The three men took their final steps, each flanked by their confessor, towards the place of execution. Maximilian turned to Mejía and Miramón, embracing them one last time. "Soon", he said, "we will see each other in heaven".[22] With their backs to an uneven adobe wall, they took their places. Before them lay the town they had struggled to hold, a crowd of onlookers, and, directly in front of the condemned, the firing squad. From their executioners' view, Maximilian was on the far right, Miramón in the middle, Mejía to the left. Turning to face straight towards his executioners, Maximilian spoke in clear, loud Spanish: "I forgive everybody, I pray that everyone may also forgive me, and I wish that my blood, which is now to be shed, may be for the good of the country. Long live Mexico, long live independence."[23]

Miramón spoke next; Mejía stayed silent. Maximilian gave some money to his executioners, telling them to aim for his heart. The firing squad was barely five paces away, but he beat his hands against his chest, indicating where they should aim. Then he glanced up at the sky. He had got his wish. It was a cloudless day.

The shots rang out. Maximilian fell to the ground, and smoke gently wisped skywards from the bullet holes in his clothes as he lay dying in the Mexican dust.

EPILOGUE

Maximilian's body was placed in a cheap wooden coffin and taken to the convent where he had been imprisoned. There it was embalmed. According to Felix Salm-Salm, the doctors treated the corpse with disdain, smoking while they prepared it. "What a delight it is for me to be able to wash my hands in the blood of an Emperor!" one remarked. When the liver, heart, and lungs were placed in a box, a guard joked that they should be fed to the dogs.[1]

On his way to Mexico City, Benito Juárez had stopped in Querétaro to see Maximilian dead, the first time the president had laid eyes on the emperor. Rather than return the body to Austria, Juárez hoped to use it as leverage to secure Franz Joseph's recognition of republican Mexico. Thus, Maximilian's clumsily embalmed and decomposing corpse was transferred to Mexico City, where it remained for months until finally permission was given to release it. On November 25, 1867, the coffin was loaded onto Maximilian's beloved ship, the *Novara*, which sailed to Europe.

On January 16, 1868, a boat covered with black velvet and decorated with the coat of arms of the Mexican empire brought the coffin to Trieste. As hundreds of onlookers watched from the wharves, it was carried onto a hearse, driven to the railway station, and put on a train for Vienna. The next day, it was delivered to the Hofburg, where Sophie, Maximilian's mother, threw herself onto the coffin, crying uncontrollably.

THE TACITEAN EPITHET—HAD he never been emperor, no one would have doubted his ability to reign—fits Maximilian perfectly. As a European prince, he was liberal, enlightened, and generous. He brought these qualities to Mexico and tried to put his beliefs into practice. He wanted to improve the lives of his subjects, to free those trapped in peonage from poverty, and make Mexico a great, powerful nation secure from US invasion. He saw himself as a modern, munificent sovereign, a patron of the sciences and the arts, and a champion of education. He even transcended some of the prejudices of his time. Unlike many of his European and, for that matter, Mexican contemporaries, he did not think the indigenous population was beneath contempt, or pre-Columbian Mexican civilisation mere barbarism. Many Mexicans from across the political spectrum supported his empire, some from party loyalty, some from self-interest, but others because they saw the emperor as a leader who could bring peace, stability, and progress after years of civil war.

Unfortunately, he was ill-suited to the task, and his third way of moderate liberalism proved woefully ineffective. In Benito Juárez, Mexican liberals had a hero of reform and civil war, and they did not want an ersatz European version. Moreover, after the civil war of 1858–1861, party hatred was visceral in Mexico. Maximilian's goal of reconciliation between the factions was admirable, but impractical. The constitution he spent so long drawing up in Europe was never implemented in Mexico because the empire never seemed stable enough.

Yet Maximilian governed as though the Mexican empire were a strong, established state, rather than a precarious edifice built by conservative émigrés and French bayonets. Foreign invasion tainted his empire in the eyes of nationalists, its reactionary conservative origins alienated liberals, and US opposition meant that it had a powerful foe north of the border. No amount of royal tours, etiquette, or personal charisma would change this.

But the emperor's hubris should not be forgotten in his downfall. This was a man divorced from reality, a man used to bending the world to his imagination, as he had creating his fairy-tale castle of Miramar. Here he received ample warning that his reign would not be welcomed in Mexico and would require force to impose it. He procrastinated for more than two years, cognisant that his first condition for accepting the crown—British support—could never be met. Perhaps he allowed himself to be convinced that the second condition—popular support—had been fulfilled because of the relentless French campaign of disinformation, but the military problems the intervention faced should have disabused him of this as well. Yet Maximilian went anyway. He had thought his Habsburg lineage might put him beyond the forces of history. As support for his regime crumbled, it showed the limits of human agency for even the most powerful of aristocrats.

By the time the French left in 1867, the showdown between Juaristas and imperialistas was a one-sided affair, one Maximilian could have avoided had he abdicated. But just as his belief in his Habsburg destiny brought him to Mexico, his veneration for Habsburg honour kept him there. When imprisoned, he was fond of quoting the sixteenth-century French king Francis I, who, after a catastrophic defeat—against a Habsburg army, no less—supposedly wrote, "All is lost save honour".[2] This idea of honour consumed Maximilian, crippling his decision making. When confronted with a choice—to take the throne, to abdicate, to escape—the question for Maximilian was always whether it was honourable. His tendency to vacillate made these decisions especially tortuous, not least for Maximilian, who suffered from depression. If the squalor of his final few months in Querétaro was far removed from the splendour of his dynasty, in his own mind his final stand was heroic.

For his mistakes, he paid the ultimate price. It is perhaps fitting then that if Maximilian is remembered at all outside of Mexico, it is for his death. In Édouard Manet's *Execution of Maximilian*, the serenity, calm, and stoicism—the honour—of Maximilian's death is what strikes the viewer. The detail of the painting is not accurate, for Maximilian did not stand in the centre, nor did he wear a sombrero, but it captures a wider truth.

BEYOND A DEPICTION of honour and dignity, Manet's painting conveyed another message Maximilian would have welcomed. The soldiers in the painting wear uniforms almost identical to French troops, and the man preparing for the coup de grâce shares the conspicuous features of Napoleon III. The implication was clear: Napoleon III had blood on his hands. Unsurprisingly, the painting was banned from public display in Paris.

When defending his government in the Corps législatif against the eviscerating attacks of opposition deputies like Jules Favre, Napoleon III's minister Eugène Rouher appealed to posterity. The idea behind the Mexican expedition, Rouher said, would one day be recognised as great. "And, if, later, someone casts their eyes on our old debates and long-forgotten arguments, if he takes the historian's pen, he will say: 'this was a man of genius'" who took France to Mexico. "Yes," concluded Rouher, "this page will be glorious and the writer who traces it will say, 'these distant expeditions begun for the reparation of our honour have ended with the triumph of our interests.'"[3]

No historian will ever write that. With Maximilian's execution, intervention in Mexico was recognised as a cataclysmic failure months after the last French soldiers returned. A monumental gamble—outrageous even by the standards of European imperialism—Napoleon III's policy unleashed yet more chaos and violence in Mexico and further impoverished a poor nation. As for the idea behind it, stopping US hegemony, it was the greatest challenge to the Monroe Doctrine until the Cuban missile crisis nearly one hundred years later; however, at the cost of billions of dollars in today's money and thousands of lives, far from checking US power, Napoleon III was merely afforded the opportunity to witness it firsthand: forced to withdraw French forces from Mexico to avoid war with its northern neighbour.

In many ways, this failure was of Napoleon III's own making. He wanted to extend French power on the cheap: Mexico would pay for the privilege of its own occupation. The Treaty of Miramar and the two loans placed burdens on Maximilian's treasury that it could not meet. Napoleon III criticised Maximilian's inability to solve Mexico's financial problems, but the Mexican budget could never have been balanced with so much debt owed to France. Napoleon III bankrupted Maximilian's empire before it began.

Mexico was not the last of the French emperor's foreign policy disasters. On July 28, 1870, Napoleon III, in excruciating agony with gallstones, left Paris to take command of his own army in a desperate attempt to save his regime after declaring war on Prussia. Like Maximilian, he ended up under siege, in the small northeastern town of Sedan. The scale may have been different—Napoleon III had some 130,000 troops under his command—but the situation was remarkably similar to what Maximilian had faced. Outnumbered and with German guns occupying the surrounding hills, the French emperor was confronted with the same choice as his Mexican counterpart. Unlike Maximilian, Napoleon III did not resist to the end, surrendering, on September 2, only days after the siege began. Two days later a republic, France's third, was proclaimed.

The former emperor was imprisoned, in far greater luxury than Maximilian had enjoyed, but escape was not necessary. He was released months later and made his way to England. There, in Chislehurst, Kent, he was reunited with wife and son. On the morning of January 9, 1873, Louis-Napoleon, as he now was again, passed away, his final thoughts also about honour: "We were not cowards at Sedan, were we?" he whispered before death.[4]

The Franco-Prussian War drew in other characters from Mexico. Felix Salm-Salm fulfilled one of Maximilian's last wishes: taking up arms against the French, having enlisted in the Prussian army. As ever, Agnes accompanied him, serving as a field nurse. Then on

August 18, 1870, Felix was mortally wounded, dying in agony three hours later; he had with him a souvenir Maximilian had given him.

The Franco-Prussian War did not end with the battle of Sedan; the newly proclaimed French republic fought on. Now commander of the Army of the Rhine, Achille Bazaine was also besieged, at Metz, with 165,000 men. With food running out, disease spreading, and little love for the new republic, Bazaine too surrendered. There were more parallels with Maximilian. After peace was signed, France needed a scapegoat for the disastrous war, and Bazaine fitted perfectly. Charged with treason, he was found guilty and sentenced to death.

This condemnation was commuted to a prison sentence on the Île Sainte-Marguerite. In August 1874, disguised as a workman, Bazaine put a sack of rubbish over his shoulder and walked out of the prison and onto a boat, where his Mexican wife, Josefa Peña, was waiting. They managed to evade the authorities, fleeing to Madrid. Josefa soon tired of Spain and returned to Mexico, leaving her husband behind. Bazaine, once the most powerful man in Mexico, spent his final years alone in abject poverty, dying in 1888. The French press reported news of his death with delight. The man who had spent his life fighting for France remained forever a traitor.

IN MEXICO, Juárez's republic dealt with its own traitorous enemies. Chief amongst them was Leonardo Márquez. He held Mexico City until June 21, 1867, two days after Maximilian's execution. Márquez ruled the capital as a personal fiefdom, extorting money from the inhabitants and giving up the struggle only when an Austrian diplomat got word to Maximilian's remaining foreign volunteers, still garrisoning the city, that their emperor was dead. Porfirio Díaz then took the capital, and imperialistas were hunted down. Santiago Vidaurri was found and promptly executed. Márquez, however, managed to evade the authorities and, after months in hiding, fled to Havana, where he died at the age of ninety-three in 1913.

José María Gutiérrez de Estrada died in Paris in 1867, supposedly of a broken heart at the collapse of the empire he had done so much to create. Juan Nepomuceno Almonte, also in France, was dead two years later. José Manuel Hidalgo y Esnaurrízar, whose dreams of a monarchy in Mexico always showed a talent for fiction, became a novelist, passing away in 1896.

Until recently, Maximilian's empire was buried in official Mexican history, dismissed as the work of fanatical reactionaries, traitors, and European imperialists. All three could be found at the heart of Maximilian's empire, but they had to work alongside many who considered themselves liberals, patriots, and heroes of Mexico's earlier wars. Caught between European and US imperialism, many were drawn to the Mexican empire, preferring the former to oppose the latter, but, with Union victory in the American Civil War and the end of Maximilian's empire, the 1860s was a crucial decade on the road to a later US-dominated world order.

When visiting Maximilian's opulent imperial rooms at Chapultepec today, therefore, this subsequent history makes them feel absurdly out of place, odd ephemera of a forgotten empire, of a European dynastic order unravelling on its own continent, let alone capable of reasserting itself across the Atlantic.

Yet the collapse of Maximilian's empire did not usher in a triumphant new era of Mexican democracy. Benito Juárez has become one of the great figures of Mexican history, perhaps the greatest. And rightly so: his bravery, courage, and unswerving belief in republicanism and liberalism saw him defeat all his foes, seemingly, at times, against impossible odds. He remains a unifying and inspirational figure in Mexico, although his victory at the time was short lived. Elected president in 1867, he stood again in 1871. Accused of accumulating too much power in his own hands, he was opposed by Porfirio Díaz. When no candidate won a majority, congress named Juárez president, but he died the next year, leaving a divided Mexico to his successor, Sebastián Lerdo de Tejada.

Having lost the 1871 election, Porfirio Díaz launched an armed revolt. In this attempt, Díaz failed, but when Lerdo de Tejada sought reelection in 1876 the general rebelled again, this time successfully. Díaz may have fought the French under the republican banner, but he would have agreed with Napoleon III that what was needed in Mexico was not parliamentary liberty, but a liberal dictatorship. That is exactly what Díaz created. He ruled for the next thirty-four years. Known as the *Porfiriato*, this regime gave Mexico a degree of political stability for the first time since independence, but under an authoritarian system where absolute power was in the former Juarista's hands.

It was also a regime in which US interests increasingly dominated. The fears of imperialistas never came to pass; there was no more US expansion at Mexico's expense. This was not because of some altruistic new policy in Washington, but rather because capital and business advanced US interests far more effectively, and profitably, than conquest. Díaz well understood this unequal relationship—the quote "Poor Mexico, so far from God, so close to the United States" is usually attributed to him—but by the end of his reign, much of Mexico was owned by US businesses. Most notoriously, Standard Oil dominated Mexico's petroleum industry, but US companies or capital controlled numerous mines, factories, railroads, department stores, and huge tracts of land. This neocolonial exploitation of Mexico's economy by Washington and Wall Street ensured that anti-Americanism went from the preserve of Catholic conservatives in the 1850s and 1860s to the liberal and radical Left in the years leading up to Díaz's fall. When he announced in 1910 that, at the age of eighty, he would run again for president, it sparked the Mexican Revolution. One year later, Díaz was forced into exile; he died in Paris in 1915.

In some ways, Mexico's subsequent relations with the United States were more fortunate than many Latin American nations. While Veracruz was briefly occupied in 1914 and two years later the

US Army spent months wandering the deserts of Chihuahua looking for the Mexican revolutionary Pancho Villa, the United States generally refrained from military interventions in Mexico. Other nations were not so lucky. In 1898 the United States confirmed itself an imperial power, invading Cuba, Puerto Rico, and the Philippines. Nor did Washington stop there, for there were numerous armed interventions in Latin American countries, especially between the years 1898 and 1933. And as the American imperial project proceeded into the twentieth century and beyond, extending farther across the globe, it would frequently deploy the strategy that failed in Mexico—regime change. The problems Maximilian and the French army faced became familiar to US commanders in Vietnam, Afghanistan, and Iraq. After all, as Carlota wrote, without the love of the people, bayonets alone can never support lost causes.

It was cold, very cold. The night before had been freezing, and in the morning the snow began to fall, covering the Belgian village of Meysse with a white shroud that thickened by the hour. Only the black branches of trees stood out against the grey sky. Nearby, the villagers lined a road that led up to a castle. They had come to watch a funeral procession. Four horses pulled the hearse, which was driven to a nearby chapel where the coffin came to rest. As mourners paid their respects, they read the inscription on the casket: "Her Majesty", Carlota, "princess of Belgium, born Laeken 7 June 1840, died Bouchout Castle 19 January 1927, widow of archduke Maximilian, emperor of Mexico."

After Carlota left Rome in October 1866, she had returned to Miramar, where doctors insisted she be kept in isolation in a small garden house on the castle grounds. It was not until July 1867 that she was moved to the palace of Laeken, the official residence of Belgian royalty. There her family was so worried about her mental health that they hid the news of Maximilian's execution. In January 1868, when Carlota was finally told that her husband was dead, she fell crying into the arms of her sister-in-law Marie-Henriette. Carlota's pain, her sister-in-law related, was offset by the thought that Maximilian had died gloriously.

It was hoped that Carlota would make a full recovery. She never did. For nearly sixty years, her life was one of lucidity interspersed with moments where she lost all reason. After Laeken, she lived in Tervuren Castle, on the outskirts of Brussels. It burned down in 1879. "How beautiful!" Carlota cried out as she watched the flames consume the building. For the rest of her long, lonely life, she lived in the austere Bouchout Castle, to the north of the capital. Sometimes she wandered its corridors, crying out "Maximilian is not here!"; once she was found at a piano, softly playing the Mexican national anthem.

She died in 1927, far outlasting Napoleon III, who continued to haunt her dreams. By that time, the Habsburg dynasty, which when she married into it seemed the most important in the world, was becoming little more than a quaint memory, having disintegrated after defeat in the First World War. When taking the decision that unleashed this conflict across Europe, the octogenarian Franz Joseph led his empire into it with words reminiscent of his younger brother: "If we must perish, we should do so with honour."[5] As for the empire Maximilian and Carlota had once ruled over a half century earlier, hardly anyone remembered it.

ACKNOWLEDGMENTS

E normous thanks are due to all those who made this book possible, including Patrick Walsh and everyone at Pew Literary as well as the fantastic people at Basic Books and Faber & Faber. Editors Claire Potter, Ella Griffiths, and Alex Bowler provided brilliant, invaluable feedback after close reading of drafts and have been extremely generous with their time. I am also tremendously grateful to Brandon Proia, who provided marvellously granular line edits, as well as all those involved in copyediting and proofing the manuscript.

There have been many brilliant academics who have contributed either in person or through their published works to my understanding of the Second Mexican Empire, but I would especially like to thank Professor Nicola Miller for all her support and guidance over the years. I also owe a great intellectual debt to Dr David Dodd and his analysis of nineteenth-century French imperialism.

Friends and family have been especially supportive while I've written this book. Long, rambling conversations—well, I say conversations, when sometimes they've been more like monologues—with Orazio, Ben, Albert, and David have been hugely enjoyable, for me at least. In fact, special thanks to David, who insisted I write a book, which I now suspect he did so I would stop talking to him about it.

ACKNOWLEDGMENTS

My father, a very talented writer and storyteller, was kind enough to bring his literary flair to the very earliest drafts of the text, while his partner, Margaret, has been very supportive over the years. Peter and Christabel too have been reassuring, helpful, and loving. Christabel helped me pursue my academic studies, and I am eternally grateful to her. My brother, Alex, similarly subjected to monologues like my friends, has been brilliantly sympathetic, kind, and encouraging along the way. I would also like to thank his wife, Helen, and wish them all the best as they look after their baby daughter, Amy May Christabel Shawcross. Without Catherine and Ian's help, it would not have been possible to write this book, and I am very appreciative of everything they have done over the years—thank you. Sadly, my mother passed away some time ago. She always provided great love and care and nurtured my interest in history. I like to think she would have been proud of this book.

Finally, to my partner, Hannah, who gave birth to our beautiful baby girl, Ena Marion Shawcross-Stone, on May 14, 2020. A global pandemic is not the easiest time to have a baby, and without Hannah's love and support it would not have been possible to write this book at the same time. I love her immensely, and this book is dedicated to my two dearly beloved treasures, Hannah and Ena.

NOTES

This work draws on some ten years of research focussed on the Second Mexican and French empires, including much time in the archives of Mexico City, Vienna, Paris, and London. Space precludes a wider bibliography, and I have kept notes to quotations only.

400AP/61-400AP/63	Campagne du Mexique, Archives nationales, Fonds Napoléon, Paris
AAE, CP Mexique	Archives des Affaires Etrangères, Correspondance Politique, Mexique, Paris
FO	Foreign Office, National Archives, London
HHStA	Haus-, Hof- und Staatsarchiv, Archiv Kaiser Maximilian von Mexiko, Vienna

CHAPTER 1: THE PLOT AGAINST MEXICO

1. Nathaniel Hughes Jr. and Timothy D. Johnson, eds., *A Fighter from Way Back: The Mexican War Diary of Lt. Daniel Harvey Hill, 4th Artillery, U.S.A.* (Kent, OH: Kent State University Press, 2002), 127.

2. José María Gutiérrez de Estrada, *Carta dirigida al Excmo. Sr. . . . necesidad de buscar en una convención el posible remedio de los males que aquejan a la república, y opiniones del autor acerca del mismo asunto* (Mexico City: Ignacio Cumplido, 1840), 58. Unless otherwise indicated, translations are the author's own.

3. Frances Erskine Inglis Calderón de la Barca, *Life in Mexico During a Two Year Residence in That Country*, 2 vols. (Boston: Charles C. Little and James Brown, 1843), 1:349, 352–353.

4. Gutiérrez de Estrada to Klemens von Metternich, March 28, 1846, in Richard Metternich to Count Johann Bernhard von Rechberg und Rothenlöwen, July 5, 1861, HHStA, 1.

5. Quoted in Josefina Zoraida Vázquez, "War and Peace with the United States," in *The Oxford History of Mexico*, edited by William Beezley and Michael Meyer (Oxford: Oxford University Press, 2010), 347.

6. Wyke to Russell, July 29, 1861, FO, 30/22/74.

7. Dubois de Saligny to Édouard Thouvenel, July 27, 1861, AAE, CP Mexique, 55.

8. Concepción Lombardo de Miramón, *Memorias de Concepción Lombardo de Miramón*, Kindle ed. (Mexico: Rosa Ma. Porrúa, Edición digital, 2020), chap. 7.

9. Philippe Séguin, *Louis Napoléon le Grand* (Paris: Bernard Grasset, 1990), 68.

10. Roger Price, *The French Second Empire: An Anatomy of Political Power* (Cambridge: Cambridge University Press, 2001), 15.

11. Alexis de Tocqueville, *Oeuvres complètes* (Paris: Gallimard 1959), 7:369; David Baguley, *Napoleon III and His Regime: An Extravaganza* (Baton Rouge: Louisiana State University Press, 2000), 36.

12. Karl Marx, *The Eighteenth Brumaire of Louis Bonaparte*, trans. Eden Paul and Cedar Paul (London: G. Allen & Unwin, 1926), 23.

13. *Le Tiers Parti et les libertés intérieures* (Paris: E. Dentu, 1866), 13.

14. James Buchanan, "Message to the Senate on the Arrest of William Walker in Nicaragua," January 7, 1858, American Presidency Project, www.presidency.ucsb.edu/documents/message-the-senate-the-arrest-william-walker-nicaragua.

15. Manuel Díez de Bonilla to Gabriac, March 2, 1854, in Gabriac to foreign minister, "Reservé et confidentielle," March 4, 1855, AAE, CP Mexique, 43.

16. Michel Chevalier, "Variétés. De l'expatriation considérée dans ses rapports économiques, politiques et moraux; par M. S. Dutot. Le Texas et sa Révolution; par M. T. Leclerc, médecin en chef de l'hôpital-général de Tours," *Journal des débats*, September 23, 1840.

17. Michel Chevalier, *Le Mexique ancien et moderne* (Paris: L. Hachette et Cie, 1863), 478–479.

18. Charles du Pin to Napoleon III, "Du Mexique dans ses rapport avec Napoléon III par le baron Charles du Pin, sénateur," November 9, 1863, AAE, Mémoires et documents, Mexique, 10.

19. Egon Caesar Corti, *Maximilian and Charlotte of Mexico*, trans. Catherine Alison, 2 vols. (New York: London: Alfred A. Knopf, 1928), 1:99–102.

CHAPTER 2: THE ARCHDUKE AND THE PRINCESS

1. John Jennings Kendall, *Mexico Under Maximilian Etc.* (London: T. Cautley Newby, 1871), 157; Sara Yorke Stevenson, *Maximilian in Mexico: A Woman's Reminiscences of the French Intervention* (New York: Century, 1899), 224; Egon Caesar Corti, *Maximilian and Charlotte of Mexico*, trans. Catherine Alison, 2 vols. (New York: London: Alfred A. Knopf, 1928), 1:44.

2. Mike Rapport, *1848, a Year of Revolution* (New York: Basic Books, 2008), 60.

3. Joan Haslip, *Imperial Adventurer: Emperor Maximilian of Mexico* (London: Cardinal, 1972), 42.

4. Maximilian, *Recollections of My Life*, 3 vols. (London: Richard Bentley, 1868), 1:197, 170.

5. Maximilian to Franz Joseph, 1856, in Corti, *Maximilian*, 1:47–55.

6. Maximilian to Franz Joseph, January 14, 1857, ibid., 69.

7. Maximilian to Franz Joseph, June 1856, ibid., 62.

8. Carlota to Madame d'Hulst, undated, H. de Reinach Foussemagne, *Charlotte de Belgique, impératrice du Mexique, etc.* (Paris: Plon-Nourrit et Cie, 1925), 35.

9. Carlota to Madame d'Hulst, December 29, 1855, February 10 and April 6, 1856, ibid., 41.

10. Carlota to Madame d'Hulst, December 29 and November 23, 1856, ibid., 63, 50.

11. Victoria to Leopold, June 16, 1857, in Arthur Christopher Benson and Reginald Baliol Brett Esher, eds., *The Letters of Queen Victoria*, 3 vols. (London: John Murray, 1907), 3:234.

12. Maximilian to Sophie, autumn 1858, in Corti, *Maximilian*, 1:83–84.

13. Maximilian, *Recollections*, 3:92.

14. Carlota to Madame d'Hulst, June 13, 1860, in Foussemagne, *Charlotte*, 106.

15. Maximilian to Carlota, January 1, 1861, in Konrad Ratz, *Correspondencia inédita entre Maximiliano y Carlota*, trans. Elsa Cecilia Frost (Mexico: Fondo Cultura Económica, 2004), 69–70.

16. Maximilian to Carlota, April 8, 1860, ibid., 56.

17. Gutiérrez de Estrada to Richard Metternich, July 4, 1861, in Metternich to Rechberg, July 5, 1861, HHStA, 1.

18. Rechberg to Metternich, July 28, 1861, HHStA, 1.

19. Corti, *Maximilian*, 1:114–145.

20. Carlota to Leopold II, January 27, 1862, in Luis Weckmann, ed., *Carlota de Bélgica: Correspondencia y escritos sobre México en los archivos europeos, 1861–1868* (Mexico City: Editorial Porrúa, 1989), 287.

21. Leopold, Duke of Brabant, to Carlota, November 1, 1861, HHStA, 1.

22. Maximilian to Gutiérrez de Estrada, November 12, 1861, HHStA, 1.

23. "Copie d'un rapport secret du Comte Mülinen en date de Paris, le 3 Novembre 1861", HHStA, 1; Napoleon III to Charles Joseph, comte de Flahaut, October 9, 1861, HHStA, 1.

24. Gutiérrez de Estrada to Maximilian, December 28, 1861, HHStA, 1.

25. Maximilian to Napoleon III, January 2, 1862, HHStA, 1.

CHAPTER 3: FRENCH INVASION

1. Palmerston to Clarendon, December 31, 1857, in Richard van Alstyne, "Anglo-American Relations, 1853–1857: British Statesmen on the Clayton-Bulwer Treaty and American Expansion," *American Historical Review* 42 (1937): 491–500; Napoleon III to Charles Joseph, comte de Flahaut, October 9, 1861, HHStA, 1.

2. "Copie d'un rapport du Comte Mülinen en date de Paris, le 15 Octobre 1861 No 63", HHStA, 1.

3. "Copie d'un rapport secret du Prince de Metternich en date de Compiègne, le 16 Novembre 1861", HHStA, 1.

4. Quoted in Carl Bock, *Prelude to Tragedy: The Negotiation and Breakdown of the Tripartite Convention of London, October 31, 1861* (Philadelphia: University of Pennsylvania Press, 1966), 231–232.

5. "Extrait d'une letter particulière du Prince de Metternich en date de Paris, 2 Décembre 1861", HHStA, 1.

6. Jurien de La Gravière to Thouvenel, December 3, 1861, AAE, CP Mexique, 57.

7. François Charles du Barail, *Mes souvenirs*, 3 vols. (Paris: E. Plon, Nourrit et Cie, 1895–1896), 2:335, 342.

8. Paul Laurent, *La Guerre du Mexique de 1862 à 1866, journal de marche du 3e chasseurs d'Afrique, notes intimes écrites au jour le jour* (Paris: Amyot, 1867), 15.

9. Napoleon III to Maximilian, January 14, 1862, HHStA, 1.

10. Hidalgo, "V", undated memo, HHStA, 1.

11. "Carta Pastoral", *La Sociedad*, October 12, 1863.

12. Napoleon III to Maximilian, March 7, 1862, in Corti, *Maximilian*, 1:370–371.

13. Napoleon III to Maximilian, June 7, 1862, ibid., 372–373.

14. "Suplemento al numero 337", *El Siglo*, December 18, 1861.

15. "The State of Mexico", *Times*, May 23, 1859.

16. José María Vigil, *La Reforma*, vol. 5 of *México a través de los siglos: Historia general y completa del desenvolvimiento social, político, religioso, militar, artístico, científico y literario de México desde la antigüedad más remota hasta la época actual*, ed. Vicente Riva Palacio, 5 vols. (Barcelona: Espasa y Compañía, 1884–1889), 516.

17. Charles Ferdinand Latrille, Comte de Lorencez, to Jacques Louis Randon, April 26, 1862, in Gustave Niox, *Expédition du Mexique, 1861–1867: Récit politique & militaire* (Paris: J. Dumaine, 1874), 155.

18. "Gloria a México", *El Siglo*, May 6, 1862; "El 'Voto del Pueblo' de Guadalajara", *El Siglo*, May 10, 1862.

19. Eugenie to Carlota, June 7, 1862, in Corti, *Maximilian*, 1:373–374.

20. "Corps législatif", *Journal des débats*, June 27, 1862.

21. Saligny to Thouvenel, May 8, 1862, AAE, CP Mexique, 58.

22. Lorencez to Randon, May 24, 1862, in Michele Cunningham, *Mexico and the Foreign Policy of Napoleon III* (Basingstoke: Palgrave, 2001), 121.

23. Lorencez to Randon, July 22, 1862, in Niox, *Expédition du Mexique*, 190.

24. "Foreign Intelligence. France", *Times*, June 19, 1862.

25. Copy of William Seward to William Dayton, March 3, 1862, HHStA, 1.

26. Carlota to Leopold, February 2, 1863, HHStA, 2.

27. Charles Bourdillon to de Pont, May 2, 1863, HHStA, 2.

28. Carlota to Leopold, June 2, 1863, HHStA, 2.

29. "Conversation avec Kint du Roodenbeck", May 31, 1863, HHStA, 2.

30. Corti, *Maximilian*, 1:195; Alfons de Pont to Gutiérrez de Estrada, January 31, 1863, HHStA, 2.

31. Maximilian to Rechberg, February 10, 1863, in Corti, *Maximilian*, 1:203.

32. De Pont to Hidalgo, February 23, 1863, HHStA, 2.

33. Niox, *Expédition du Mexique*, 237; Barail, *Mes souvenirs*, 2:397.

34. Charles Blanchot, *L'Intervention française au Mexique: Mémoires*, 3 vols. (Paris: E. Nourry, 1911), 1:384–385; Barail, *Mes souvenirs*, 2:444.

35. Sara Yorke Stevenson, *Maximilian in Mexico: A Woman's Reminiscences of the French Intervention* (New York: Century, 1899), 87.

36. "Editorial", *El Monitor Republicano*, May 30, 1863.

37. Niceto de Zamacois, *Historia de Méjico, desde sus tiempos más remotos hasta nuestros días*, 18 vols. (Barcelona–Mexico City: J. F. Párres, 1877–1882), 16:518.

38. Ibid., 525.

39. Blanchot, *L'Intervention française au Mexique*, 1:414; Stevenson, *Maximilian in Mexico*, 93.

40. Forey to Randon, June 14, 1864, in Niox, *Expédition du Mexique*, 288.

41. Barail, *Mes souvenirs*, 2:468.

CHAPTER 4: THE MEXICAN CROWN

1. Emanuel Domenech, *Histoire du Mexique: Juarez et Maximilien, correspondances inédites, etc.*, 3 vols. (Paris: Librairie Internationale, 1868), 3:117.

2. Egon Caesar Corti, *Maximilian and Charlotte of Mexico*, trans. Catherine Alison, 2 vols. (New York: London: Alfred A. Knopf, 1928), 1:277–279.

3. Franz Joseph to Maximilian, October 4, 1863, ibid., 262.

4. Maximilian to Napoleon III, June 12, 1863, ibid., 375–376.

5. James Williams to Maximilian, December 9 and September 6, 1863, HHStA, 6, 3; Maximilian to Rose O'Neal Greenhow, December 28, 1863, HHStA, 6.

6. Napoleon III to Maximilian, September 19, 1863, in Corti, *Maximilian*, I:384–385.

7. Maximilian to Rechberg, December 16, 1863, ibid., 297.

8. Maximilian to Franz Joseph, October 27, 1863; Maximilian to Rechberg, October 27, 1863, ibid., 280–281.

9. Carlota to Sophie, September 1, 1863, HHStA, 3.

10. Carlota to Madame d'Hulst, October 11, 1863; Carlota to Marie-Amelie, January 31, 1864, in H. de Reinach Foussemagne, *Charlotte de*

Belgique, impératrice du Mexique, etc. (Paris: Plon-Nourrit et Cie, 1925), 136–141.

11. Carlota to Maximilian, September 12, 1863, in Corti, *Maximilian*, 1:250–252.

12. Napoleon III to Maximilian, October 2, 1863, ibid., 389–390.

13. Charles Bourdillon to Maximilian, November 26, 1863, HHStA, 5.

14. Napoleon III to Bazaine, September 12, 1863, in Genaro García and Carlos Pereyra, eds., *Documentos inéditos ó muy raros para la historia de México*, 36 vols. (Mexico City: Vda. de C. Bouret, 1905–1911), 16:34–36.

15. Joseph de Maistre, *St Petersburg Dialogues*, trans. Richard Lebrun (Montreal: McGill-Queen's University Press, 1993), 217.

16. Bazaine to Napoleon III, October 25, 1863, in García and Pereyra, *Documentos*, 15:133–144.

17. Francisco de Paula Arrangoiz y Berzábal, *Méjico desde 1808 hasta 1867: Relación de los principales acontecimientos . . . desde la prison del Virey Iturrigaray hasta la caida del segundo imperio. Con una noticia preliminar del sistema general de gobierno que regia en 1808, etc.*, 4 vols. (Madrid: A. Pérez Dubrull, 1871–1872), 3:159.

18. Napoleon III to Bazaine, September 12, 1863, in García and Pereyra, *Documentos*, 16:34–36.

19. Charles du Barail, *Mes souvenirs*, 3 vols. (Paris: E. Plon, Nourrit et Cie, 1895–1896), 2:490.

20. Ibid., 495.

21. Juárez to Doblado, January 20, 1864, in José María Vigil, *La Reforma*, vol. 5 of *México a través de los siglos: Historia general y completa del desenvolvimiento social, político, religioso, militar, artístico, científico y literario de México desde la antigüedad más remota hasta la época actual*, ed. Vicente Riva Palacio, 5 vols. (Barcelona: Espasa y Compañía, 1884–1889), 627–628.

22. Metternich to Rechberg, March 14, 1864, in Corti, *Maximilian*, I:329; Napoleon III to Maximilian, March 18, 1864, ibid., 398.

23. Queen Victoria's Journals, RA VIC/MAIN/QVJ (W), March 14, 1864 (Princess Beatrice's copies), http://qvj.chadwyck.com/home.do?instit 1=peking&instit2=p3k1ng, retrieved August 23, 2020; Émile Ollivier, *L'Empire liberal*, 18 vols. (Paris: Garnier frères, 1895–1915), 6:579.

24. Franz Joseph to Maximilian, March 22, 1864, in Corti, *Maximilian*, 1:333–334.

25. Maximilian to Franz Joseph, March 22, 1864, ibid., 334.

26. Eugenie to Metternich, March 27, 1864, ibid., 338–339.

27. Metternich to Rechberg, March 27 and 28, 1864, ibid., 339.

28. Napoleon III to Maximilian, March 28, 1864; Carlota to Eugenie (unsent), March 28, 1864; and Maximilian to Napoleon III, March 29, 1864, ibid., 399–400.

29. Ollivier, *L'Empire liberal*, 6:584.

30. Leopold to Carlota (telegram), April 6, 1864, in Corti, *Maximilian*, 1:350.

31. Maximilian to Napoleon III, April 8, 1864; and Napoleon III to Maximilian (telegram), April 10, 1864, ibid., 402.

32. Sophie to Maximilian, April 11, 1864, ibid., 359.

33. Carlota to Marie-Amelie, April 24, 1864, in Foussemagne, *Charlotte*, 171.

CHAPTER 5: EMPEROR AND EMPRESS

1. Carlota to Marie-Amelie, May 28, 1864, in H. de Reinach Foussemagne, *Charlotte de Belgique, impératrice du Mexique, etc.* (Paris: Plon-Nourrit et Cie, 1925), 178–179.

2. Carlota to the Empress Eugenie, June 18, 1864, in Egon Caesar Corti, *Maximilian and Charlotte of Mexico*, trans. Catherine Alison, 2 vols. (New York: London: Alfred A. Knopf, 1928), 2:836–837.

3. "The Emperor Maximilian in Mexico—from Our Own Correspondent", *Times*, July 30, 1864.

4. Carlota to Eugenie, June 18, 1864, in Corti, *Maximilian*, 2:837.

5. Niceto de Zamacois, *Historia de Méjico, desde sus tiempos más remotos hasta nuestros días*, 18 vols. (Barcelona–Mexico City: J. F. Párres, 1877–1882), 17:273–276; François Charles du Barail, *Mes souvenirs*, 3 vols. (Paris: E. Plon, Nourrit et Cie, 1895–1896), 2:483–484.

6. Maximilian to Karl Ludwig, July 26, 1864, in Corti, *Maximilian*, 2:431.

7. José Luis Blasio, *Maximilian, Emperor of Mexico: Memoirs of His Private Secretary*, trans. Robert Hammond Murray (New Haven, CT: Yale University Press, 1934), 38–40.

8. Carlota to Maximilian, August 15, 1864, in Konrad Ratz, *Correspondencia inédita entre Maximiliano y Carlota*, trans. Elsa Cecilia Frost (Mexico: Fondo Cultura Económica, 2004), 115–116.

9. Blasio, *Maximilian*, 39.

10. Francisco de Paula Arrangoiz y Berzabal, *Méjico desde 1808 hasta 1867: Relacion de los principales acontecimientos . . . desde la prison del Virey Iturrigaray hasta la caida del segundo imperio. Con una noticia preliminar del*

sistema general de gobierno que regia en 1808, etc., 4 vols. (Madrid: A. Pérez Dubrull, 1871–1872), 3:219–220.

11. Arrangoiz, *Méjico*, 3:220–221.

12. Blasio, *Maximilian*, 4.

13. Carlota to Marie-Amelie, June 26, 1864, in Foussemagne, *Charlotte*, 202.

14. Maximilian to Napoleon III, August 9, 1864, in Corti, *Maximilian*, 2:845.

15. Ratz, *Correspondencia*, 138–139.

16. Maximilian to Archduke Karl Ludwig, September 21, 1864, in Corti, *Maximilian*, 2:434.

17. Antonio Riba y Echeverria to Romero de Terreros, Mexico, September 28, 1864, in Manual Romero de Terreros, *Maximiliano y el Imperio segun correspondencias contemporaneas que publica por primera vez* (Mexico: Cultura, 1926), 36–37; Arrangoiz, *Méjico*, 3:228–229.

18. Maximilian to Carlota, October 11, 1864, in Ratz, *Correspondencia*, 156; Blasio, *Maximilian*, 51.

19. Quoted in Brian Hamnett, *Juárez* (London: Longman, 1993), 183.

20. Éric Taladoire, *Les contre-guérillas françaises dans les terres chaudes du Mexique (1862–1867): Des forces spéciales au XIXe siècle* (Paris: L'Harmattan, 2016), 70–72.

21. Émile de Kératry, *L'Élévation et la chute de l'empire Maximilien: Intervention française au Mexique, 1861–1867* (Paris: A. Lacroix, Verboeckhoven et Cie, 1867), 41, 179.

22. Napoleon III to Maximilian, November 16, 1864, in Corti, *Maximilian*, 2:852–855; Eugenie to Carlota, November 16 and December 15, 1864, ibid., 855–856, 859.

23. Quoted in Thomas David Schoonover, *Dollars over Dominion: The Triumph of Liberalism in Mexican–United States Relations* (Baton Rouge: Louisiana State University Press, 1978), 121–122.

CHAPTER 6: LIBERAL EMPIRE

1. Pius IX, 1864, "The Syllabus of Errors", Papal Encyclicals Online: www.papalencyclicals.net/pius09/p9syll.htm.

2. Carlota to Eugenie, December 27, 1864, in Egon Caesar Corti, *Maximilian and Charlotte of Mexico*, trans. Catherine Alison, 2 vols. (New York: London: Alfred A. Knopf, 1928), 2:862–868.

3. Carlota to Eugenie, January 9 and 26, 1865, ibid., 868–870, 872–875.

4. Ibid., 474–475.

5. Niceto de Zamacois, *Historia de Méjico, desde sus tiempos más remotos hasta nuestros días*, 18 vols. (Barcelona–Mexico City: J. F. Párres, 1877–1882), 17:1022; Francisco de Paula Arrangoiz y Berzabal, *Méjico desde 1808 hasta 1867: Relacion de los principales acontecimientos . . . desde la prison del Virey Iturrigaray hasta la caida del segundo imperio. Con una noticia preliminar del sistema general de gobierno que regia en 1808, etc.*, 4 vols. (Madrid: A. Pérez Dubrull, 1871–1872), 3:266.

6. Juarista quoted in Robert Duncan, "Maximilian and the Construction of the Liberal States," in *The Divine Charter: Constitutionalism and Liberalism in Nineteenth-Century Mexico*, ed. Jaime E. Rodríguez (Lanham, MD: Rowman & Littlefield, 2005), 151; Maximilian quoted in "Actualidades", *La Sociedad*, September 17, 1865.

7. "Discurso Pronunciado por S. M. el Emperador en la solemne instalación de la Academia de Ciencias y Literatura, día de su cumpleaños", *El Pájaro Verde*, July 13, 1865.

8. Dano to de Lhuys, October 10, 1865, AAE, CP Mexique, 65; Maximilian to Jilek, February 10, 1865, in Corti, *Maximilian*, 2:466.

9. De Pont to unnamed, March 16, 1864, in *Executive Documents Printed by, Order of the House of Representatives, During the First Session of the Thirty-Ninth Congress, 1865–'66* (Washington, DC: Government Printing Office, 1866), 679–680.

10. Carlota to Maximilian, May 5, 1865, in Konrad Ratz, *Correspondencia inédita entre Maximiliano y Carlota*, trans. Elsa Cecilia Frost (Mexico: Fondo Cultura Económica, 2004), 187–188.

11. Carlota to Marie-Amelie, September 10, 1864, in H. de Reinach Foussemagne, *Charlotte de Belgique, impératrice du Mexique, etc.* (Paris: Plon-Nourrit et Cie, 1925), 205; Carlota to Maximilian, May 13, April 23, and May 4, 1865, in Ratz, *Correspondencia*, 197, 168, 186–187.

12. Maximilian to Karl Ludwig, February 24, 1865, in Ratz, *Correspondencia*, 465.

13. Charles Blanchot, *L'intervention française au Mexique: Mémoires*, 3 vols. (Paris: E. Nourry, 1911), 2:264–265.

14. Carlota to Maximilian, May 1 and 4, 1865, in Ratz, *Correspondencia*, 178–179, 183–185.

15. Maximilian to Carlota, May 25, 1865, ibid., 208–209.

16. Dano to de Lhuys, July 29, 1865, AAE, CP Mexique, 64.

17. Carlota to Maximilian, May 1, 1865, ibid., 178–179.

18. De Lhuys to Dano, August 15, 1865, AAE, CP Mexique, 64; Napoleon III to Maximilian, April 16, 1865, in Corti, *Maximilian*, 2:901–903.

19. Sara Yorke Stevenson, *Maximilian in Mexico: A Woman's Reminiscences of the French Intervention* (New York: Century, 1899), 139–140.

20. Carlota to Eugenie, January 26 and April 14, 1865, in Corti, *Maximilian*, 2:872–876, 896–901.

21. Carlota to Eugenie, February 3, 1865, in Corti, *Maximilian*, 2:878–883.

22. "Général du Martray, Lettres du Mexique", *Carnet de la Sabretache* 50 (1922): 398; Henri Augustin Brincourt, *Lettres du Général Brincourt, 1823–1909: Publiées par son fils, le Commandant Charles Brincourt* (Paris: Carnet de la Sabretache, 1923), 339–340.

23. Stevenson, *Maximilian in Mexico*, 135.

24. Maximilian to Karl Ludwig, June 20, 1865, in Corti, *Maximilian*, 2:507.

25. Maximilian to Carlota, April 27, 1865, in Ratz, *Correspondencia*, 173–174.

26. Brincourt to Randon, July 8, 1865, in Genaro García and Carlos Pereyra, eds., *Documentos inéditos ó muy raros para la historia de México*, 36 vols. (Mexico City: Vda. de C. Bouret, 1905–1911), 30:124–125.

27. Brincourt, *Lettres*, 337; Gustave Niox, *Expédition du Mexique, 1861–1867: Récit politique & militaire* (Paris: J. Dumaine, 1874), 519.

28. Paul Gaulot, *L'Expédition du Mexique (1861–1867) d'après les documents et souvenirs de Ernst Louet . . . Nouvelle èdition*, 3 vols. (Paris: P. Ollendorff, 1906), 2:167–168.

29. Carlota to Maximilian, April 29, 1865, in Ratz, *Correspondencia*, 177–178; Carlota to Madame de Grünne, March 14, 1865, in Foussemagne, *Charlotte*, 219.

30. *Mexican Times*, September 9, 1865.

31. Garcia and Pereyra, *Documentos*, 30:250.

32. John Bigelow, "The Heir-Presumptive to the Imperial Crown of Mexico. Don Augustin de Iturbide", *Harper's Weekly*, April 1883, 743.

33. Carlota to Marie-Amelie, September 29, 1865, in Foussemagne, *Charlotte*, 233.

34. Bigelow, "Heir-Presumptive to the Imperial Crown", 741.

35. Dano to de Lhuys, September 19 and October 10, 1865, AAE, CP Mexique, 64, 65; Maximilian to Napoleon III, December 27, 1865, in Corti, *Maximilian*, 2:925–930.

36. Carlota to Maximilian, November 10, 1865, in Ratz, *Corresponden-cia*, 225–227.

37. Quoted in Henry Flint, *Mexico Under Maximilian* (Philadelphia: National, 1867), 129.

38. Maximilian to Carlota, December 19, 1865, in Ratz, *Correspondencia*, 252.

39. Maximilian to Napoleon III, December 27, 1865, in Corti, *Maximil-ian*, 2:925–930.

CHAPTER 7: THE END OF THE AFFAIR

1. Quoted in James McMillan, *Napoleon III* (London: Longman, 1991), 121.

2. Jules Favre, *Discours parlementaires, publiés par Mme. Vve. J. Favre*, 4 vols. (Paris: E. Plon, 1881), 2:178–179.

3. Ibid., 352.

4. Louis-Napoléon Bonaparte, *Oeuvres de Napoléon III*, 5 vols. (Paris: Amyot, 1854–1869), 5:225.

5. Favre, *Discours*, 2:540–570.

6. "Chronique de la quinzaine—31 décembre 1865", *Revue des deux mondes* 61 (1866): 241–272.

7. Grant quoted in Thomas David Schoonover, *Dollars over Dominion: The Triumph of Liberalism in Mexican–United States Relations* (Baton Rouge: Louisiana State University Press, 1978), 215; Andrew Johnson, "First Annual Message", December 4, 1865, American Presidency Project, www.presidency.ucsb.edu/node/201985.

8. John McAllister Schofield, *Forty-Six Years in the Army* (New York: Century, 1897), 385–386.

9. Napoleon III to Maximilian, January 15, 1866, in Egon Caesar Corti, *Maximilian and Charlotte of Mexico*, trans. Catherine Alison, 2 vols. (New York: London: Alfred A. Knopf, 1928), 2:930–931.

10. Napoleon III, *Oeuvres de Napoléon III*, 5:252–253.

11. José Luis Blasio, *Maximilian, Emperor of Mexico: Memoirs of His Private Secretary*, trans. Robert Hammond Murray (New Haven, CT: Yale University Press, 1934), 65.

12. Corti, *Maximilian*, 2:571.

13. Carl von Malortie, *'Twixt Old Times and New* (London: Ward & Downey, 1892), 287–290.

14. Blasio, *Maximilian*, 70.

15. Ibid., 76–77.

16. Scarlett to Clarendon, January 27, 1866, FO, 50/394.

17. Dano to Drouyn de Lhuys, January 18, 1866, AAE, CP Mexique, 66.

18. Maximilian to Napoleon III, February 18, 1866, in Corti, *Maximilian*, 2:931–932.

19. "EXTÉRIEUR. France. Correspondence particulière", *Journal de Bruxelles*, April 7, 1866.

20. Maximilian to Duran, March 16, 1866, in Corti, *Maximilian*, 2:587.

21. Napoleon III to Maximilian, April 12, 1866, ibid., 933–934.

22. Maximilian to Carlota, February 9, 1866, in Konrad Ratz, *Correspondencia inédita entre Maximiliano y Carlota*, trans. Elsa Cecilia Frost (Mexico: Fondo Cultura Económica, 2004), 260.

23. Maximilian to Degollado, March 8, 1866, in Corti, *Maximilian*, 2:605.

24. Émile de Kératry, *The Rise and Fall of the Emperor Maximilian: A Narrative of the Mexican Empire, 1861–7*, trans. G. H. Venables (London: Sampson Low, Son, and Marston, 1868), 107.

25. Eloin to Emperor Maximilian, March 30, 1866, in Corti, *Maximilian*, 2:583–584.

26. Lhuys to Dano, May 30, 1866, AAE, CP Mexique, 67.

27. Maximilian to Barandiaran, June 16, 1866, in Corti, *Maximilian*, 2:626–627.

28. Maximilian to Hadik, February 3, 1866, ibid., 572; Maximilian to de Pont, September 19, 1865, ibid., 531.

29. Ibid., 638–641; Émile Ollivier, *L'Empire liberal*, 18 vols. (Paris: Garnier frères, 1895–1915), 9:73.

30. Carlota to Madame d'Hulst, March 18, 1866, in H. de Reinach Foussemagne, *Charlotte de Belgique, impératrice du Mexique, etc.* (Paris: Plon-Nourrit et Cie, 1925), 273–274.

31. Maximilian to Carlota, August 7, 1866, in Ratz, *Correspondencia*, 312–314.

32. Corti, *Maximilian*, 2:671.

33. Ibid., 671–672.

34. Carlota to Maximilian, August 15, 1866, ibid., 681.

35. Ibid., 684.

36. Carlota to Maximilian, August 22, 1866, ibid., 685–687.

37. Carlota to Maximilian, September 9, 1866, ibid., 699–701.

38. Blasio, *Maximilian*, 92.

39. Carlota to Maximilian, September 26, 1866, in Ratz, *Corresponden-cia*, 331–333.

40. Carlota to Maximilian, October 1, 1866, ibid., 335.

41. Corti, *Maximilian*, 2:712.

42. Blasio, *Maximilian*, 106–107.

CHAPTER 8: ABDICATION CRISIS

1. Ernst Pitner, *Maximilian's Lieutenant: A Personal History of the Mexican Campaign, 1864–7*, trans. Gordon Etherington-Smith (Albuquerque: University of New Mexico Press, 1993), 120–140.

2. Printed and translated in *Executive Documents Printed by, Order of the House of Representatives, 1866–'67* (Washington, DC: Government Printing Office, 1867), 199.

3. Maximilian to Carlota, September 20, 1866, in Konrad Ratz, *Correspondencia inédita entre Maximiliano y Carlota*, trans. Elsa Cecilia Frost (Mexico: Fondo Cultura Económica, 2004), 329–331.

4. Sara Yorke Stevenson, *Maximilian in Mexico: A Woman's Reminiscences of the French Intervention* (New York: Century, 1899), 236.

5. Maximilian to Bombelles, September 20, 1866, in Egon Caesar Corti, *Maximilian and Charlotte of Mexico*, trans. Catherine Alison, 2 vols. (New York: London: Alfred A. Knopf, 1928), 2:723–724.

6. Maximilian to Carlota, August 24, 1866, in Ratz, *Correspondencia*, 321–323.

7. Maximilian to Carlota, September 20, 1866, ibid., 329–331.

8. Samuel Basch, *Memories of Mexico: A History of the Last Ten Months of the Empire*, trans. Hugh McAden Oechler (San Antonio: Trinity University Press, 1973), 13–14.

9. Maximilian to Carlota, September 20, 1866, in Ratz, *Corresponden-cia*, 329–331.

10. Napoleon III to Maximilian, August 29, 1866, in Corti, *Maximilian*, 2:945–946.

11. Maximilian to Carlota, October 5, 1866, in ibid., 731–732.

12. Basch, *Memories of Mexico*, 23–24.

13. Herzfeld to Bazaine, October 20, 1866, in Émile de Kératry, *The Rise and Fall of the Emperor Maximilian: A Narrative of the Mexican Empire, 1861–7*, trans. G. H. Venables (London: Sampson Low, Son, and Marston, 1868), 202.

14. Castelnau to Napoleon III, October 28 and November 9, 1866, 400AP/61, Dossier 3.

15. Maximilian to Bazaine, November 12, 1866, in Kératry, *Rise and Fall*, 234–236.

16. Herzfeld to Fischer, November 5, 1866, in Corti, *Maximilian*, 2:741–742.

17. Scarlett to Stanley, October 3, 1866, FO, 50/397.

18. Scarlett to Stanley, November 5, 1866, FO, 50/397.

19. Scarlett to Maximilian, November 4, 1866, in Scarlett to Stanley, November 5, 1866, FO, 50/397.

20. Scarlett to Stanley, November 11, 1866, FO, 50/397.

21. Scarlett to Fischer, November 6, 1866, in Corti, *Maximilian*, 2:746–747.

22. Maximilian to Bazaine, November 18, 1866, in Kératry, *Rise and Fall*, 239.

23. Gutiérrez de Estrada to Maximilian, November 28, 1866, in Corti, *Maximilian*, 2:752.

24. Basch, *Memories of Mexico*, 56–57; Niceto de Zamacois, *Historia de Méjico, desde sus tiempos más remotos hasta nuestros días*, 18 vols. (Barcelona–Mexico City: J. F. Párres, 1877–1882), 18:679–680.

25. "Prensa de la Capital", "Orizaba", "Regreso del Emperador", and "Nueva faz del imperio", *La Sociedad*, December 5, 6, and 7, 1866.

26. Basch, *Memories of Mexico*, 49–50.

27. Napoleon III to Castelnau, December 13, 1866, in Paul Gaulot, *L'Expédition du Mexique (1861–1867) d'après les documents et souvenirs de Ernst Louet . . . Nouvelle èdition*, 3 vols. (Paris: P. Ollendorff, 1906), 2:447.

28. Castelnau to Napoleon III, December 28, 1866, 400AP/61, Dossier 3.

29. Castelnau to Napoleon III, December 9, 1866, 400AP/61, Dossier 3.

30. Castelnau to Napoleon III, January 28, 1867, 400AP/61, Dossier 3.

31. Basch, *Memories of Mexico*, 82–83.

CHAPTER 9: UNDER SIEGE

1. Sophie to Maximilian, January 9, 1867, in Egon Caesar Corti, *Maximilian and Charlotte of Mexico*, trans. Catherine Alison, 2 vols. (New York: London: Alfred A. Knopf, 1928), 2:770–771; Karl Ludwig to Maximilian, January 9, 1867, ibid., 771–772.

2. Castelnau to Napoleon III, January 9, 1867, 400AP/61, Dossier 3.

3. Niceto de Zamacois, *Historia de Méjico, desde sus tiempos más remotos hasta nuestros días*, 18 vols. (Barcelona–Mexico City: J. F. Párres, 1877–1882), 18:867.

4. Sara Yorke Stevenson, *Maximilian in Mexico: A Woman's Reminiscences of the French Intervention* (New York: Century, 1899), 258.

5. Émile de Kératry, *The Rise and Fall of the Emperor Maximilian: A Narrative of the Mexican Empire, 1861–7*, trans. G. H. Venables (London: Sampson Low, Son, and Marston, 1868), 290; Charles Blanchot, *L'intervention française au Mexique: mémoires*, 3 vols. (Paris: E. Nourry, 1911), 3:408–409.

6. José Luis Blasio, *Maximilian, Emperor of Mexico: Memoirs of His Private Secretary*, trans. Robert Hammond Murray (New Haven, CT: Yale University Press, 1934), 127.

7. "Actualidades", *La Sociedad*, February 6, 1867.

8. Zamacois, *Historia de Méjico*, 18:934.

9. Paul Gaulot, *L'Expédition du Mexique (1861–1867) d'après les documents et souvenirs de Ernst Louet . . . Nouvelle èdition*, 3 vols. (Paris: P. Ollendorff, 1906), 2:491.

10. Samuel Basch, *Memories of Mexico: A History of the Last Ten Months of the Empire*, trans. Hugh McAden Oechler (San Antonio: Trinity University Press, 1973), 95–96.

11. Blasio, *Maximilian*, 133.

12. Basch, *Memories*, 109–110, 101–102.

13. Ibid., 119–120.

14. Felix Salm-Salm, *My Diary in Mexico in 1867*, 2 vols. (London: Richard Bentley, 1868), 1:64.

15. Albert Hans, *Querétaro: Souvenirs d'un officier de l'empereur Maximilien* (Paris: E. Dentu, 1869), 149.

16. Basch, *Memories*, 128–129.

17. Zamacois, *Historia de Méjico*, 18:1201–1202.

18. Blasio, *Maximilian*, 151.

19. F. Salm-Salm, *My Diary*, 1:144, 152.

20. Basch, *Memories*, 158–159, 162.

21. F. Salm-Salm, *My Diary*, 1:167–168.

22. Blasio, *Maximilian*, 149.

23. F. Salm-Salm, *My Diary*, 1:190.

24. Basch, *Memories*, 175–176; F. Salm-Salm, *My Diary*, 1:191–194.

25. Zamacois, *Historia de Méjico*, 18:1345.

26. Blasio, *Maximilian*, 162.

27. F. Salm-Salm, *My Diary*, 1:198.

28. Blasio, *Maximilian*, 164; F. Salm-Salm, *My Diary*, 1:199.

29. Basch, *Memories*, 181.

CHAPTER 10: THE TRIAL

1. Samuel Basch, *Memories of Mexico: A History of the Last Ten Months of the Empire*, trans. Hugh McAden Oechler (San Antonio: Trinity University Press, 1973), 187.

2. Agnes Salm-Salm, *Ten Years of My Life* (Detroit: Belford Brothers, 1877), 190.

3. José María Vigil, *La Reforma*, vol. 5 of *México a través de los siglos: Historia general y completa del desenvolvimiento social, político, religioso, militar, artístico, científico y literario de México desde la antigüedad más remota hasta la época actual*, ed. Vicente Riva Palacio, 5 vols. (Barcelona: Espasa y Compañía, 1884–1889), 848–849.

4. Basch, *Memories of Mexico*, 196.

5. Felix Salm-Salm, *My Diary in Mexico in 1867*, 2 vols. (London: Richard Bentley, 1868), 1:238–239.

6. A. Salm-Salm, *Ten Years of My Life*, 198–199; F. Salm-Salm, *My Diary*, 1:240–241.

7. F. Salm-Salm, *My Diary*, 1:249–250.

8. José Luis Blasio, *Maximilian, Emperor of Mexico: Memoirs of His Private Secretary*, trans. Robert Hammond Murray (New Haven, CT: Yale University Press, 1934), 172–173.

9. Antoine Forest to Dano, June 30, 1867, in Dano to Lionel de Moustier, September 1, 1867, AAE, CP Mexique, 69.

10. Forest to Dano, June 30, 1867, AAE, CP Mexique, 69.

11. As reported in Egon Caesar Corti, *Maximilian and Charlotte of Mexico*, trans. Catherine Alison, 2 vols. (New York: London: Alfred A. Knopf, 1928), 2:812. Agnes Salm-Salm did not speak Spanish; if it took place, this exchange must have relied heavily on body language.

12. Basch, *Memories of Mexico*, 213.

13. A. Salm-Salm, *Ten Years of My Life*, 214.

14. Basch, *Memories of Mexico*, 214.

15. William Harris Chynoweth, *The Fall of Maximilian, Late Emperor of Mexico* (London: published by the author, 1872), 164.

16. Corti, *Maximilian*, 2:817n46; Basch, *Memories of Mexico*, 215.

17. Chynoweth, *Fall of Maximilian*, 170.

18. A. Salm-Salm, *Ten Years of My Life*, 223.

19. Chynoweth, *Fall of Maximilian*, 174–175.

20. Konrad Ratz, *El ocaso del imperio de Maximiliano visto por un diplomático prusiano* (Mexico City: Siglo XXI, 2011), Kindle edition, San Luis Potosí, August 17, 1867.

21. "Mexique", *Le Mémorial diplomatique*, October 10, 1867.

22. Niceto de Zamacois, *Historia de Méjico, desde sus tiempos más remotos hasta nuestros días*, 18 vols. (Barcelona–Mexico City: J. F. Párres, 1877–1882), 18:1512.

23. Corti, *Maximilian*, 2:822.

EPILOGUE

1. Felix Salm-Salm, *My Diary in Mexico in 1867*, 2 vols. (London: Richard Bentley, 1868), 1:312.

2. In fact, Francis I wrote, "Of all I had, only honour and life have been spared."

3. "Corps législatif", *Supplement au Journal des débats*, January 28, 1864.

4. Quoted in Louis Girard, *Napoléon III* (Paris: Fayard, 1986), 501.

5. Quoted in Martyn Rady, *The Habsburgs: The Rise and Fall of a World Power* (London: Allen Lane, 2020), 315.

INDEX